D1279325

Ticking Along Too

Cover artwork by Cornelia Ziegler, Basel.
Sketches throughout book by Joseph Caruso, Zurich.

Published by: Bergli Books AG
                     CH-6353 Weggis, Switzerland

Layout and Design: CGD Computer Graphic Design AG,
                     CH-8037 Zurich, Switzerland

ISBN   3-9520002-1-3

TABLE OF CONTENTS

INTRODUCTION

If you've picked up this book hoping to plan your next trip around Switzerland, you'll be surprised that it includes no maps and few sightseeing recommendations. This is not a travel guide. But it will take you to viewpoints that may only be reached after years of exploration in this small but many-faceted country of world-wide significance.

Maybe you are a newcomer to Switzerland and you hope this book will give you lots of facts and suggestions so that you can feel at home here within 30 days. After reading only a few pages, you may want to allow yourself 30 years to reach that goal.

Perhaps you are Swiss and you enjoy reading and learning English. Maybe you are tired of grammar exercises, comprehension questions and texts in English about far-away places. Maybe you'll find yourself in this book. May I assure you that I and all the authors hope you enjoy the portraits.

You might have read my first collection of stories 'Ticking Along with the Swiss' and be eager for more of the same. There are similarities. A quick glance at the 'List of Authors' at the back of the book will show that the authors are of various nationalities and have come to Switzerland for a broad variety of reasons. Some are even Swiss. No author claims to be an authority on this country or its people. Nobody wants to teach you anything nor sell you anything. This is not a collection from a writers' workshop or some club project. The authors do not know each other and have not exchanged opinions. Some authors are professional writers, editors, translators or journalists. Others have never published a sentence in their lives. They may be businessmen or business women, homemakers, teachers, artists or entertainers. As you read through their experiences in this country, you may agree with me that for such a small country, Switzerland has mountains of impressions and that you should beware of anyone claiming to know everything about it. May this book help you feel part of the crowd here.

Most of these articles were written in response to 'Ticking Along with the Swiss' published in 1988. Those stories seemed to motivate readers to take pen in hand and write down their own personal experiences with the Swiss. Many of these letters and sagas sent to me were very touching. It seemed only natural to continue this project of publishing articles for the enjoyment of all those readers who are fascinated by intercultural encounters.

Many people have helped make this second collection possible. ''Just do it!'' is what Roger Bonner said to me when we came up with the idea to publish personal stories about living in Switzerland resulting in 'Ticking Along with the Swiss'. A few weeks ago I was startled to hear him say those three little words again while we were discussing if this second collection will receive such a good response. Thanks Roger, those sparks of ideas from you have kept me at it. I'm a soft-hearted editor and would have liked to publish almost all the anecdotes sent to me, but the book would have been too heavy to hold. Besides Roger Bonner, a number of 'sample readers' reviewed the most appropriate stories and their evaluations have helped make the final selections for 'Ticking Along Too'. I wish to express my sincerest thanks to the following 'sample readers': to Barbara Grinbergs, a newcomer to Switzerland, for her valuable viewpoints and help with typing; to Annette Keller for playing the role of a sensitive Swiss, to Gill Uster for recognizing entertainment value and to Steve Gregoris for his colorful evaluations and suggestions, to Stanley Hubbard for his expert advice on English usage, to Betty Nauta and Jackie Primiano for their British points of view. Many thanks too are due to all of you who shared your stories with me. You prove how inspiring yet how tough writing is. Keep at it! This whole project would not be possible without the constant support and encouragement of my husband Walter Kiefer, son Martin and daughter Loretta who are my most precious Swiss friends.

May 1990
Weggis, Switzerland   Dianne Dicks

AN UNFORGETABLE GREAT MYTH

by Adham Loutfi

One spring day during a college semester abroad in Switzerland, I took a train from Zurich to the town of Schwyz, which lent its name to this country some 700 years ago. My idea was to do a day-hike up to the top of Gross Mythen, or Great Myths, a 6,000 foot mountain near the town.

Despite the fact that it was a beautiful, mild day, there were very few people on the trail, and soon I'd left most traces of humanity far behind, or so I thought.

After a few hours of walking up through forests and alpine meadows, I was pretty proud of myself. The higher up I went, the more the mountain range stretched in panorama before me. Soon it was time for lunch, and I saw a clearing coming up on the trail ahead, not far from the summit. The strange thing was that there were also voices coming from the clearing. It had been an hour since I'd seen someone on the trail, and since I'd started early in the morning, I was curious to see who'd made it there before me.

Nuns. Actually, about a dozen of them, mostly 50 to 60 years old with a few quite a bit older. My pride at having conquered the treacherous trail evaporated immediately. I was as shocked to see them as they were delighted to share their picnic lunch with me.

It turned out that they were from a nunnery in the valley, and often came up here for lunch when the weather was fine. We had a great conversation, about the mountains, Switzerland, and current events. Soon they were heading back down, and I continued on to the top, from where I could just barely make out 12 dark blue dots moving down the trail, and when the wind was right, a peal of laughter.

1

DEAD ON TIME

by Gay Scott O'Connor

The Swiss and I do not understand each other. Swiss sobriety and Jamaican insouciance appear to have no common ground. Even the grave does not unite us, and our shared life is an exasperating muddle of hurt feelings and pained surprise. No wonder! What are the earnest Swiss, with their reverence for their fatherland, to make of the Jamaicans' cheerful disrespect for fatherland and everything else?

When the Swiss want to sell something successfully to their countrymen they proudly stamp it, in large letters, 'Swiss Made'. Jamaicans in the same position will gleefully brand it, in even larger letters, 'Imported'. Fellow Jamaicans will flock to buy it.

The funniest Jamaican jokes are homegrown and everyone grumbles about everything under the Jamaican sun. But who dares carp or giggle at the Swiss? Foreigners may not - that is impertinent and resented. But the Swiss may not either and any newspaper that makes the mistake of doing so will be inundated with irate letters accusing it of *Nestbeschmutzen* (fouling one's own nest).

The Swiss aren't super patriots, exactly. In the seventeen years I've lived here, I've never been able to track down one specimen who could sing the national anthem. Half of them don't even know the name of their current federal president. Ignorance of Switzerland is tolerated. Poking fun at her is not.

But a sense of humour is essential if we are all to survive each other's peculiarities. Humour is far more important to the human race than all those incredible nuclear shelters that the Swiss keep building. (We've just got a letter about ours; they want us to install bunk beds in it. AND a portable WC).

Some cross-cultural misunderstandings can be so funny that it seems a shame to explain them. The imposing building in your

Swiss town mysteriously labelled *Rathaus* does not house rats. It is the local town hall. And the Swiss gentleman whose car sports a blatant VD on the license plate is not sharing his sex problems with you. He merely lives in the Canton of Vaud. I hoard and gloat over such absurdities. They make me rich.

Swiss visitors to Jamaica may be alarmed at the sight of the locals hurtling gaily over the pot-holes with varnished coffins roped to the roofs of incredibly decrepit cars. The Swiss may wag their fingers, and shake their heads, at what they consider to be unpardonably native excesses. How much better it would be to find us funny, and to enjoy us instead. After all, are the Swiss themselves really any better?

Consider the disconcerting Swiss habit of digging up the dead and turfing them out after twenty-five cosy years in situ. This is recycling with a vengeance. The Swiss are economical, land is scarce, and great aunt's tombstone can be taken home and turned into a birdbath. What happens to the excavated bits? (Very substantial bits in some cases, I understand.) No-one seems to know. And amazingly, no-one seems to care. I've asked lots of people about this, but all I've ever got are vague shrugs and mumbles about possible mass graves (where?) or maybe cremation. (What happens to the ash?) What comes through loud and clear is that they don't WANT to know, which I find unnerving.

This quaint little folk custom and I got off on the wrong foot anyway. When we first came to Switzerland, my Swiss husband and I lived in a small flat with no garden and I used to take our children for walks to the local church. It was pretty, and green, and there were benches. I was somewhat puzzled that, although the church was quite old, the earliest graves didn't date before the nineteen fifties. Had some natural disaster destroyed the original graves? Geography presumably ruled out the hurricanes of my childhood, but what about earthquakes? Perhaps

3

an avalanche? However, babies, housework and valiant efforts to conform kept me busy and I didn't get around to tracking down an explanation.

Then came the day when I arrived with pram and kids to find a lot of graves missing. At first I thought I must be in the wrong walkway and tried vainly to find the right one. Round and round we went, while the awful truth dawned: rows and rows of graves had disappeared! Horrors! How could graves disappear? Graves were permanent, marble monuments that outlasted time while poets sat on them, composing elegies in the sunset. But these graves were nowhere. I was in my own personal Twilight Zone. Hysterically I cantered home, shrieking "Walti! Walti! The graves are gone!"

My husband enlightened me. I don't think, actually, that it made me feel any better.

I'm not particularly neurotic and I don't much mind what happens to me when I'm dead. You can entomb me or embalm me. Cremate me with incense and sprinkle me in the Ganges. Hoist me, Parsee-like, heavenwards, and let the birds get on with it. But I've travelled too much in my life to want to move house when I'm dead.

Please don't bury me in Switzerland.

PINCHES OF CULINARY SWISSNESS

by Ken Becker

Living in Switzerland, as in any foreign country, also means eating your way into it. That's not the same as eating your way through it, which can be done on a culinary binge. At a more leisurely pace, as you lunch and nibble here and there, you accumulate some mouthfuls at least of what Swissness is all about. For what the Swiss put on the table is not just food, but part of their world and way of life.

An unforgettable experience of this sort was my first encounter with *Raclette*. "Have you ever eaten *Raclette*?" a colleague asked me at a parish festival.

Still green to Swiss living, I had no notion of what *Raclette* was, much less whether it could be eaten. An irate tennis player might eat his racket, perhaps, but *Raclette*...? "No, what's that?" I returned.

"Come on down to the *Raclettestube* and I'll buy you some. It's a great Swiss specialty."

That sounded appealing, even exciting, a plunge into the exotic depths of Swiss cuisine art. Vague visions floated up of something exquisite, complex, and subtle - worthy of a place with other national dishes such as beef Stroganoff, *spaghetti al pesto, paella*, Hungarian *goulash, pulgogeh, and sukiyaki*. Or at least different and unique, like the leaden potato dumplings my Swedish grandmother used to make.

I almost laughed out loud in amazement, then, when I got to the *Raclettestube* and saw what *Raclette* really was: melted cheese (a particular sort of cheese, *Raclette* cheese, to be sure) poured onto potatoes (the younger and smaller the better) boiled with their skins on. That's all! - except for a dill pickle and a couple of cocktail onions to punctuate the mixture, accompanied by Fendant, a fine white wine from the Valais region. So simple - even primitive, I thought.

Perhaps that is the key to it, why it is indeed a national specialty. It captures in a culinary way a certain Swiss simplicity and efficiency, as well as their ability to make something big and complicated out of something little and simple just by paying attention to it.

5

Raclette also expresses its Swiss origins, or rather the origins of the Swiss, in simple, frugal peasant life. This peasant influence lives on not only in Swiss cuisine. It is heard in their dialects and their way of expressing themselves. It underlies the Swiss sense of village democracy and politics even on the level of high finance and federal officialdom. Most probably it also shapes their way of dealing with poverty and wealth (they tend to hide both).

My most authentic and delicious experience of *Raclette* was right at its peasant roots, in a vineyard in Valais. I had helped the vintner and his family pick grapes all morning. At noon we gathered at one of the trails through the vineyard. He piled up some dried vines and made a fire, unwrapped a half-wheel of *Raclette* cheese, and melted the open side at the fire. We ate it, not on potatoes, but on bread, washed down with Fendant from his own vineyard.

Even when not playing their role in *Raclette*, boiled potatoes in their skins are no ordinary, nondescript item in the Swiss diet. They are dignified with their own name, *Gschwellti*, which is also the name of a whole meal when they are accompanied by a plate of cold cheese - a sign of how important this simple dish is to the Swiss. True to typical Swiss regional diversity, over the hill from me these boiled potatoes aren't *Gschwellti*, but *hültsche Gummel*. Whatever they are called, I like them, and am delighted that *Gschwellti* get served so often.

Another potato dish, *Rösti* (something like hash browns), serves to define the whole German-speaking area of Switzerland, especially as distinguished from the French-speaking area. These two regions are separated by the *Rösti* trench. Their differences are vastly more complex than a plate of potatoes implies, of course. The Swiss nonetheless sum up the matter in a tasty and substantial regional dish.

With my image of Switzerland as a cool northern country of high mountain pastures, I was amazed to discover that many an excellent wine is produced here. I was also surprised to see how alcoholic beverages are used - namely, on all occasions. Where in the U.S. the standard offering may be coffee - with a meal, before a meal, after a meal, with cake for a social evening - in Switzerland the proffered beverage may be wine. Not only fund-raising dinners and festivals, but even church breakfasts and *apéros* (a morning social snack after the service) serve wine, beer, and *Schnaps* (any distilled liquor, usually from fruit). Coffee is often accompanied by a *Schnaps* - alongside it or dumped right in, and there are stronger variants of this as well. By no means do I want to give the impression that the Swiss go around drunk. But perhaps this broad application of alcohol helps a coolish, reserved national character warm up and enjoy life a bit more. (*Schnaps* is also used externally as a disinfectant, I learned when a farmer's dog bit me and I stopped to complain.)

Though the Swiss are a prosperous people and consider themselves highly civilized, when they eat their cheese *Fondue* (bite-sized pieces of bread dipped in melted cheese) they arm themselves with long forks and eat out of a common pot, like in some more primitive world before plates and bowls or concern about hygiene. My conjecture is that *Fondue*, as well as *Raclette*, originated in homely kitchens where Swiss peasants invented different ways to serve what staples they had - cheese, potatoes, bread, and more cheese. To make a good *Fondue* with the right taste and consistency is a fine art sometimes cited to distinguish the true Swiss from the non-Swiss. (The distinction doesn't hold, of course, as I can attest from a variety of uneven *Fondue* experiences.)

There is a simple, jovial spirit at the table when people gather around the common *Fondue* pot - maybe this setting could be used as an image of Swiss democracy, at least as such a democracy should be. A *Schnaps* (usually *Kirsch*, made from cherries) is almost obligatory with *Fondue*. *Schnaps* not only facilitates the joviality, but helps dissolve the big wad of cheese in your stomach after you've eaten too much *Fondue* (as all too readily happens).

What can their honey and tea tell us about the Swiss? During my first months in Switzerland several people advised me that honey was good against headaches, and so was black tea. Odd - I'd never heard anyone recommend foods for headaches before, or even refer to headaches that much. In Switzerland, however, many people suffer from a particular sort of headache. It is caused by the *Föhn*, an atmospheric pressure that pushes down from the Alps and creates weather conditions ranging from a surrealistically clear calm to a ferocious wind. The *Föhn* somehow invades the body and the nervous system, causes heart attacks, strokes, nervousness, traffic accidents, euphoria, and all those Swiss headaches.

To understand people in Switzerland and especially how they act on some days, therefore, you must realize how they can be affected by the *Föhn*. If you get *Föhn* headaches, you can be sure that you are not alone. Hundreds of thousands of people are suffering with you. That is often an important consolation, since it assures you that you neither have a brain tumor nor are going insane. All will be well with the next rain. In the meantime a strong black tea brewed briefly may help.

Along with my tea and honey, I enjoy good bread, especially graham and whole-grain varieties. Switzerland has lots of it, in a wonderful assortment, and it's fresh every day if you plan your shopping right. During my first stay in Zurich, therefore, I was puzzled when on Sunday the wonderful breads disappeared (except perhaps for some pieces left over from Saturday), replaced by a twisted loaf that was depressingly white and discouragingly dry. Why do these people go out of their way to serve the worst bread on Sunday, when I would serve something better than everyday fare? It seemed an irreverent contradiction. After a while, however, I learned that in almost every German Swiss household the same sort of loaf, the *Zopf* ('braid' - the dough is braided before baking), appeared on the breakfast table every Sunday morning. That it is white and braided and made with milk makes it their finer bread, no matter how inferior it seems to me. There would be loud protests if the *Zopf* were missing - it is indispensable in the observance of Sunday. The consoling side of this custom of white bread on Sunday is that not all *Zöpfe* are of the dry, uninteresting quality I first encountered - my Swiss wife makes a terrific *Zopf*.

My grandfather used to say that you don't know people until you've eaten a barrel of salt with them. What I've shared with you is just some sprinkles from the first few handfuls here among the Swiss. It's been interesting, I certainly haven't starved to death, and I'm still eating with them. Maybe it would do us all good to see life more as a common fondue pot. Cheese has a lot of salt in it, too.

THE WORD STARTS WITH 'S'

by Gillian Uster

Something Soothing:

What do you do when you need to solve a minor medical problem (without consulting a doctor) in Switzerland? Where I come from in South Africa you simply pop down to the local chemist, explain your problem and hey presto, off you go with pills or cream. Not that easy in Switzerland though!

My minor medical problem, haemorrhoids to be more precise, decided to flare up within a couple of days after my arrival in Ebertswil (ever heard of the place? - not many have) in Canton Zurich. My German was non-existent, my *Schwizerdütsch* - well at that point I did not know the difference between the two.

My Swiss husband, Kurt, had more than enough on his plate. He'd recently taken over a failing family business, had secured us a very large Swiss home, was busy with all the paper-work that involved bringing a foreign wife and baby into the country, and was not about to play family doctor to his haemorrhoid-suffering wife!

"There's a *Drogerie* in the next village. Go there and I will tell you what to say," said Kurt.

He explained that the matter was really very simple. A haemorrhoid is pronounced the same in English and German and the word for cream was *Salbe* - so what more did I need to know - I simply had to say *Haemorrhoid-Salbe bitte* (please).

Little did I bargain for my introduction to Herr Rütimann, the owner of the Drogerie in the next village of Hausen a. Albis. (We had in ours no shops apart from a *Molkerei* (dairy) and a Post Office).

I set off driving carefully on the right-hand side of the road, for this was also a new venture for me, and pulled up outside Drogerie Rütimann.

I walked in as casually as possible to be greeted by a cheerful *Grüetzi*.

I received a few interested stares from the customers, presumably regulars exchanging local gossip while Herr and Frau Rütimann dispensed their potions, pills and even to my surprise, wine and pet food!

Herr Rütimann eventually approached me and rattled off something - I never discovered what - but nevertheless I proudly launched into my limited German.

"Ich habe Haemorrhoids," said I. The conversation of those around me immediately ceased and I was given a few interested stares. Herr Rütimann appeared slightly ill at ease and simply stared at me, (probably wishing he'd left me to the mercy of his devoted *Frau*).

I plunged on. *"Ich hätte gern..."* and then the word *Salbe* vanished clean out of my head. I thought desperately - I knew the word began with S.

Herr Rütimann had not taken his eyes off me and the crowd in the shop were eagerly awaiting my next words. Then it came back to me. Of course, how could I forget?

"Ich hätte gern Senf," I said proudly.

"Senf?" said Herr Rütimann in utter amazement.

"Ja, ja," I said smiling, proud that I had remembered just in time to save myself the embarrassment.

I noticed Frau Rütimann disappearing behind a curtain at the back of the shop and I heard a stifled laugh. Meantime Herr Rütimann had gone a little red in the face, but was sorting through a drawer full of tubes of cream.

Finally he placed a tube on the counter. I saw the word haemorrhoid and quietly congratulated myself. Not so bad after all! He handed the tube to me and my eye caught the word *Salbe*...

Oh how silly I felt, how could I possibly have forgotten the word! "You must not put *Senf*, you put this," said Herr Rütimann in broken English.

I took the tube of cream, paid for it and fled. Now where had I seen the word *Senf*? Of course, at breakfast, my husband was squeezing mustard all over his Swiss sausage. Funny what they sell in tubes these days!

My little story made me quite a celebrity in Hausen a. Albis. Herr and Frau Rütimann never forgot me and I became a good customer. A few years later I was to make a good friend in Hausen and she even knew the *Senf* for my haemorrhoids story, as she was a good friend of the Rütimann's too.

What of my haemorrhoids? Well the *Salbe* did the trick!

Something Sporty:

I'm a bit of a keep-fit fanatic and before arriving in the land of cheese and chocolate, I attended regular classes in South Africa, Tokyo, and Malaysia. Having no international friends close by, I decided to do my workout alone at home.

If you want to do the workout in a proper manner, you must dress accordingly - bright red and blue tights and a leotard, in my case, with lively disco music to set the pace.

My first incident occurred around 8:30 one June morning on a beautiful summer day. Martin, my young son, who was just a toddler, was playing outside in his sandpit and all was well.

I did my warm-ups and swung into my arm exercises when the front door bell rang. Throwing a dressing gown over my leotard, I opened the door to discover nobody there. Martin was having a great game with his Mum. I was annoyed and told him I was not to be disturbed until I had done my exercises and back I went to concentrate on my hips and thighs.

A few minutes later, the bell rang once again. This time I was going to surprise my little monkey, thought I. I bounced down the stairs, flung the door open wide and did great arm circle movements...

My arms suddenly stopped in mid-circle, for there was no Martin at the door, but a perfect stranger - a middle-aged man who looked like he had had the surprise of his life!

"Frau Uster," he managed to stammer in utmost disbelief, probably wondering why ladies with respectable Swiss names were not 'putzing' (cleaning) or fixing *Znüni* (a nine o'clock snack) at this time of the morning.

He introduced himself as Herr Zimmermann and handed me a card which informed me he was employed by a glazing company. I suddenly remembered my husband's mentioning that he wanted a quote for a new glass sliding door on our patio. So I ushered Herr Zimmermann in and showed him our party room.

I also remembered that Kurt had said I must offer all workmen coffee if it was around 9 am and mineral water or beer if it was later in the day. Undaunted I prepared for a small German conversation, clad only in my leotard. After all, he'd already seen all there was to see of me, so what was the point in getting modest and covering up. *"Hast Du gern Kaffee?"* I asked.

I noticed Mr. Zimmermann flinch awkwardly.

"Nein, nein," he said reaching for his measuring tape and glasses. So as not to appear too forward, I retired to continue with my workout. I waited about 10 minutes, this time I put on my dressing gown and wandered back to the patio to see how Mr. Zimmermann was progressing. But, much to my amazement, he was gone. My bird had simply flown away. The patio door was open and Mr. Zimmermann had made his exit across the front lawn. "How strange, how rude," I thought.

Needless to say, when I recounted the story to Kurt later that evening, he just rolled his eyes.

"You said *Du* to him and were dressed the way you were? No wonder the poor man fled," said Kurt.

We received a fairly reasonable quote though and Mr. Zimmermann's company did the job. When they did the work, I was properly dressed. But alas, there was no sign of Mr. Zimmermann.

A few months later, having made a few friends and getting heavily involved in *Schwizerdütsch,* I continued my aerobics classes in my spacious attic with the local hairdresser and a nearby farmer's wife as my two willing pupils.

Margot (the hairdresser), Therese (the farmer's wife) and I did our routine twice a week and enjoyed coffee and a chat around the kitchen table afterwards. I could improve my language skills and they could keep fit.

My second aerobics incident took place in January during the heavy snowfalls of winter. Margot, Therese and I shed our track suits and swung into step in the chilly attic. Martin was playing happily in his bedroom with his toys - it was 10 am.

Half-way through the workout, Martin appeared in the attic in search of a diversion, but he soon got cold and wandered back to his bedroom. I failed to notice that when he closed the attic door, he had locked us in!

At 10:45 am we were finished and eagerly awaiting our quick coffee and chat before preparing our noon-time Swiss lunches. Imagine my concern when I tried the door and found it locked!

I managed to attract Martin's attention by banging loudly on the door, but when he realised what he had done, he burst into tears and was of no use at all. Worse still, he could not even slide the key under the door, as there was not a centimetre to spare. (The Swiss do not like icy draughts from attics entering their homes!)

Meanwhile, Margot, Therese and I were feeling the cold. A leotard and thin track-suit were certainly not enough cover in an unheated attic of minus 3 degrees centigrade.

Another dreadful thought struck me. My husband was not coming home for lunch that day. We were truly trapped. Martin was too small to use a telephone and there was no way I could send him out to get help.

Margot offered some hope. Her 105 kg husband, Manfi, always came home at 11:30 for his lunch. If there were no Margot and no food, he'd surely search for her and he was aware of our aerobics class! But, then again, how was he to get into my house? All the doors were locked. Talk about panic stations!

We simply had to do something. After a quick discussion and much giggling (whether from nervousness or sheer mirth, I was not sure), it was decided that I was to climb through the glass trap-door in my roof and stand on the roof and shout for help. We found a chair in the attic for me to stand on to make my exit into the below zero temperature outside.

Our house was fairly close to a busy road. We hoped somebody would come to our rescue. I gingerly climbed out on the roof wearing only my aerobics shoes. I was terrified I would slip as there was a good cover of snow on the roof.

A few trucks and cars swept by, I waved. No luck. I gave up and came in from the freezing cold. Martin was screaming hysterically at the locked door. It was 11:15. I prayed Manfi would pass by.

Then, what I can only describe as a miracle happened. Along came Herr Wolfisberg, a nearby farmer, on his tractor complete with a *Gülle* container (liquid fertilizer tank). He was off to fertilize his fields of snow.

What made him look up to my roof I'll never know, but I swear he nearly fell clean out of his tractor seat when he saw me up there. He stopped immediately and I sent Margot up onto the roof to describe our predicament as my language skills were far too limited to describe our dire situation.

Being a man of means, he was able to gain access to my house through the kitchen and within minutes he rescued three freezing keep-fit fanatics and calmed Martin down.

There was no time for coffee, but we had it all the same, only too relieved to be in the warm kitchen once more.

The next day we baked Mr. Wolfisberg a large tart to offer our heartfelt thanks and sent it over to him. I often wonder what he must have said to his wife....

"A funny thing happened to me on the way to doing the *Gülle* today, dear."

That fateful attic key was promptly removed from the door and only replaced three years later when we moved from Ebertswil to Baar, Canton Zug.

Swiss Surprises:

Getting used to new kitchen appliances which keep breaking down can be a bind, especially if you cannot communicate with the repairman.

My dishwasher kept throwing in the towel. First it was the pump and my kitchen floor was awash with soapy suds. Then it was the motor....

The agents dispatched a repairman, Mr. Dudle, to solve my problems, but to no avail! Mr. Dudle was a large rotund Swiss man with a black beard, and I soon learned he enjoyed a beer, both before and after lunch.

In fact he became a regular guest at my kitchen table while he chatted away describing my domestic dilemmas. I'm not sure what dialect he spoke, but I never could understand him and getting rid of him after one beer became a bit of a problem.

When my machine broke down for the third time, I urged my husband to get another repairman, or just simply to get the spare part and try to do the job himself. Mr. Dudle was making me most agitated.

Then a few days later, just after Kurt had left for the office and I had finished doing the dishes by hand, I heard a car drive up. I was upstairs in my bedroom and I could see the large rotund man with the black beard getting out of his car. He was carrying a small box.

"Ah, Mr. Dudle and the spare part," I said to myself. This time there would be no beer for him. I made a quick plan.

I opened the window and shouted *"Grüetzi"* (hello). He looked up in surprise and appeared confused. He said something which I could not understand, but I was quite adamant that I was not letting him in.

"Mein Mann flick Machine selber," (my husband will fix the machine himself) I said and I clapped my hands so that he would simply throw the box up to me on the second floor. I would then have the spare part and Mr. Dudle could depart....simple as that.

The man looked most surprised, but I continued to clap my hands and point to the box. Talk about having a thick skin! Finally he got the message and threw the box up to the second floor. I caught it, said my thanks and drew the net curtain across the window.

He just stood there for a few seconds before slowly climbing back into his car and driving off. I waited at the window until he departed.

My toddler son, on hearing the conversation, came into the bedroom and demanded to see what was in the box.

"It's only a part for my dishwasher which Daddy will fix," I said handing him the box.

"Martin like *Zopf,*" said a small voice.

I stared in disbelief. In the box was a small plaited bread and a tiny packet which I quickly discovered was salt. There was a letter as well and I quickly opened it. It was in German, but the letterhead carried a cross and an address in Hausen a.Albis.

"Oh boy, I've done it again," I thought.

When poor Kurt arrived home later that evening, he read the letter and let out a low moan. He explained it was a letter to welcome us to the community from the Catholic Church and my 'Mr. Dudle' was none other than the local father. He was offering us the bread and salt of life as a symbol and this was especially for newcomers.

Since we are not Catholic, we took the matter no further for Kurt was fast becoming embarrassed by my escapades.

Our dishwasher was finally repaired. The part arrived in the post! The father is still at the Catholic Church. We saw him when we attended a recent funeral (fortunately he never recognised me). I wonder if he knows that his double is a guy called Dudle?

TEXAS RANCHERS IN SWISS FARM COUNTRY

by Catherine P. Studer

Most American tourists come to Switzerland to see beautiful mountains and old towns, museums, castles and other tourist attractions. Liz and Ed were different. They are from Texas, where they live on a ranch and own a sizeable herd of Brahman and other cattle. This summer they visited Europe for the first time, and after they had spent a few days in Germany, we were going to show them a bit of Swiss farm country.

"We haven't seen any cows yet!" Liz told us when we met her and Ed at the railway-station in Lucerne. We explained that many of our cows spend their summers up on Alpine pastures and promised them that they would see some cows - many of them in fact - the next day.

Our destination was a tiny mountain village not far from Interlaken. In the 'Alpenrose' up there, we were welcomed by a group of very merry villagers. During dinner quite a singing contest developed between the villagers and a choir of guests, interspersed with some real yodelling on the one hand, and some well-known American folksongs on the other. "You never know what's in store for you when you come up here," we had warned our friends from Texas, who enjoyed the singing a great deal, but did not quite dare to join in the competition as a third, US chorus.

The next morning we took a two hour hike up to a high Alpine pasture where we hoped to be able to watch the herdsmen making cheese. On the way through the village our Texans were surprised by the huge 'bluebonnets' in many of the pretty farm gardens: lupines in all colors. What astonished them even more were all the mountain brooks and waterfalls coming down from all sides of the valley. "What an abundance of water!" Ed exclaimed. He didn't even mind the cool and rather wet weather, knowing that a few days later they'd be back in the hot Texas sunshine.

Soon the first herd of heifers welcomed us from behind a cattle gate: many Simmentalers, some Swiss brown and a few Holstein cows, but no Brahmans, of course. Liz and Ed were beginning to feel very much at home. But these cows were all wearing bells, a thing unheard of in Texas. "I can't imagine how I'd get bells on my cows!'' While cattle in Texas generally are quite wild, Swiss cows are very domesticated. In fact, each one is personally known to the farmer by its name and character. And while the Texas cows roam about on the range and generally take care of themselves - so we were told - these Swiss dairy cows need a lot of attention. They spend much of their time in barns and have to be milked twice a day.

''Why do the cows wear bells? And don't those bells bother them?'' Liz wanted to know. Up on the Alpine pastures the bells are essential because the cows can roam around freely and sometimes you have to look for them. The sound of the bell helps find them. But also in the lower country, where the cows graze more or less around the house, the farmer likes them to wear their bells. Even without really listening all the time, he is constantly aware of what the cattle are doing out there. He notices if there is some unusual commotion or if a cowbell is tinkling somewhere - for instance in the vegetable plot - where the cow should not go. And then, of course, those bells are an old, cherished tradition.

''The bells that the cows wear everyday do not bother them,'' the herdsman assured us. ''Some heifers even graze better to the rhythm of the bell. The huge parade bells which some lead cows wear at special occasions - like when they go up to the higher Alpine pastures or come down again - are different. Those are heavy and bothersome, but they are just for show. Sometimes the cows seem to know that only the best may wear such beautiful big bells and they give the impression of being even proud to wear one for a short time.''

But now, the climb up to the high Alpine pastures started in earnest. This too was a new experience for our Texas ranchers who are used to being in much flatter country and riding in their pickup trucks. But they made it in good time and couldn't believe it, when, indeed, they arrived at the top. They were rewarded by the spectacular mountain scenery and the beautiful flowers - everything so different from South Texas. ''Back home, nobody will believe that we've been here!''

In the *Sennhütte* (the Alpine hut) the cheese making was in full progress. It is a very old building and they make the cheese in a huge 200 gallon kettle over the open fire. We could watch every stage of the process and were spellbound. This was going to be the same kind of cheese we had enjoyed for breakfast at the 'Alpenrose'.

Later we looked for a place near the mountain brook to have a picnic. While we were sitting there among the Alpine roses, the herdsmen let all the cattle out of the cow-sheds. They came, scores of them, filling the place, with bells ringing. And by the time we had roasted our 'wieners' *(Cervelats)*, a bunch of curious cows had joined us and we all had a merry time together. Liz kept saying, "This is the nicest picnic we've ever had!"

On the way back to the village, Ed, who is an expert at hay baling in Texas, watched the hay making business with special interest. It had come to a standstill because of the rain. He looked sadly at the hay which was lying wet and soggy on a few of the slopes.

"It will turn bad - they can't use that hay anymore!"

"Oh yes, we can," a local farmer explained, "we keep turning it over and over until someday it will have a chance to dry. And it will be very clean by then!"

Making hay in Texas surely is much easier than in a Swiss mountain village. Not only the sunshine, but also the terrain makes farming easier for the Texas farmer. Our friends were impressed by the strenuous work of making hay on these steep Swiss slopes, storing the hay in those little hay shacks high up on the hillsides and getting it down again in winter with big bob-sleds. ''You should have miniature hay balers,'' Ed suggested, ''It would make the gathering and storing of hay so much easier.''

Two days later we took our friends from Texas to visit a farm in Baselland. Making hay there was more to Ed's liking. He even found a New Holland hay baler parked in front of the farmhouse - the same kind he owns back in Texas! And Hans, the Swiss farmer, smiled at how expertly his American colleague handled it.

He and Ed also compared notes on the prices of cows. Whereas a good cow can easily cost Sfr. 4000 (about $2600) here, Ed gets about $750 (about Sfr. 1250) for a cow in Texas. And Liz finally got an answer to a question which had bothered her for a while: ''Where are the calves?'' In Texas, the cow and her calf form an important unit. The cow is supposed to rear her calf.

In Switzerland, the farmer's income comes mostly from cows' milk. The barns are built so that it is convenient to milk the cows. Also, the cows are used to being milked by milking machines. Therefore, for practical reasons, the calves are taken away from the cows after birth and are fed by the farmer with the same milk they'd get from their mothers. We were astonished to hear that in Texas the calves might drink from their mothers for as long as nine months.

It was fascinating to hear those farm people compare notes! We tried to figure out the relationship between an American acre and a Swiss hectare. As two and a half acres amount to about one hectare, Ed must own about fourteen times as much land in Texas as Hans does in Baselland. This is why Hans has to make the most of his property by tending to all kinds of different crops in addition to his milk cows.

It was cherry-picking season, so we all tasted some of the dark red cherries for which Baselland is famous. Cherry picking looks like a pleasurable job. You can sit in the trees and eat as many cherries as you like while you are picking. In reality, the fun is not so great if you have to do nothing else for weeks on end, or if heavy rain destroys the cherries which were supposed to bring in part of your yearly income. Also, cherry picking is a risky business. Each year many bad accidents occur when ladders slip or tree limbs break.

Later, we were invited to the farmhouse and sat all together around the table in their cosy *Stube* (living room). Almost half of the room was taken up by an old *Kachelofen*, an enormous tiled stove, built-in between the living room and kitchen, such as are frequently found in old farmhouses here. The kitchen part of the stove can be used for cooking and baking. Many farm wives still bake in it, though they prefer to do their regular cooking on a modern kitchen stove. Hans' wife Annette had just baked a few four-pound loaves of delicious farmbread and a huge *Gugelhopf* - "A mountain cake!" Liz exclaimed. Since our friends from Texas had not been able to see any snow mountains because of the cloudy weather, this was at least a bit of a compensation. The bread, cheese, cake and homemade cider were delicious. And there was so much to talk about. Hans' precious jumping horses, as compared to Ed's cowboy horses; or Ed's tales about rattlesnakes, armadillos and coyotes, against Hans' troubles with wild boars ravaging his crops.

We could have spent hours and hours talking and enjoying ourselves. But farmers have a lot of work to do and never enough time. Hans and Annette had to go back to their cherry trees and Ed and Liz were getting anxious about all the hay waiting for them back home in Texas.

Our American friends were sorry to leave Switzerland the next day. "I think I would like to spend a summer working on an Alp or helping Annette pick those cherries," Liz mused. And Ed sighed, "If only I could take a big bag of this nice fresh, cool air back home!"

BEHIND THOSE CLOSED CURTAINS

by Susan Tuttle-Laube

When we moved into a semi-detached house in the suburbs I felt that I had finally moved into Swiss life. It was a real neighborhood - older, one-family houses with red tiled roofs, tidy gardens, swept walk-ways and PTT-approved mailboxes at each front gate. No traffic, no anonymous apartment blocks and, as it turned out, no other foreigners but us. No one really noticed us at first. But something was askew. We weren't doing some things right. My trash would appear curbside earlier than that of my neighbors. My children would occasionally appear on the street still clad in PJ's, or even less. I would arrive home with a week's worth of groceries in the car instead of the daily shopping caddy full. And I just couldn't keep up with the leaves which accumulated on our walk-way, let alone the weeds which overtook our garden. I might never have given these things a second thought had I not felt myself observed, watched, checked. I realized that I had drawn attention to myself and that I was suspect because I was different. And suspicion is what guided the hand behind the white mesh curtain of my neighbor's window.

I would be unloading the car, yelling for kids to get in the house when my eye would detect that curtain move. I'd come out at 6:30 am dressed in my nightgown to grab the paper from the mailbox and again, I'd see someone behind that curtain. Every visit to the car, the street or the mailbox, I'd find myself being observed. Early morning, midday or evening, someone was watching.

It started to get to me. I began to look for the shadowy figure behind that curtain. I became conscious of my actions and I felt myself getting annoyed. Then finally, the events of one Sunday morning motivated me into taking action. We were outside readying the bikes for a family bike ride. One child's bike seat still needed attaching, so my husband got out the drill in order to make one hole in the bike frame. The sound of the drill lasted 20 seconds. The seat was mounted, the tools put away and just as we were about to embark a policeman walked up to my husband. ''We had a report that someone was working.'' We explained what we had done, the policeman shrugged and said ''that's not work'' and he left. I looked to my neighbor's house and that curtain moved.

The next day I put my plan into action. I instructed my older son to wave whenever he spotted our neighbor behind the curtain. I did the same. I wouldn't let whoever it was continue to feel invisible. Our waves were always accompanied by our big smiles - welcoming, not malicious. The first few times the curtains moved abruptly, the shadowy figure retreating. But eventually the figure remained. And then finally the curtain was cautiously pulled aside and there was a hesitant wave. Then one day a smile. A chance meeting, a greeting, a small chat. The children served as go-betweens, a kind of safe, neutral meeting place, an excuse to talk.

Since that time we have become neighbors. Herr and Frau Ernst are in their eighties. No children, very little family left and they are outliving all their friends. They built their house 50 years ago and moved in when they were newlyweds. They told me about the time that the lot on which our house stands was still a cornfield. About how difficult it was to get a house built during the war years. They built their house with a family in mind - unfinished rooms on the second story were to be children's bedrooms. But the children just never arrived and the Ernsts lived on alone on one story while the years passed and the neighborhood grew. Their original neighbors who built next door, on the cornfield and down the street, grew old and moved out, or passed away. They watched new, young families move in, take over and suddenly, they were strangers. Then one day over coffee they confessed to me that they didn't feel at home anymore. They had become isolated and mistrustful, daring only to look at the world from behind closed curtains.

The Ernsts don't hide anymore. When I'm at the car or the mailbox they still observe me, but now they'll open the window and chat. We greet each other nearly every day. They give the kids chocolates. I shop for them. We look out for each other, smile a lot and share bits of our daily lives. Maybe they feel a little more at home now in their old neighborhood. I'm glad that they are there, watching, interested. If it weren't for their looking out from behind those curtains I might never have gotten a chance to know them. And that would have been too bad for all of us because the feeling of home extends beyond walls. And the feeling of home is what I've been looking for.

LEISURE TIME: HOW DO THE SWISS SPEND THEIRS?

by Patricia Highsmith

Every country and folk has a favorite way, maybe several ways, of spending its free time. If asked, some individuals will say at once, ''Oh, I go fishing, weather and season permitting.'' Or ''I fool around with my stamp collection.'' Or a type apt to be French or English: ''My garden demands a lot and I love it. It's at the back of my house. Then there's reading.'' An English man or woman: ''A walk in the Green Park, then tea at the Ritz with a friend. Jokes and gossip. Sheer indulgence and loads of fun.''

When I decided to take a look at what I know about Swiss free time and to inquire into their way of spending it, I found the answers a bit slow in coming. The Swiss man or woman seemed to ponder, as if asking themselves, ''Have I any free time?'' Maybe they were asking themselves, ''What is free time?'' The answer to that surely must be when one is not working or doing chores.

At last the Swiss man or woman could come up with an answer: they had their *Verein* or club. (This turned up frequently.) Maybe it was a *Turnverein* (athletics), maybe a singing club, or a religious club. Perhaps they met once a week, and if so it was regular and at a certain time. Afterward, the members of the club might get together at a nearby restaurant or bar-café for drinks or coffee, but not for long if the club members had to get to work the next morning.

Then of course skiing, the aristocrat of sports among the Swiss, it would seem. One doesn't need a club or ski society to go skiing, just buy a pair of skis and a railway ticket, and off you go, let us suppose with a few ski lessons beforehand. And how about talk and chatter before and after skiing? An exchange of ideas, maybe? An exchange also of addresses?

And hiking, a splendid exercise and a wonderful way to see the countryside, trees, wild flowers, and to collect odd stones, fir cones and chestnuts in autumn. Like-minded friends can pull a watercolor set out of a backpack, perch on a rock or a fallen tree, and create another amateur masterpiece to take back home.

In New York for example, where skiing and the singing clubs do not play such a big role, there are the museums, the Frick, the Metropolitan, the Museum of Modern Art. One Sunday recently I rang up an old friend in New York, and we tried for the J.S. Sargent exhibition at the Frick: no luck, the queue went round the corner. We went to the Met instead, and the afternoon was still a success. A coffee and a talk afterward, a total of at least three hours, some exercise involved too, albeit not strenuous.

What may make the Swiss hesitate when asked about leisure is that they associate it with organized hours and activities, whereas the English and Americans value leisure and free time mainly because it is not, in theory or practice, organized. An outing may be spontaneous. Its proposal evokes a smile and "All right, let's!" A visit to the zoo, a boat ride around Manhattan, or a ferry to Staten Island on a Sunday afternoon? "Fine, let's go!"

Even the *Verein* meetings, I am told, often involve tea and cake, and members are encouraged to bring something.

Far more dampening as to casual get-togethers after work hours, say on the way home, around 6 pm, is the fact that the habit hasn't taken root in Switzerland. I have been living in Switzerland for seven years now. A person can't say "Come in for a drink (or a fruit juice) around six-thirty, if you can. We have an interesting houseguest from France." No, the person invited probably has a spouse waiting at home, and - it seems - the evening meal has to be at the same time as usual.

The three-quarters of an hour after work and before home-and-spouse (of course spouse could join in too, if so inclined) are of some importance in Paris, London and New York, in regard to change-of-atmosphere, getting new ideas, meeting new people. Meeting new people, like them or not, is stimulating.

But the Swiss - I speak of the German-Swiss and the Ticino parts, I am not familiar with Geneva social life - seem truly burdened by the obligation of laying on a whole meal for their invited. And why shouldn't they feel burdened, if their obligation is to prepare a sit-down meal? A meal for two or four involves hours of preparation, and perhaps even part of the day before spent in shopping. In the Ticino, at least, a buffet won't do. It has to be sit-down and three courses.

I know from a friend and neighbour that the three courses are daunting. I suggested buying the first course - cold cuts, olives, for instance, something with mayonnaise from a delicatessen - and preparing the other two courses herself. She works half the day, anyway, cooks for husband and two children, surely she can be forgiven for buying a first course? It depressed me, I confess, to learn that the three-course obligation had put off some dinner parties (I prefer to call them get-togethers) which my friend, American by the way, believes should be based on friendship, talk, laughter, argument maybe, the lending and borrowing of books. But no, the three-course business reigns, and there can't be 'an evening' without it.

The non-planners - it seems that they are not in the majority in Switzerland - are the chance-takers. Of course something may go wrong, such as two of a happy gathering of four having to disappear by 8 pm, maybe to mom's, maybe to a date. But the planned can be a bore too, as anyone who has ever sat through a rather silent three-courser at a Swiss restaurant knows. The food often seems of more interest than the conversation or jokes, if any. Then the slow second helpings. The meal can last slightly more than two hours.

However, since leisure is by definition a free time, each country, including Switzerland, surely spends it in a manner to its liking. If even easy-walking-distance neighbours do not ring up and ask if they can pop in for a minute around 6 pm, it is because they (each of the parties concerned) don't need this brief pick-up. If leisure is free time, it is also the freedom to choose how to spend it.

THE SHOCK

by Jean Bonjour

The characters in this story are fictitious. Any resemblance to actual persons is INTENTIONAL!

For the past few years, companies with branches in foreign countries have observed that the success or failure of their operation is often based on the well-being and adjustment of the entire family sent abroad.

Formerly, an aspiring businessman was chosen for his ability and personality. His family was plucked from familiar roots and flown to wherever he was transferred. Adaptation to a new environment was not automatic. Something eventually named 'Culture Shock' struck some member of these families.

Sue and Tom were typical transferees. They had met and married while both were working for a large Midwest company. Sue continued to work as a secretary. She liked her work and felt she was an efficient member of the office staff.

Just before their second anniversary, Tom received a notice to report to his boss. That night Tom said, "Jordan wants to see me tomorrow. The secretary said it was important. Maybe they need a new vice-president."

Sue laughed, "If you skip over the heads of five department managers, you can ask for me to be your secretary."

The next evening Sue rushed out to the car.

Tom grinned and said, "Sorry, they didn't put me on the Board."

"Oh Tom, stop teasing. What is it?"

"Susie, I can see the headlines 'Popular young suburbanites departing for foreign assignment'. Would that please you?"

Sue beamed, "I'd love it. Where are we going? When do we leave? Who shall we tell first?"

In four short weeks Sue and Tom had sold their car, found a home for Luella, their canary, packed their belongings and made quick trips to visit family and friends.

The first month they lived in a hotel while they searched for a place of their own. Tom had to begin working and Sue was left to find an apartment. She learned very quickly that they could not afford a house even if they could find one for rent. She looked at a few furnished places, but they seemed to be filled with generations of cast-off pieces. She finally found an apartment on the top floor of a private home. The owner lived on the ground floor.

At first Sue was busy making the apartment into a home and trying to find the right ingredients for cooking. This soon became routine and only took a couple of hours of her time.

Discontentment began to erode her enthusiasm. She missed the life she had led before they had come overseas. There had always been someone around with whom she could talk, share a coffee or share a joke.

Sue regarded herself as an equal partner in their marriage. She began to resent having nothing interesting to do while Tom spent long hours in his new job. She grumbled and became suspicious. She was sure the butcher had cheated her. She didn't understand the cuts of meat. The refrigerator was too small. There was no dish-washer. She hated to have to clean the outside stairs to the apart-ment. She never knew if she should shake hands. She could only use the washing machine at certain times and there was no tumbler. The list grew.

The house owner had shown her how to put up the outside clothesline. She waited until she was alone and put it up her own way. A half hour later she looked out and saw three of Tom's shirts trailing on the ground. She sneaked down to get them and saw a neighbor in the window. The woman smiled and raised her hand. This added to the humiliation and anger Sue felt. She washed the shirts again and sat down and cried.

Tom suggested that she take a course in the language she was always complaining about. She kept procrastinating and said she would do it soon.

Each evening when Tom came home he found a discontented wife. They bickered over unimportant matters. He was tired and annoyed and felt guilty about Sue.

One Friday evening Tom came home with a surprise. He had bought bicycles for both of them. Sue was thrilled with hers and rode it every day. The newness wore off and she found she didn't like to ride alone or the weather was too bad to go out. She only used it to go to the local market.

One day she left it leaning against the front gate. When she went to get it, it was gone. She was sure someone had stolen it. The landlady came and said she had put it in the shade.

That night Sue complained to Tom that the woman should not have touched her bicycle. If she wanted to leave it in the sun it was her own business.

"She watches everything I do. She is nosy. She brings the mail up and probably hopes I'll invite her in, then she can see if I'm keeping the place clean. The women here only think about washing and cooking and cleaning these awful hardwood floors. I won't live like that. They do things the way their grandmothers did."

Tom was concerned, "Sue, you should remember that we are foreigners here. They are not going to change their way of living because of us. I worry about you and it isn't helping either of us. You used to have a good sense of humor. Try to find it again."

Sue felt hurt and resentful that he did not give her the sympathy she felt she deserved.

The next day Sue rode her bicycle down to the market. She bought a kilo of potatoes and fastened them on the backrack of her bicycle. She started up the hill. A bus behind her sounded the horn. She moved over. The driver blew the horn again and she got off her bicycle and glared at him. He had switched the door open and called out. He pointed back the way she had come. She looked behind her and saw she had been strewing potatoes for half a block. She felt a wave of shame. The bus had continued on and the only thanks the thoughtful driver had received was her scowl of hostility.

Leaning the bicycle against a lamppost, she went back to retrieve her lost potatoes. A young woman had started to pick them up for her.

She was embarrassed but forced a smile and said, "Thank you."

"Oh you're English," the woman said.

"No, I'm a misplaced American," Sue replied.

It was an introduction.

They walked up the hill together and talked as people do when they feel they might be friends. At the gate the woman invited Sue to come home with her for a coffee. For the next couple of hours they had a lot to say to each other. As Sue reluctantly prepared to leave, her new friend asked, "Do you think you have enough time to join our English conversation group? We are five friends and have such fun. Our only trouble is we don't have much chance to speak English. It would be such a help if you could."

Sue didn't hesitate to answer that she would be happy to join them.

When she got home the landlady told her she had taken two letters up for her. She thanked her pleasantly.

Her cure had begun. She had passed the crisis of her personal 'Culture Shock'.

That evening a surprised Tom was met at the door. Sue threw her arms around his neck and said, "Oh Tom, the most wonderful thing happened to me today."

"What?" Tom asked.

Sue burst out laughing, "I lost a kilo of potatoes!"

スイス語、話しますか ？

DO YOU SPEAK *SCHWIZERDÜTSCH?*

by Masako S. Uzawa

I once read a story about a Russian linguist who spoke many languages. He was having a nightcap in a pub in Irkutsk when he overheard men chatting in a strange language he had never heard. He listened intently but could not recognize it, to his disgrace. Curiosity took him over to ask them. Those men had been speaking *Schwizerdütsch*, of course!

It was a blessing to read this, balm for the pains in my neck trying to keep my head above Swiss water. If a world-famous linguist has trouble with Swiss German, why shouldn't I? But then, my trouble does not end here. It begins. For I live where this strange language is spoken.

Schwizerdütsch, as I understand, has historical origins and stems from the medieval German language, an ancestor of present High German. It is not just a countryish dialect of 'Good German'. The real trouble with *Schwizerdütsch* is that there is no Standard Swiss German. 'Candy' is *Däfi* in Basle, *Zältli* in Zurich, *Dröpsli* in Lucerne, and *Suisserli* I don't know where. In the Basle area where I live, there are dialects of the city and of the rural area, the latter further differentiated in upper and lower. I wouldn't be surprised to learn there is a middle one too. The Basle dialect involves not only a certain pronunciation but also the many customs and attitudes that go with it. For instance, real Baslers are supposed to greet you with *"Guetenoobe"* (good evening) from 2 pm on, which seems, even without summer time, a bit untimely to me.

Local dialect is a proud heritage and means of identity for Swiss people. The autonomy of cantons and communities is reflected in the dialects spoken. You'll hear Swiss say, ''He is a real Basler,'' ''He is clearly a Berner,'' or ''He must come from somewhere in the Northeastern Region.'' The Swiss can distinguish the slightest accent. A local dialect is rooted so deep in those born and raised here that 'foreigners' can usually be spotted the moment they open their mouths.

I play guessing games with my Swiss husband at times, but with little success. I can tell a Berner with his slow and distinctly Bernese accent. I still have trouble being able to spot a Basler even though I have been around this town a long time. Basle is so cosmopolitan. I can hit or miss with the dialects of a few other cantons. This summer we were in Hammerfest, Norway, to see the midnight sun. In a small remote restaurant, we overheard the people at the next table. "Swiss!" I said. "Yes, from Aargau." my Swiss husband elaborated. You do hear *Schwizerdütsch* in the most out-of-the-way places on the globe!

Schwizerdütsch is a spoken language, rarely written. I once collected Basle *Fasnacht* verses but I could neither read nor make sense out of them. You can only learn *Schwizerdütsch* by listening. My pseudo-*Schwizerdütsch* is the concoction of many teachers; my children (with Basel-Stadt and Basel-Land accents), my in-laws (with Lucerne accents), and my neighbours and friends from various other regions. My husband has long given up on me on this subject in order to save our marriage. Since I have a Japanese accent and, besides, a Southern drawl which I picked up in Chapel Hill, North Carolina, I am apparently a difficult case. I get myself tangled up in all kinds of communication problems. When I speak *Schwizerdütsch* and my listener looks confused, I try to switch to High German. When this sounds too high-brow, I have to give up and speak English. I have a feeling that the Swiss prefer my English to my 'Good German'. This problem inhibits somewhat my chances of developing any linguistic talents in this multilingual country.

It took a whole year for me to see through the mist of *Schwizerdütsch*. I've learned it the hard way. My parents-in-law were determined to orient their Oriental daughter-in-law into the Swiss way-of-living. They spoke no English with me, though later I heard them converse with English guests in their beautiful royal English. It is considered good Swiss manners to speak the language of the person you are speaking to, but in my case learning to speak *Schwizerdütsch* was a prerequisite for me to be accepted in my husband's family. My mother-in-law gave me a few good lessons. There are three basic key words to open the narrow gate to this wonderland:

Ha is *haben* (have),
gha is *gehabt* (had) and
gsi is *gewesen* (been).
Those are the secrets of it all. Thus, *ha gha* is 'have had' which
must be reversed to *gha ha* in subordinate clauses. You should say
"I bi gsi" (I have been), not *"I ha gsi"*. It's a Swiss word puzzle.
You are 'in' if you can do it.

When in Switzerland, do as the Swiss do! I have found that the
slightest efforts to speak the local language are appreciated and
complimented. So after I had my 'German for beginners' course
behind me, I decided to have a try at learning the Swiss version of
this language and take a course in *Schwizerdütsch*. I found several
other brave, admirable foreigners gathered to adapt themselves to
their host country. People from Germany living in Switzerland are
reputed by many not to want to condescend to speaking this
countryish dialect. But most of my classmates were German couples
who wanted to become naturalized citizens of this peaceful neutrality. I was also surprised to find some French-speaking businessmen
in the class, since the French are supposed to expect the whole world
to speak their language. There were also British people, Canadians,
but no Americans. I was the only Japanese. There were no Italians
- perhaps they knew better how to enjoy their evenings.

The German people had to learn to slur down their clear, fricative,
staccato tones, into soft diphthongs and to sing folk songs. The
French speakers had to be brain-washed to pronounce H as *Hin-
terem Huus het's Hüener* (Behind the house there are chickens).
The English speakers had to work on their Zs: *Zyschtig Znacht
zwische Zwölfi und Zwei* (Tuesday night between twelve and two).
Being Japanese, I had to work on my infamous 'L' and 'R': *"Lueg
in die richtigi Richtig, links und rechts"* (look in the right direction,
right and left).

This difficult language of *Schwizerdütsch* has one big advantage
over High German. When you are uncertain about whether a word
should have *der, die, das, dem, den* in front of it, you can confidently slur a 'd' and not worry about the rest. You can also just
swallow the endings on words with *...er, ...en, ...em, ...es* when you
are not sure about them.

"You have to be musically talented to get the right intonation or
melody of *Schwizerdütsch*," my husband claims, "and to be able

to hear the subtle off-key, 1/8 tone in the rhythm.'' He must be right as I know a Japanese music student who was able to speak the Basle dialect without difficulties after being here only two years. He was working as a newspaper boy for extra money between 4 and 5 in the morning and I doubt that he met anyone to communicate with at that hour. But of course he must have been very talented as he played baroque music on a zither! I guess I am not musical. Maybe I'm tone deaf! The best compliment to my musical ability was a comment by a German businessman about my High German having a heavy *Schwizerdütsch* accent.

Even though you have to learn the Swiss tongue by listening, it may not always be wise to repeat what you hear. Once I mimicked how my children used to speak. They were horrified to hear me say *"Wenn's schifft, hock i vor em Fernseh, suff Coki und gaff.''* I shall try to translate this as lady-like as I can with the help of my American Slang Dictionary and Roget's Thesaurus: ''When it piddles outside, I squat in front of the TV and guzzle Coke and gape.'' Children may talk like that but ladies shouldn't!

Besides, adjectives are most irregular. The degree of intoxication, for instance, goes like this: *beschwipst* is tipsy, *besoffen* is drunk and *voll* is under the table. I've never forgotten one of my very first and most embarrassing lessons learned 30 years ago at dinner. My mother-in-law asked me graciously if I wanted another helping, I politely declined saying in my best German, ''No thank you, I am *voll.''*

I have come a long way since then and have become very fond of this curious language. I love its slow, folksy melodious tone, putting a sweet 'li' at the end of names and *'gäll?'* or *'oder?'* at the end of sentences. *Schwizerdütsch* grows on you. It suits the Swiss - their faces, tempo, scenery and in fact the whole atmosphere in this country. Switzerland would not be the same without it. Now, neither would I.

今日は、皆さん ！

"Grüezi Mitenand"

グリュツィ ミッテナント ！

FANFARE

by Barry Tunick

We were spending the summer with my wife's family in Cormoret which lies between Biel and La Chaux-de-Fonds in the Jura. Besides being the village cheesemaker, Trudi's brother Hans-Ueli was the assistant director of the 'Fanfare', the village band. She asked him if our 15-year-old son Danny, who'd been taking drum lessons, could play with them during a rehearsal. One day he told us the drummer was on vacation and Danny could sit in that night.

A few minutes before 8 pm, Danny and I walked down the hill to the 'college' or school, where the 'Fanfare' rehearsed. He carried his sticks.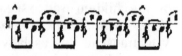
I was a bit apprehensive; I didn't know how he felt because he never shows his feelings. Here he was, going to play music he'd never seen or heard with people he'd never performed with. Besides, that night Hans-Ueli couldn't be there.

We climbed the steps to the rehearsal room. Fifteen or so brass and woodwind players (by day farmers and factory and office workers) sat on folding chairs in a white room. I introduced myself and Danny to the director, a small unsmiling man who made an effort to respond to my French (they usually speak Swiss-German). Oh boy, now Danny'd have to take directions in a language he didn't know.

Some of the musicians seemed skeptical. I deciphered the Swiss-German words for "little boy from America" muttered in a cynical tone of voice. They seemed resigned to tolerate a bumbling performance.

The director handed Danny the drummer's part, a little four-page booklet of lines and notes for a Swiss march. He skimmed through it in about ten seconds. I asked him if he had any questions I could relay to the director. "No, it's OK," he said, sitting down and giving the snare drum a few taps to test its tension.

That was all the preparation he got, because the director started the count, "*Eins, zwei, drei...*" and they were off. Musical notation must be universal, because Danny didn't miss a beat. I assume the rest of the 'Fanfare' played well, but I was focusing on the drum part, which was crisp and clear.

At the end of the march, the director smiled for the first time and said "*Très bien, monsieur,*" to Danny as the band members applauded. I wanted to applaud, but feared it might be inappropriate. The director asked if Danny could play with the 'Fanfare' at the next weekend's festival in Courtelary, the larger village to the east. Of course he could.

I thanked the director and the 'Fanfare' members. Then I put my arm around my son's shoulders, and we walked quietly through the warm night back to the chalet.

DEAR DISTINGUISHED AND GENTLE DRIVER...

by Jan Lane

I began driving a car 32 years ago. I love to drive and have been told I'm rather good at it. I've never had an accident and only one minor traffic ticket. Unfortunately, for the past seven years, since I've lived in Switzerland, I haven't had a car and am obliged to walk to most places.

Ticino, the Italian-speaking part of Switzerland, like the rest of this beautiful country, is a walker's paradise ... that is, as long as you don't have to deal with cars.

To venture out of the house on foot in the Ticino is not for daydreamers. It must be undertaken while fully alert. Something happens to the people here when they get into their automobiles. All that famous Swiss diplomatic charm goes right out the window and they become driven ... literally. It is as if the automobile has a life force of its own and might abandon the driver if there's an attempt to control it. Perhaps it is best to view this behavior positively - as a necessary release for pent-up emotions. Otherwise why would people who live in such a small country, with no place to go that takes more than a few hours, drive like this?

Your attitude as a pedestrian is critical if you are to survive a venture on foot. It is highly important that you have a good imagination. You must have a willingness to imagine you are at the Indianapolis 500 or the Monte Carlo Grand Prix when approaching a crosswalk. With this outlook, you won't be terrified when the yellow lines of the crosswalk and any human beings on them are ignored by the approaching drivers. In fact, with this outlook, you'll understand the speed and aggression of the drivers, tolerate them and perhaps even applaud their expertise. The more experienced the driver, the more adept he is at swerving into the oncoming traffic lane and around any pedestrian who happens to be in the middle of the crosswalk. Less skilled drivers chicken out by applying their brakes at the last possible moment, screaming profanities and gesturing wildly that the pedestrian has disrupted the flow of traffic. The reflexes of these drivers are nothing short of awe-inspiring. Years of practice have gone into developing the ability to stop at the last possible moment without killing a single pedestrian. Imagine the sacrifice of time and effort. Some of these drivers must only get out of their cars to eat and sleep.

Walking in the rain is never fun in a city and can be especially discouraging if you have to do it daily to get to and from work. The narrow streets in the Ticino have extremely narrow sidewalks, if any at all. This means pedestrians often have to hover up next to the walls of houses and buildings. Walking along such streets while an automobile race is going on leaves the pedestrian in a rather vulnerable position, to say the least. However, if you are prepared, any number of approaches can be explored. For example, save water and time by forgoing your morning bath and allowing the passing automobiles to provide it. Or, if you have both hands free and acrobatic talent, you can take two umbrellas - one for over your head and the other to minimize the amount of water that hits you from the side as cars pass. Or add variety to your appearance by taking along an entire change of clothes and by wearing a motorcycle helmet to protect your glasses.

On sunny days you may also wish to take along a change of clothes in case you have to squeeze by automobiles and trucks parked on the sidewalk by impatient drivers who felt they didn't have the time or the desire to look for a parking place in the street. There is usually only a foot-wide passage way between these vehicles and buildings. Despite the compulsive cleanliness of the Swiss, I always find my clothing covered with dirt after I've struggled through one of these auto-lined sidewalk passages.

Let me warn you that during the tourist season, if there isn't an auto race, cars are usually bumper to bumper. The fumes are unbelievable. You might want to carry a gas mask. You can pretend you have emphysema and are taking your oxygen.

Contrary to what you might think, in bumper to bumper traffic it is almost impossible to cross the street. For some reason drivers don't like to leave any space between cars. This situation demands you use all your theatrical talents to succeed in crossing the street. I use my 'New York City tough stance' - the one New Yorkers use to discourage muggers and rapists. The head is held high and confident with an aggressive, determined gait that says, ''Don't mess with me or you may not live to regret it.'' This is how I cross the street, hoping no *Ticinese* driver recognizes me as a foreigner and decides to accidently dent me to score points with fellow

Ticinesi. In this part of the world, the natives are very proud to be Swiss. It's just that anyone who isn't *Ticinese* is considered a foreigner - French and German-speaking Swiss included.

A final word of advice: Carry along a fold-up sign that you can pull out and display when attempting to cross a street. Don't put "STOP DAMN IT" on it like you would if you were in the States. Write something that appeals to the drivers' pride and sense of cul- ture, something gently persuasive and dip- lomatic like,

DEAR DISTINGUISHED AND GENTLE DRIVER: WOULD YOU BE SO KIND AS TO CONSIDER ALLOWING ME THE POSSIBILITY OF CROSSING THIS STREET? OF COURSE IF YOU'RE IN STRESS AND HAVEN'T TIME TO STOP I TOTALLY UNDERSTAND AND WOULDN'T DREAM OF DETAINING YOU. ON THE OTHER HAND, IF YOU ARE OPEN TO THE POSSIBILITY OF MY CROSSING THIS STREET PERHAPS YOU'D CONSIDER JOINING ME AT THE CORNER BAR TO DISCUSS IT OVER A BOCCALINO OF MERLOT.

This sign might really do the trick, but be sure to have it translated into the local Italian dialect.

You probably think I'm exaggerating. To be fair, I do admit that there are considerate and courteous drivers in the Ticino. I know at least 5.

SERVING SWISS TIME

by Leslie Bachmann

Serving time. Marking time or doing time? We are all doing time of sorts. It is a pity not to use our time, wherever we are, for joy and growth. I, for example, chose a life sentence in Switzerland when I married a Swiss and I know what I want to do with this time. Some people, however, get their lives in a muddle at one point and find themselves doing time in a dull and lonely prison cell.

I visited a prisoner in a Geneva prison last week who said, ''I'm going to use this place as a sanatorium. By prison rules, for one thing, I have had no alcohol since I came here a year ago. I get up early every day, shave, put on nice clothes, listen to half an hour of classical music, jog, cycle and take courses. I'm improving my chess game, too.'' That man does not need AUXILIA. In fact, as he works to cheer up other men in his block, he could be considered part of our team.

AUXILIA is a voluntary organization through which I give correspondence courses in English as a foreign language to prisoners all over Switzerland. Most of the people I hear about or deal with on this programme are bored, depressed, confused, homesick. They turned to theft or drug traffic as a better way of making money than what their trade skills or the economic system of their country would allow. Or they rebelled against unfeeling people of their past. Now they find drug traffic even easier, and moral support even rarer inside prison than outside. I am convinced that the combination of contact with someone who cares plus developing a taste for study are what can help these people change their attitudes while they are 'doing time'.

What a pleasure teaching these men and women is for me. Some of their work stagnates and we just enjoy exchanging short notes. But others grow in enthusiasm over the months. Here is what one of my students wrote about his English lessons:

```
''I don't know where she lives. Her address
still remains the same: an anonymous post
office box in Berne. Mine has already changed
a few times. In England I would be a G.H.M. -
Guest of Her Majesty...
```

"As a guest of the Swiss tax-payers, I've got some free time to spend in prison. So I decided to carry on with English when I heard about AUXILIA. I learned the basics of English at school.

"Hi, Mrs Bachmann," I say about twice a month (it depends on my degree of laziness) and she listens to my voice, recorded on a tape. Already I'm looking forward to getting my homework back and listening to her voice, her comments. There's something about the teacher-student relationship and the friendship. She lives 'outside'...

"As most of my homework is made of written exercises, it happens she draws a 'Smiley' beside one of my sentences. I lost my freedom but I try to keep a certain sense of humour...

"When the humour is as scarce as a stain on a Swiss car, learning and studying English becomes, for me at least, a part of a dream. Because one day ... one day I'll be free. I'd like to travel! I'm learning the value of freedom..."

(signed)
one among others

Another of my students wrote the following comments:

"Through AUXILIA I've met teachers who have given me the taste and desire to study. I'm thinking that if in my youth I had had such positive teachers, surely today I would not be in jail. They always correct my work with a lot of explanations and always add encouragement and friendly words, which are for me like the cherries on a cake.

"I don't know how to thank Mrs Simone Payne, AUXILIA Manager who, in addition to her administration work, has sent extra work to me for a year; my English teacher who is most friendly and takes infinite patience to explain the satanic pronunciation; and Mrs Chamat, my Spanish teacher, who always adds typical South

```
American songs or music on the cassettes.
''I don't know how to thank them for spending
part of their free time to help prisoners.''
```

He says the extra pleasures in his work are like cherries on a cake. Well, there are cherries on MY cake, too. The biggest and reddest ones are the unusual tales students tell me. Subjects for composition often sound very commonplace, but the rich life of the illegal world yields up some pretty surprising treatment of them. One prisoner, when asked to relate a car journey, for example, tells of trying to drive from Paris to Marseilles in four and a half hours on a bet! Instead of describing a painting as asked in an exercise, another tells me of a vision he had while under the influence of marijuana. In response to the question of Christmas menus they report about unheard of seafood dishes with accompanying Portuguese wines, snakes in Africa or tortillas on the beach in Mexico.

There is a textbook exercise with the instructions: "You are swapping houses for a month with another family who will arrive after you have left. Write a note for them, explaining where things are." It is intended for practice of such expressions as 'under the stairs,' 'on the top shelf,' 'in the drawer on the right.' One fellow sarcastically wrote the following, even though I said he could write about a house he had lived in before:

```
''The single drinking glass is on the right
side of the lone wash-basin and the one and only
mirror is above it. The only table is in the
centre of the room under the only light bulb...
You may read my comics which are on the one and
only shelf in the back left corner of the room
but please don't steal them.
''Have a good time, Mr. ......''
```

... and named a man who was in the headlines of the local press that week and whom, I suppose, he would have rejoiced to see behind bars.

41

On the subject of painting, another student insisted that I see the Gauguin exhibition in Paris even if it meant spending half the day on the train. So it is thanks to a prisoner that I went to Paris and back in one day and thrilled to all the colour, warmth and vibrance of Gauguin's paintings.

In the chapter on dogs there is a very unassuming question: Are you afraid of dogs? By return of post that week I was told that if I wanted to disarm a frightening dog, I should get down on my hands and knees. Nobody told me about the dog's reaction, however. Perhaps dogs have an unwritten law that they should be lower than humans. Anyway, there we were, a little dog and I on the beach at St. Sulpice a while after I got that letter. The dog came running and barking furiously at me. I got down on all fours as my student had advised. After I got down, the dog stopped barking and got down even lower till its belly was wriggling and rubbing a hollow in the sand. When I stopped moving, it stopped and did not inch forward until I did. I giggled to myself and thought, ''Who, apart from this prisoner, has ever got me playing such a crazy game?''

Sometimes the enjoyment I get out of working for AUXILIA comes from the imaginative changes I myself make in the exercises. Our course books are attractive; accompanying workbooks, cassettes, and French translations present the language very methodically. Yet some exercises are still not suitable for correspondence courses. One such exercise is the budget form. How can I ask a man in a bolted cell about the amount he spends on heating or on bus fare to school? Here is a case where I treat myself to a bit of creativity. I put happy, relaxing music on the tape and instruct the student to ''lie back and escape to that part of your mind that can look at a photograph of someone very very different from you and feel what it is like to be that person. To each of my detailed questions about this person, accept any answers that float up with the music. What is his name? Where is he from and what does his house look like?'' Prisoners' imaginations, thus guided, have produced some very exotic characters with equally amusing budgets.

If prisoners can imagine a different life in this exercise, are they not also capable of imagining a more positive way of life after they get back into society? This may be a lofty ideal, and I may never reach it, but I am having a lot of fun trying.

HOW SWITZERLAND BECAME CLEAN

by Mavis Guinard

Switzerland, just as I had been told, was immaculate. I admired the snowy napkins as much as the starchy mountains. I discovered new standards of housewifery. Spring-cleaning lasted all year round. I was fascinated by my neighbor who rose early to festoon her windows with sheets and quilts. Her days followed a set routine. On Mondays, she aired the family's Sunday best, adding her husband's uniform from time to time. When we met, she told me the chimney sweep would be coming and advised me to buy huge over-slippers for him to wear as he padded from fireplace to attic.

My kids learned fast. By the time they acquired a smattering of French at school, they taught me to pocket candy wrappers and never toss a butt away. I could never figure out what the orange-clad workmen with their huge vacuum cleaners ever found along the gutters. On May Day, just behind the red banners and chanting marchers, sweeping machines as big as tanks close the parade, guzzling tracts as casually as they guzzle cabbage leaves after the weekly markets.

It was not always like this. I was delighted to discover this fact from sociologist Genevieve de Heller's thesis on how Switzerland became clean. In fact, foreigners had a lot to do with it.

Halfway into the 19th century, Switzerland was about as dirty as the average European country, pretty dirty indeed. Early Christian morality and barbarian invasions had wiped out the Romans' bathing habits. It took the Crusaders to rediscover Turkish baths, strict monastic rule to set fresh standards. But such undue concern for the body was denounced by religious reformers and counter-reformers alike.

Fear of syphilis dealt a blow to cozily permissive bath-houses. Out with promiscuity went the bathwater. Louis XIV lavished much water on his Versailles fountains, little on himself. Until the 19th century, most Europeans felt secure in an *'étui de crasse'*, a protective sheath of grubbiness.

43

According to de Heller, to make Switzerland clean took the combined pressure of tourism and the fear of epidemics. The pursuit of cleanliness found such a favorable terrain here that it became compulsive.

Early tourists recommended the inns of the German-speaking cantons or along well-traveled roads as quite clean. As they ventured off the beaten track, things were far different. Murray's 1838 HANDBOOK FOR TRAVELERS IN SWITZERLAND praised the farmers for keeping milk pails shiny but warned that their chalets would probably be filthy.

Some of these well-located chalets became luxurious hotels by the second half of the 19th century. Tutored by the valets of gentlemen like Byron or Ruskin, Swiss innkeepers tried to keep up with the demands of their new clients. English visitors thought nothing of loading a metal tub on a mule and wanting a hot bath at the end of the Alpine trail. Though less fussy than the French about food, they insisted on other niceties besides spotless napery. Four years after Edison invented the light bulb, hotels in Vevey and Montreux advertised that they had electricity, elevators, imported bathrooms and toilets.

Everything had to be squeaky clean. Contamination was a phobia. Lethal epidemics of cholera and typhoid, brought from the colonies, had swept through Europe. Doctors campaigned for slum clearance and sewers. Sanitary housing regulations were passed.

Philanthropist William Haldimand, a close friend of Charles Dickens, gave Lausanne its first public baths. But, as in other towns, people clung to that snug coat of dirt: wasn't it well known that washing the feet weakened the eyes? Ten baths for all Lausanne were plenty. In nearby Germany, Oscar Lassar, the man who invented shower baths, had calculated that Germans bathed once every 30 years: for 32 million people there were only 1,032 baths.

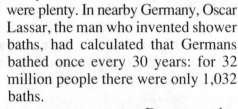

Doctors decided that for the world to be made safe from epidemics, the lower classes had to be taught to wash. Switzerland began on military recruits and schoolchildren. From 1890 to World War I, new schools were equipped with showers. Once a week, classes were marched in to undress and soap themselves. Then, the teacher turned the single faucet. The last rinse was Spartan cold.

Cold water was good for you. Cold baths, cold milk and black-bread treatments worked miracles. Hot water was good: thermal springs the Romans had discovered in the Alps reopened as modish spas in Baden, Loèche and St Moritz. Altitude was good. Doctors found that the pure air relieved tuberculosis.

Enter the Magic Mountain. With it came a new fear of contamination from patients who lived in regular hotels before sanatoriums were built. The concern for clean rooms and bed-linen increased. Once a rich man's privilege, spotlessness became a tourist's right.

Pasteur's little germs plagued housewives and hotel keepers. The hand that held the broom could sweep society of many evils. To keep her husband out of the café and her daughter off the streets, a woman only had to make her home clean and inviting.

Before getting busy on political matters, literary women spent a lot of time educating their servants and sisters on their daily tasks. Before writing UNCLE TOM'S CABIN, Harriet Beecher Stowe did a book on housekeeping. About the same time, domestic science was introduced to Swiss schools. These practical courses had a nice spin off. They furnished a yearly contingent of willing domestic help for Swiss housewives to 'train' at home, who were expected to apply what they had learned in booklets like the one used in Valaisan schools. On page 16 it detailed the fine care of a broom: "Remove the dust and imbedded threads, wash the brush and handle in a solution of ammonia, comb the fibers out-of-doors but in the shade. Wax the handle."

When feminists became more articulate in Switzerland, some wondered out loud if the cleaning habit had not become too ingrained. Sociologist de Heller's 230-page thesis on the development of cleanliness in the Canton of Vaud was published in 1979. After explaining the historical reasons for Switzerland's cleanliness, it raised the question if collective cleanliness does not have another side: "What lies under the immaculate surface?"

News reports revealed some rebellion. When Swiss women finally obtained federal voting rights in 1971 and equal rights ten years later, feminists denounced a systematic bent to keep them at home to polish it into a "museum of domestic stupidity." Girls began to boycott domestic science courses. One was kept in jail overnight for refusing to pay the alternative fine for non-attendance. Though cooking and housekeeping courses are still on the school program, they have been opened to boys.

Spotless hotels, trains and streets depend on foreign help for the dirty work. Because of tight quotas for foreign workers, many are here illegally and live in squalor. Real estate dealers invoke sanitary rules to tear down or convert low-rent housing into sleek high rises. Rebellious young squatters move into these abandoned buildings, taunting police to use force to evacuate them. Bulldozers have been used to raze dilapidated centers. Swift, neat and clean operations. But have they answered the underlying problems?

Modern Swiss women accuse compulsive housewives of paying too much attention to spit and polish, feeling that this cleaning mania distracts from fulfilling the real needs of a family. Does an excessive concern with surface cleanliness also distract Switzerland from the needs of people who live here?

I have come to love this spanking clean country and I wonder.

FROM HOLLYWOOD TO AN ALPINE HAMLET

by Don Wells

Employing somewhat of a Bruce Springsteen-type lyrical statement, I WAS born in the USA and raised in a 'tough-man cow town'. It was John Steinbeck's birthplace in California, Salinas. It sits at one lush agricultural end of the locale of one of his noted books, THE LONG VALLEY.

Augmenting the cowboys and their cattle were many dairymen who had migrated from Switzerland and settled there. With their frugality and a helluva lot of hard work, they built some very successful dairy enterprises. A few are still in the original family's hands.

That was then...this is now! In a 'migration reversal', my wife and I took up permanent residence in another 'cow town' - a Swiss village where those milk-delivering animals are as vital to the economy as they are in California.

When I reached 65 and began retirement after a lengthy career of broadcasting professional sports, my wife and I decided to join our son and his family in Switzerland. We had lost our ever-so-loving and multi-talented Swiss daughter-in-law to the ravages of cancer. Therefore we wanted to erase a 6,000 mile separation and be able to watch our grandsons grow. Our friends in the United States understood our mission but that didn't ease the oh-so-many tearful farewells.

This decision meant that, late in life, we would be thrusting ourselves into an entirely different life-style. At first Switzerland seemed to be a half-dozen light years removed from all we had possessed and cherished back home. We had enjoyed Los Angeles, despite all its smog-saturation and bumper-to-bumper traffic. Because of our earlier visits to the Swiss village of Aeschi, we were partially prepared. However, this time, it would not be just another vacation. This move had all the permanence of the Jungfrau mountain!

One of the immediate needs in dealing with such a transition is to make every effort to eliminate impatient American attitudes. They can lead to what I classify as the 'O-Level' of conduct. 'O' for obnoxiousness, a label that fits many American 'invaders' and other aggravating *Ausländers*. That leads to another adjustment

47

need of ignoring what some of your traveling friends may have said about the Swiss: that they are a 'difficult' people, too 'stand-offish', not very accommodating and, oftentimes, as cold as their winter weather. During our initial visit, it took us only a day and a half to discover there wasn't any truth to those assessments.

Accepting and respecting the customs of your 'new land' is a must, especially in villages. In hamlets everywhere in this world, gossip is the 'nectar of the nosy' and my wife and I have made it a policy not to supply any subject matter.

Exhibiting a feeling of friendliness, mixed with a sense of humor, is vital no matter where you travel or ultimately reside. As an example, my wife easily generated laughter in her initial and repeat visits to village shops when she would come in contact with products she had never dealt with before. That's when, in her early and limited use of the native language, she openly made fun of herself for not being more knowledgeable. She would begin to laugh - and shop employees would do the same - not in a belittling way but in warm appreciation of an outsider making every effort to learn how to become part of their community.

On the subject of humor, I have to relate what we encountered upon registering with the US Embassy in Berne. With the return of our passports, they also included a listing of American and Swiss-American organizations. I'm sure many of these serve worthwhile purposes. However, there was one entry I found hard to believe or take too seriously. I beg the forgiveness of its founder but I still have to laugh at the thought of a 'Sons of the American Revolution Society' existing in Switzerland with fifteen members and listing its major purpose for existence as "being patriotic". What a wacky world!

There are many Americans who dislike having their country criticized. To me, those are the tunnel-vision, we're-right-and-you're-wrong types. That's a frame of mind that requires some sensible adjustment. One of our friends, who teaches English and other languages in the village secondary school, is a sometimes slightly overheated critic of the United States' foreign policy and other matters. For me, mentally 'fencing' with Franz is a refreshment. Of course, in our spirited exchanges, I don't hesitate to point out Switzerland's problems, for ours is a world without any lily-white countries. Despite our occasional disagreements, Franz and I share the hope that the village bomb shelter will remain as empty tomorrow as it is today!

Speaking of bomb shelters, my wife and I never thought a home of ours would include one, but now we have a *Luftschutzkeller*. Many years ago, they were 'panic popular' in the United States because of uneasy relations with the Soviet Union, but that was short-lived. Many people here in Switzerland joke about this building requirement. I tell them there is no international guarantee that the future will be one of permanent peace and devoid of human errors when it comes to 'trigger fingers'. Of course, these rooms also make wonderful wine cellars!

During my wife's first days in her Swiss kitchen, I recall how she contemplated the preparation of a beef entree, *Einfache Burgunderplätzli*, as the culinary delight of the evening. It's a heavenly dish but she discovered you can go through hell in the kitchen trying, for the first time, to determine the ingredients and quantities involved. An 8.6 on her Richter Scale of 'earthquake emotion' was created by 'messing' with the metric system for the first time, after a lengthy lifetime of using a half pound of this, two cups of that and an ounce of whatever. When she reached the height of frustration, I didn't blame her for closing her *Kochbuch*, sitting back and enjoying a *Wodka mit Eis*!

Those frustrations were also eased by the helpfulness of others and an accumulation of friends. So many times during confusing language situations, someone will suddenly appear at your elbow and volunteer translation help. That has then led to even more friendships. In the bewildering language department, I have some knowledge of French but Swiss-German or German poses countless problems. Fortunately, there are some English and German word similarities that help at trying times and 'sign language' aids as well. However, there are times when I feel like Marcel Marceau pantomiming my need for perhaps a personal hygiene product. That's when I hope some of my more dramatic gestures won't be misinterpreted.

In the cleanliness of Disneyland in Southern California, people will go out of their way to deposit trash in receptacles. However, once they leave those immaculate grounds, there is no limit to what they dispose of on streets and beaches. Now my wife and I are residing in an environmental Eden. It is especially clean here in the

Berner Oberland. Swiss self-discipline may fail occasionally but I can't help admiring their spotlessness. A young friend's profession deals with what humans do to mistreat the quality of water and what can be done to eliminate those crimes against nature. Maintaining the purity of water is an endless study for Adrian and others in Switzerland. This world of trash-littered lakes and polluted beaches overburdened with mankind's refuse can learn much from what the Swiss have been able to accomplish in a variety of environmental matters.

We have to walk nimbly and cautiously, however, on Swiss cow-*Strassen*. Those massive milk-wagon animals with their quadruple faucets dispensing nature's perfect food seem to disdain neatness. Their souvenirs are dropped indiscriminately, making visual alertness a must. As children in America playing baseball in farmers' fields, we uttered the warning cry: "Watch out where you're steppin' for that ain't second base!" When the Swiss farmers march their often-meandering animals to different alpine altitudes at different seasons of the year, the village streets and sidewalks suffer the blight. Some side-stepping pedestrian skills are needed.

My wife and I are occasionally asked about homesickness and how much we miss life in the United States. Our policy has been to never look back for too long. However, there have been interesting reminders. One day, our youngest grandson was playing his home computer sports game. Outdoors, it was snowing. Indoors, he was skateboarding in sunny Southern California. Serving as a colorful background on the small computer screen was the famed Hollywood sign. I had worked almost in its shadow for many years. Another surprising reminder of what we had left behind came when a class in the village secondary school (all twelve students, with no help from their teacher) staged 'American Day' in the *Gemeindesaal*. American flags were flying. There were text and photo exhibits ranging from politics to aviation, space travel and the history of the American Indian, sports, National Parks and even the world of Walt Disney. To complete the treat, a disco featured music from the US and, in a classroom converted into a café, they sold hot dogs, hamburgers and apple pie! What a treat those very imaginative Swiss youngsters had created!

Although I have always felt shackled to lower levels, I have long admired those alpinists who have successfully challenged the sheer face of the Eiger or muscled and maneuvered their way up the

Matterhorn. Some ignore the more precipitous peaks and seek a less treacherous way of spending a few hours in the solitude and splendor of a high-altitude Alpine scene. A friend in our village is one of those. Recently, he asked if, one day, I might join him and take a look at life from above, far removed from the world's confusion, cacophony, chaos and clutter. I thanked Edi for the invitation. I told him that climbing stairs is challenge aplenty for this ex-resident of sea-level Los Angeles. It helps me avoid the *Bergkrankheit*, mountain sickness. Actually, I still prefer escalators!

In our village there is an honor system of sorts that is rarely dishonored. I am referring to the high respect people have here for property belonging to others. I see merchandise displayed in the open, without all the surveillance systems I was accustomed to in the United States. Infants are left unattended in prams at shops while mothers go about their buying business. Motor-bikes and bicycles are left unsecured and autos unlocked. Coats hang on common racks in restaurants. These would all be open invitations to crime in my old hometown!

On many occasions in the village, I have been aware of one particular passer-by, an elderly lady. To me, she seems to typify the spirit of the Swiss, their drive and their determination. A white cloche snugly fits her head like a fresh 'hat' of snow perched on the peak of the nearby Morgenberghorn. This wee, heavily wrinkled and seemingly fragile figure walks not with ease but with obvious determination. With all the passing years, her body has been bent to withstand the winds of life's challenges. She pauses on Zwygartenstrasse and, with her cane, begins to probe some fallen leaves. Is it a coin she sees? A shimmering stone? Or, a rusted key to a trove of treasure? It is a search without satisfaction but the frustration will not be a deterrent. There will be other inquisitive times. In a sense, all our existences are conducted in such a fashion as we poke our canes into life's many riddles and mysteries and hope for rewarding discoveries.

My wife and I plan to continue our 'search' in Switzerland. It has already been rewarding, thanks to our family and thanks to the friends we have already made here and thanks to our confidence that there will be a growing number of new friends in the future.

'Tis a grand place to spend the golden years of our lives!

SWEEPING DIFFERENCES

by Gay Scott O'Connor

God must be an optimist. No-one else would have dared to create people in so many different colours. For with the joy of diversity comes the risk of prejudice. Did He foresee ghastly systems like apartheid? I don't know. But I'm willing to bet that when He got to creating Swiss mothers-in-law and their sons' Jamaican wives, He must have had an inkling that some sort of segregation might be advisable, if only to keep the peace. Separate, but equal. Or separate but not equal. No-one is quite as equal as a Swiss mother-in-law.

Being a daughter-in-law can be tricky at the best of times. But become daughter-in-law to a Swiss polisher and you've lost before you start. If my own mother-in-law had to complete a 'least wanted' list, a Jamaican *Schwiegertochter* would top it, ahead of leprosy, lockjaw, and ring-around-the-collar. You name it, I couldn't do it right.

I arrived in Switzerland with nothing more than good intentions and woefully ill-equipped to deal with Swiss domestic reality. Nothing mattered but being a good *Hausfrau*, which I certainly wasn't. (If the kids saw me cleaning up, they asked who was coming.) But I had many other qualities. Surely they counted? No, they didn't, and what's more, they seemed to add insult to injury. My mother-in-law said I had been wrongly educated. Study was not good for girls. What mattered were scrubbing, polishing and crocheting. She told me I came from the jungle, an accusation that sat oddly with the charge of my being over-educated. The way I brought the kids up was wrong too but here her arguments were particularly eccentric. She disapproved of the drinking of plain water and prophesied dire diseases and inflammation of the kidneys unless it was flavoured with sinister-looking teas, or, idiotically, a tooth-rotting syrup. And the same woman who abused me for not washing my floors daily, objected to my bathing the kids every night. She said it was neurotic and possibly unhealthy and what was wrong with once a week? Some people's priorities defy comprehension.

I remember the day my mother-in-law discovered I was planning to get a dishwasher. She made a rapid tally of all the females living in our house and came up with a grand total of five: two pre-school daughters, two indolent Jamaican cousins, and me. This, she stated flatly, made a dishwasher unnecessary. Had the house been full of BOYS she might have excused it. But with so many girls, no. Dishwashing was our duty. To refuse was to be unfeminine. I got the impression that God had spent most of the pre-Eden period designing girls for just this activity and that even incompetent Jamaicans should shrink from trying to frustrate divine purpose.

Before battle lines could be fully drawn up, one of our recurrent family disasters intervened and the dishwasher had to be postponed. Two years later, oh joy, I finally got my dishwasher. I have lived hand in hand with it ever since and if we ever had to part I would go back to Jamaica and make the kids eat off banana leaves. Oddly enough, and in the face of my mother-in-law's theories, not-washing-up hasn't made me feel unfeminine. Actually, I feel more feminine than ever. I would ask her about this, but unfortunately we are no longer on such terms.

I have heard through the grapevine, however, that her attitude to dishwashers has mellowed. She now lives alone in a spanking new flat with a nondescript dog and has a magnificent dishwasher all to herself. What she does with it I do not know. Perhaps, like the bathtub, it is used once a week.

Looking back, I must concede that my mother-in-law's best effort, and the one which most neatly summed up her opinion of Jamaicans in general, was the day she pointedly offered a black friend of ours a banana. (Perhaps I should explain that I am white. Yes Virginia, there are white Jamaicans. And not only black and white and brown ones, but Chinese and Indian ones too. We like it that way.)

It's probably easier being a white Jamaican in Switzerland than a black one. I'm sure my welcome would have been even bleaker had I arrived trailing coffee-coloured offspring. My friend Maureen, who is black, got so tired of people asking her if she was a prostitute or a go-go dancer that she finally left. The fact that she was an attractive young black woman seemed, in many austere Swiss eyes, to preclude her being anything else. I've never had this problem.

No-one has ever accused me of being a prostitute. Not even my mother-in-law.

But there are drawbacks, nevertheless. I get very homesick not only for the place, but also for the mentality in which I grew up. But because I'm not black, people find it difficult to believe I really am Jamaican. I, apparently, have no excuse for being so different, so tropical, so disreputably non-Swiss. My falling short of Swiss standards is even more harshly judged than Maureen's. I don't know what the answer is. Perhaps I should be zebra-striped.

I ache to go home, to see my family. But where, after seventeen Swiss years, is home? And where, oh Lord, is my family? My Jamaican relatives, like fleas, have got everywhere. My father and a mixed bag of relations still hold the fort in Jamaica. But the rest? At present a good handful of cousins enliven Toronto, a few more have overflowed to Calgary, while my sister and her sons flourish in upstate New York. Cross the Atlantic, and England is generously sprinkled with relatives from London to Norfolk, while my dearest cousin Bronny, targeted for washing-up all those years ago by my mother-in-law in my Swiss kitchen, is now married to a policeman in Wales where she has two children. And a dishwasher.

So where would I go? The children, after all, have grown up here. And I too, after so many years, have hacked out my own little niche in the rock of Swiss tradition. Some time ago the local school hired a new handicrafts teacher. The day she arrived she tracked my daughters down in the playground. ''So!'' she cried triumphantly, ''You are the two with the mother WHO CAN'T KNIT!'' Maybe I should give autographs.

My mother-in-law and I have survived each other, but only just. Our differences are far more basic than those of nationality. Not all Swiss women today are prepared to limit their horizons to their kitchen sinks. But the *Hausfrauen* are still the majority and a woman's worth too frequently judged by her ability to sweep and scrub. What a shame! Life is too short and too precious to be squandered waging war on dust. After all, to a sympathetic eye, even dust has its uses. Had there been no dust in Eden for God to work with, none of us would have been created in the first place.

CAWFEE AND *RÖSTI*

by Susan Tuttle-Laube

I was born in New Jersey to a Swiss father and, by birthright, a German mother. But my mother grew up in New 'Joyzee' which becomes evident when she is 'tawking', making 'cawfee', or going to see a movie at the 'thayater'. Nevertheless, she makes *Rösti, Fleischkäse* and *Bauernbrot* for my father when he's home on Saturdays watching baseball on TV.

I never gave much thought to my multi-national background. In the States lots of people can lay claim to a mix of cultures in their home life. I considered myself American. But somehow I became curious about my Swiss roots, about this nationality I possessed complete with a red passport and a *Heimatort* simply because my father was Swiss. I moved to Switzerland.

Armed with a little high school German and a name with authentic ethnic origins, I quickly realized that I needed more to break into a culture which I had thought belonged somewhat to me. My American-ness, even though somewhat softened by the European base of my upbringing, suddenly became an issue worthy of every neighbor's attention. In Switzerland they regarded me as *Fremde*, a foreigner.

Things got a bit complicated when I, as a Swiss who had grown up in America, fell in love with an American who had, coincidentally, been brought up in Switzerland. Everyone had always thought he was Swiss so when we got married they presumed I had become Swiss only through him. Trying to clarify this at times was often very confusing. Our friends laughed and called us the 'odd couple' - a Swiss who could hardly speak a Swiss language marrying an American who had always passed as a Swiss.

Now after nine years, I get along pretty well with the language. I can read the newspapers and carry on a conversation in Swiss-German. But sometimes there is a catch in the level of my understanding. It SEEMS as if I'm quite fluent at times. That will then give the person who is speaking to me the confidence to rattle on, forgetful that my language skills might be lagging behind a bit. Then I have to concentrate to catch the surface meaning and I may not be able to grasp any deeper significance of their intonation or choice of words.

Sometimes having to clarify the meaning of what someone is telling me is to my advantage. I may only want to ask what a word means and check that I understood something correctly. But my questions are often misinterpreted as much deeper interest in whatever topic is at hand. People appreciate that. They like me because this gives them the impression that I'm a very good listener.

But being liked for being a good listener (to Frau Müller's latest illness and Frau Schmidt's problem with the *Waschküche* schedule) is not as rewarding as being liked for who you are. This is difficult because I just don't feel like myself when I speak German. I'm not aware of my accent in German but I know those listening to me are. How does it change their impression of me? I dread the idea of sounding 'cute' with my errors. I don't want to be tedious or make people have to work hard to understand me.

I can't be very humorous or spontaneous in German and I can't seem to include subtle nuances of meaning. I'm restricted to communication in a basic form, void of personal touches. I suspect that true fluency includes one's personality as well as one's linguistic skills. I do not feel I am that fluent yet. Is it possible to reach this level in a foreign language? The union of thought and word is comfortably and intimately rooted in my mind in English. Even if I could lay claim to fluency in another language, my true vehicle of expression would still be English. And American English at that. Living here with another language is like being put in exile.

Written expression is also very important to me. I like to write, to pick out an image, an idea or an object, bring it to some poetic light and then let my readers have the pleasant surprise of identification as they suddenly realize that they've seen that, been there or felt the same once. The reader of what I write is an essential part of my writing. When I wrote in America, I depended on the audience sharing with me a common bank of knowledge, feelings and experiences from which I could draw my inspiration.

But for whom do I write in Switzerland? What do I share with my audience here that I can offer them back in prose or poetry? Writing as an American in Switzerland, I would always be the foreigner. Can I write as a Swiss for the Swiss in English? I am still the foreigner.

Is it language alone which perpetuates this feeling of 'foreigness'? Or is there something else to it? How does one get 'in'? It seems as if language could be blamed for a lot of my troubles with expression, being understood and understanding. But perhaps the real root of the problem lies in having two cultures without calling either one home. Maybe I really am a Swiss who has simply been away too long and sometimes I realize that I'm not letting Switzerland in for cawfee or for *Rösti*. The American voice inside me says, "Come on in, the door's open!" But my Swiss voice says, "Do I know you?"

*****

When our son Lucas was 12 days old, I packed him into a *Snuggli* and 'went public'. An old woman on the sidewalk walked up to me and peered into the *Snuggli*. I obligingly lifted Lucas' hat a bit so that she could see him better. With a clucking sound she shook her head and pronounced with all authority that I was crippling the child for life. I was shattered. What did I know? What else was I doing wrong?

Well, his hands were too cold or too warm and I shouldn't prop him up like that in the carriage. I should disinfect before nursing and weigh him before and after to be sure he got enough. Keep him out of drafts but nap him outside. And I was unable to catch onto the idea of putting underpants over the diaper (under the tights). Was the idea to train him (at 8 weeks old) to wear underpants? It reminded me somehow of training bras.

The months passed and I adapted to my surroundings, my baby and the peculiarities of Swiss motherhood. Then, on a visit back to the States I horrified my female friends and relatives with my Swiss ways. "Solids at three months?!? He sleeps on a SHEEP SKIN?! And why is a BOY wearing tights?" I was saying "hoop-la" for "whoopsy-daisy" and "goo-goos" for "peek-a-boo". An American failure. One friend confidentially asked if they had pediatricians OVER THERE. I suppose it's the new mother's plight to have lots of advice to add to the insecurities. But on two continents no less!

Fortunately Lucas' goos and gurgles helped bridge any gap HE may have been experiencing. And that did it for me too.

TANGIBLES AND INTANGIBLES

by Steven Gregoris

The first things you notice are the intangibles. It 'feels' different, things 'aren't the same'. But then it becomes familiar: the neighbours; the sharp, focussed Alps on a clear morning; train schedules; the Michettis arguing upstairs. You locate yourself. And when you're no longer a stranger to your environment, you begin to feel at home. I call this my initiation, and, like all cultural and political processes here, it is taking a long time.

It all began, from a purely practical point of view, with the first task we had here: getting an apartment. Despite the fact that my wife is Swiss, "foreigner with cat" tends to wipe out any plus points fairly quickly. People with very foreign-sounding names like mine either serve Swiss customers in Swiss restaurants and hotels, or serve Swiss customers in restaurants in their own country, where the pay is lower.

About a month after having arrived and naively answering a zillion ads for apartments in a tight market, we got one. Under the counter. The boyfriend of a colleague of my sister-in-law's was moving out of his very cheap apartment to go to Zurich. It was a one-bedroom, smallish place, simple, and would we like to come and have a look? We were there the next night.

I remember the tangibles pretty well. A fridge the size of a hat-box; the washroom bigger but without a tub, shower, sink or electrical outlet, just a toilet (but brand new!); running water in the kitchen only; hammock hooks in the living room walls. Okay, I said to myself, how does one wash, pray tell? Down we went into the basement, which was a lot like a cave - damp, dark, the sound of dripping water - except for the floor, which was poured concrete. We felt our way into an adjacent cave that opened into an unfinished bathroom. It had what the upstairs one didn't: a tap, hot-and-cold running water, a big porcelain sink waiting to be installed, and a shiny new medicine cabinet complete with electrical outlet. At the end of the narrow, whitewashed room was the shower.

In this dog-eat-owner world, if the price is right, so are the goods; we moved in three weeks later. Now it feels like we've been in a movie: young couple moves into grotty flat and a few scenes later

- presto! - the place is warm and bright and livable. Except it's been five years. But we ARE at home here now, my initiation plodding along like the legislation of a left-wing initiative.

One day while we were puttering around the place fairly aimlessly, a man knocked at our door, which happens to be odd for two reasons. First, the door to the house could be, and often is, mistaken for a door that might lead into someone's front hall or living room. We occupy the second floor of the house, above Madelaine and below the Michettis, so the man had obviously braved the image and ascended, seeking us. Outside of our friends, the only people that find us are Jehovah's Witnesses and the mailman. The man who knocked was alone (couldn't be the former) and didn't have a uniform on (or the latter). He was wearing a drab, baggy, military-looking coat and was smiling. With his eyes.

It turned out he was a member of the Aare Valley Ornithological Association and wasn't selling Christmas cards. What he did have were a few questions about the history of our house. Apparently, the bird-watchers were putting together an exhibition on this part of the valley and needed some information. This wasn't an everyday occurrence; we invited him in for coffee.

He pulled out two blown-up, aerial photographs of our neighbourhood taken sometime early this century. The big difference was that it was a real neighbourhood then, not merely part of a uniform urban sprawl. Wide open fields surrounding a tight cluster of nine eclectic houses, the crescent-shaped street defining them like a lasso. Ours, the ninth, was just being finished, squeezed in on one corner. Construction had been halted, and because of the uncertain date of the picture, it may have been the First World War that caused the stoppage.

Our ornithologist told us that this grouping was called the *Negerli-Quartier*, which set it apart socially as well as architecturally. It housed nurses and orderlies working at the psychiatric hospital that our town is, well, let's say known for. The nine are unique, not only because of their age, but because they are all constructed in different styles and stand out among boxy, concrete low-rises and neat, practically identical single-family dwellings. Our number 51 rises up like a gaunt tower, somewhat ramshackle, and even looks a little mysterious on a full-moon night. But just a little.

A lot of different people live in the *Negerli-Quartier*. Two houses down from us lives a gardener who has three long hothouses full of constantly blooming flowers where his front lawn should be. There is also a man who never smiles; he winces every time you say something to him, as if he were in constant pain. He belongs to a religious sect and has a kind of Frankenstein leg he can't bend at the knee. And he spends his days in his basement-cum-garage weaving wicker baskets. His wife does the shopping with her slow, heavy, three-speed bicycle and their son is getting married and moving out this summer.

Behind us are the Garden People, who rent our front yard and have turned it into a vegetable garden. Their own front yard is a vegetable garden, too, and their backyard has been paved over and a concrete garage plunked down (neatly) in one corner. They spend hours dealing with stones, snails, weeds and hoeing. At appropriate junctures in the growing season, Mr. Garden sprays his potatoes and cabbages with a copper solution, a source of some dissention. Then there's Walter, the retired carpenter, who has a complete workshop in his garage, who calls everybody by their first name and stops the garbagemen on Fridays and invites them in for a beer, which they never refuse. Or Hans, who's an orderly at the hospital and twice a day, without fail, rings his bicycle bell when he gets in front of the house so Elsbeth will know he's home. Their son is a chimney sweep and plays hockey, and Karin, their daughter, always has boyfriends with very impressive cars.

Two and half hours after he had come, the bird-watcher thanked us for having given him coffee, cake and no useful information whatsoever. He had knocked on our door because Madelaine wasn't home.

If we hadn't been home, he probably would have gone up another flight of stairs and met the Michettis, who came from southern Italy 25 years ago and are still very much southern Italians. They spend hundreds of francs on telephone calls, mostly to their eldest son, who lives with an aunt in Italy. He has recently finished his military service, has a steady job and is engaged to a lovely Italian girl whose father is a doctor, I'm told. All is well.

Mrs. Michetti, who must be no more than half an inch over official midget height and whose body churns her ahead a good twelve inches a step, cooks rich Italian food. Always. Every day. Lots of olive oil and butter, garlic, basil and rosemary. This is reflected in

Enrico's body. Enrico is eighteen and lives with his parents. He once broke his leg because he lost his balance and fell down. Husband Dino, who is surprisingly thin, breeds canaries in his spare time. Last year he managed to hatch three eggs and had five wonderfully delicate birds singing at the top of their tiny lungs. But then the Michettis went on their annual pilgrimage to the old country. They only go second class and don't reserve *couchettes* for the 24-hour trip. I once asked them why not. The answer, it seems, is tradition: they've never reserved *couchettes* before. North Americans, I keep getting told, have no sense of tradition. Dino has, however, made one concession to modern-day travel; he now reserves seats.

Well, the Michettis went down to Gran Sasso d'Italia and, as always, asked someone in the house to take care of their canaries. Madelaine, who is conscientious, makes no noise, lives alone on the ground floor, loves to play board games and is Swiss, was asked to look after the plants and birds. That's tradition, too: she always does it. But what she did this time that she'd never done before was to forget to feed either the plants or the canaries for about a week and a half. The plants survived; the canaries didn't. This caused some consternation. The Michettis returned as the Michettis do, loaded with wine, oil, cured meats, cheese, more wine, hot sausages in jars of oil tucked away in socks, a ghetto blaster, a folding bicycle and a new birdcage. Their anger and sadness were short-lived, as Madelaine tells it, and before long things were on an even keel again.

Dino and Giulia and Enrico are realists, and Dino just made up his mind to try again this coming breeding season. Madelaine bought them a new pair of mates, and Dino has been busy cleaning out the spacious new birdcage. They have, after all, been here for 25 years.

The Michettis are also the official heralds of Christmas. It begins when they begin celebrating. They invited us up again at Christmas this year. Once upstairs, we sat down to coffee and thick slices of panettone. But this time I noticed a new something on a crocheted doily on the glass-topped coffee table: a small, plastic duck with an oversized beak standing near a gold-coloured treasure chest. When I asked about it, Dino eagerly gave a demonstration. He pressed a hidden button and the duck slid forward. Out of the chest a drawer full of cigarettes opened, the duck bent over, plucked one out with its beak, and slid back. We all got a kick out of it, especially Giulia, who giggled wildly and told us to eat more panettone.

It isn't the only plaything they have in their home. Their one-bedroom apartment is chock-full of technology. The Michettis own 2 TV sets, 2 VCRs, 2 tape deck/stereo systems (one with a built-in miniature TV), a portable oven and a video camera, not counting the tape deck and radio in Enrico's room. My wife thinks that by buying all these things, they're satisfying a desire to turn their earnings into something tangible, something more concrete than a bankbook to show for their toil. But there seems to be something else hidden amidst the toggle switches, hospitality and aroma of strong coffee.

In the course of the evening, Dino repeats something he's said a hundred times before - that when they go back for good they'll be taking all this with them to southern Italy. As we sit in their apartment, the only one on the street with Christmas lights blinking out onto the neighbours' houses like wondering eyes, I can't help saying to myself: "Not when, Dino, but if you ever go back for good."

For all their 'foreignness', the Michettis belong to the initiated. They belong here just as much as the Man-With-The-Frankenstein-Leg, or the Garden People. They're part of a world my home is in, a world where tangibles gradually dissolve like cubes of sugar in hot tea. Where 'things' aren't different or the same any more. They just are. Like sweet tea.

スイスの屋根の下で

UNDER THE SWISS ROOF

by Masako S. Uzawa

Intercultural marriages inevitably bring a lot of foreigners like me into Switzerland. A random sampling of official marriage announcements in the newspaper will confirm that about 20% of the Swiss marry a foreigner. Foreign marriage partners, men or women, used to come from neighbouring countries, with few exceptions. Presently, the marriage market has broadened to all over Europe, North and South America, and further to the Far East. Japanese wives are old-timers by now. More exotic types, Vietnamese, Philippinos and even Africans are being brought into Switzerland as wives.

Once an elderly, single Swiss woman teased me, "You foreign women take all our men away." What could I say but "Sorry, I did not mean to..?" I never intended to be a threat to their marriage market. Nor did I consider myself as part of social or political issues later.

When I came to Switzerland in 1959 there were only two other Japanese women in Basle who had married Swiss men. We were rare specimens. People were curious about us and wondered where in the world we came from. They adored our *siidige* (cute) children and even a customs officer asked my husband where he had met me, adding "although it's none of my business." Those were the good old days. As the number of foreign wives increased, I lost my popularity. So did our children, although they luckily regained their fame for being exotic beauties as teenagers.

As I look back, I was upgraded from *Fremde* (stranger) to *Ausländerin* (foreigner) around 1970 when Japan became familiar to the Swiss through the Winter Olympics in Sapporo. Swiss victory has reflected its glory upon me too. Being born near Sapporo, I earned some recognition. Now, with economic advancements, the Japanese image has changed from cheap toys "made in Japan" to sophisticated cars, cameras, etc. Business people began to come to Switzerland, and more Japanese women married Swiss.

There are now about 60 Japanese families living in Basle. In about half of these, both partners are Japanese, with the husband working either for Swiss or Japanese companies located here. These couples are here temporarily and will eventually go back to Japan and not crowd up Swiss territory. Six couples are made up of Japanese husbands and Swiss wives. There are about 20 families with Swiss husbands and Japanese wives where the Swiss men might have believed in the old, perhaps a bit out-dated saying, "Chinese food, Japanese wife, American salary and European house make the luckiest man." Times have changed and so have the roles of many wives.

Once a sympathetic neighbour asked me, "Don't you get home-sick?" I was amazed myself at my own spontaneous response, "No, not really, my home is here where my husband and children are." My after-thought was that it had taken me ten years of apprenticeship to utter such a statement. Occasional outbursts of acute homesickness have with time turned into a kind of dull chronic nostalgia. I shouldn't admit it, but my nostalgia is gastro-nomic, as I see Japanese islands in all forms of fish in my day-dreams. My husband tells me man does not live by bread alone and in Switzerland there is always cheese to go with it. In the beginning I reacted to cheese as many Swiss may react to eating raw fish. I have survived hundreds of well-meant *Fondue* and *Raclette* parties over the years. Now I've even developed a taste for cheese.

One of the problems for Japanese wives is that we miss seafood in this landlocked mountainous country. We are 'in the same boat', feeling like fish out of water sometimes. This mutuality brings us together in camaraderie. When our husbands are away on military duty, we get spurts of creative impulses and use the few ingredients available here to cook up 'fishy' dishes which may be unpalatable to our husbands. These dinners are our gastro-psychological holi-days when we chat about everything under the Helvetian sun.

Although I became Swiss by marriage, for a long time I felt like a guest in this country. I wanted to be a gracious one with plenty of *Grüezi's, Merci viilmol's, Exgysi's* and lots of small talk on weather or compliments about babies. I think I began to feel more at home once I made a conscious effort to establish contacts with my neighbours. Many times I started chatting on trains to break the dead silence, and that seemed to open the door for friendly conversation. Now I realize that the Swiss may not have the courage to talk to me because they assume I don't understand their language. Besides, now I know that until recently many Swiss have been brought up not to speak unless spoken to. But once I have taken the initiative, they often start talking to me in English and soon we are exchanging our life stories.

Tourist offices in Switzerland have found out about me and other Japanese wives who have lived here a long time and manage the language fairly well. They round us up and brand us as interpreters and guides to herd Japanese tourists around Switzerland. This keeps us busy, away from tedious housework, and enables us to earn a bit of financial independence. No tourists are so curious as the studious Japanese. Their 'Study Tours' include going to fairs and exhibitions, touring Swiss firms, farms, kindergartens, old people's homes, even cemeteries and especially, of course, chocolate and cheese factories. I might not have been to many other places of interest in Switzerland if it were not for these excursions.

I have lost count of the times I have shown Japanese tourists the Jungfrau and the Matterhorn in the clouds or a snow storm. The Japanese spend their hard-earned lifetime savings to see their dream of the Jungfrau or Matterhorn in reality. I realize it is their first time, last time and once-in-a-lifetime trip. What can I say to them when their dreams are hidden behind clouds?

Whenever an issue occurs pitting Japan against Switzerland, I find myself taking the Swiss side, contrary to what I used to do. Sometimes it requires quick and witty explanations to answer all the questions curious tourists put to me. How am I to explain Swiss timing, for instance, when a Swiss train is late? "You see, this is an international train from Milan to Amsterdam. The Swiss railway cannot prevent delays in Italy or other countries." Another tourist who was shocked by the toilets on Swiss trains exclaimed, "But I thought the Swiss had a high standard of living!" I tried my best to pacify him, "It's nature preservation due to natural organic fertilizer!"

Among many other excursions that made a Swiss out of me was an agricultural trip. I accompanied a Japanese professor to visit Swiss and other European farms. I learned about the importance of Swiss agriculture with regard to national political economics, especially in relation to the European Common Market. Since then

I buy Swiss products even though they are more expensive than imported goods. Now that my children have flown away from my parental wings, I can afford to be patriotic, a precious matter in Switzerland.

A few years ago, a small group of Japanese women came to Basle. It was a pilgrimage to study Johann Jakob Bachofen, whose *'Mutterrecht'* (Mothers' Rights) in 1861 marked the beginning of studies on women's rights. I had not heard much about him before in Basle and I re-imported more information about him from the Japanese researchers than they got from me. A week with this group, however, going around tracing the footsteps of Bachofen, was a study tour for me. I learned interesting facts about ancient Roman settlements and translated old documents about the renowned silk-ribbon families of Basle. Since then I have become very interested in the history of Basle. Perhaps I've even become a bit of a *Baslerin* myself.

That's the way life has been for me under the Swiss roof. Swiss people seem reserved at first and hesitant to make friends. But once you get to know them they may turn out to be your life-long friends. Japan has somehow faded away to become a dearly remembered place, a childhood memory. I like to visit occasionally for old times' sake. Each time I go back to Japan I realize just how Swiss I have become. I don't know whether I have changed or whether life in Japan has changed - probably both. I feel lost as a stranger in the labyrinths of the rushy subways in Tokyo. When I come back to Switzerland, I feel at home again.

MUSICAL CHAIRS
by Drew Keeling

Carmen stretched and yawned. The endless cascade of baggage passed her bleary eyes. PanColumbian had left JFK three hours late and now it seemed to be taking forever for her bags to appear.

She gazed, through the glass partition, at the rest of the airport terminal and felt a surge of enthusiasm rouse her from drowsiness. Minutes away lay Zurich; bedazzling mixture of Finance, Power, and Discretion. Mexico City, despite its larger size, seemed a barbaric village by comparison, although it would always be home.

"Hi Carmen."

She looked up at the young, bearded, All-American athlete next to her. "Oh, good morning ... uuh.."

"Dave."

"Right ... uuh ... from LA?" she half-remembered.

"You got it! But now it's 'Engadine, here I come!'"

They had met only the night before at JFK's check-in when she had laughed out loud at the sight of him struggling under his expedition-sized backpack with criss-crossed cross-country skis strapped to it. He had noticed her long dark hair and green eyes which flashed determination.

"Tired?" he asked with a smile.

"Yes," she laughed. "Too excited to sleep. It's hard to believe I'm going to be a Swiss banker. After Zurich you can go anywhere: London, Paris, Tokyo, New York. If my friends could see 'little Carmencita' now. But where is my PC?"

The baggage conveyor belt had come to what uncomfortably appeared to be a final stop. Dave's skis were also missing. They filled out the forms at Lost and Found, walked through customs and sat down in the airport restaurant for coffee, awaiting the next PanColumbian flight (scheduled to contain her personal computer and his skis).

67

"Can't wait to try out my waxable skis here," declared Dave whose real passion was 'long-distance mountain running'. "The Evolution Valley Open four years ago really got me hooked," he reminisced. "The LeMarck Col drop-off was a killer but the boulder-hopping and snow-chute glissading were awesome. The Swiss are really starting to get into the long distance stuff now, you know, and there's a radical shortage of experienced trainers."

Carmen got up to phone her Swiss uncle. She had spent summers with him during high school. It was he who had arranged to get her the new job at Creditvereingesellschaft Bank in Zurich which would start next week. She returned as Dave was ordering refills of coffee.

The restaurant was then suddenly swamped by a deluge of attaché cases and pin-striped suits from a rescheduled Ecu Airways flight. A young couple appeared from the other direction. He was a well-groomed, dark-complexioned man whose only stylistic inexactitude was the calculator bulging in his breast pocket. She was a tall blonde whose long legs took rapid strides towards the two remaining empty seats at Dave and Carmen's table. *"Sinds noo freie?"* asked the man, struggling to hide a British accent.

"Yes, yes, please sit down," answered Carmen whose Swiss uncle had not only taught her Swiss-German dialect, but also how to instantly distinguish native-English-speakers from all other Swiss-dialect-attempting foreigners.

Carmen and Dave introduced themselves to Mohamed (the well-dressed dark man) and Rosemarie (the long-legged blonde) who were both waiting for the *Grenz-saität* to open so they could take the tuberculosis tests. They had both moved very recently to Zurich; Mohamed from Pakistan and Rosemarie from England. They had met, by chance, that very morning at the *Fremdenpolizei* (Aliens Police Station) where they had gone to register as new foreign residents. The *Fremdenpolizei* had instructed them in no uncertain terms to proceed immediately to the *Grenzsanität* for their TB tests, which, it was pointed out several times, were normally required of all resident foreigners PRIOR to entry into Switzerland.

Rosemarie had just graduated from Oxford in art. Her blond hair seemed to reflect her sparkling eyes. Dave found himself looking at her without listening to her.

"All my oils were shipped from Twekesbury. Lord knows when they'll arrive. Long after your bags show up, no doubt," she said, glancing at Dave and Carmen. "I'm dying to get out my canvases and start on some Alpine winterscapes."

Carmen nodded approvingly but thought, "Oh god, another bohemian. Art is such a waste of time."

Mohamed had been a computer programmer for Swiss companies in Karachi.

"The first I've met who isn't an absolutely dreadful bore," exclaimed Rosemarie in mock horror. "But that's Switzerland for you. Day after day, I'm astonished at the talented people I meet here."

Gebrueder Braun und Wyss had hired Mohamed to work in their mechanical engineering division. He tackled life the way he attacked a programming challenge - with a seemingly effortless resourcefulness. He was also quite entertaining in his imitations of airline crew speech and movements, especially his "Ladies and Gentlemen, we are now going to demonstrate how to use oxygen masks."

The four young foreigners laughed together, each thinking "What an interesting international mix of people, but after all, that's Switzerland."

"So you've only just arrived?" Rosemarie asked Carmen and Dave. "How long will you stay?"

"A year, maybe two ... long enough to learn the basics of the banking business," Carmen answered, almost perfunctorily, and looked at Dave.

"Forever, man," he said and shrugged. "Or, least I've got no intention of leaving. For mountain sports the Alps are it."

"I could stay for years too," Rosemarie continued. "It will take ages just to paint the high peaks of the Valais."

"I think I will stay not more than 18 months," offered Mohamed, matter-of-factly and put his pocket calculator into a perfectly balanced spin on the table, like a top.

There they sat: Dave, the bearded Californian and future Swiss long-distance champ and coach; Carmen, the green-eyed Mexican girl who detested art, in Zurich to get a year or two of experience before moving on to High Finance in London and New York; Rosemarie, the blond Oxford graduate who would paint the Alps forever; and Mohamed, the dark, well-dressed, gregarious computer programmer from Pakistan, on an 18-month stay.

Three rounds of coffee were finished by the time the PanColumbian flight arrived and the *Grenzsanität* opened for the afternoon shift. Before splitting the bill, they exchanged addresses.

*****

Dave stood on the Bahnhofbrücke. The dark shiny water was like smooth satin. Only where the eddies formed around the bridge pillars could you really see just how swift-flowing it was.

He thought back to his first day on that bridge, five years ago. He had walked with Rosemarie and Mohamed over the bridge the day after they'd met at the airport. They'd had lunch together.

So much had changed. With a wry smile, he recalled the thrill he had felt five years ago at breathing in the cool breeze off the lake and mountains; the thought was like the memory of an old lost sweetheart - gone, but still cherished.

He glanced at his Taiwanese watch and quickly ran to jump into the rustic, wooden interior of a number 6 tram. In five minutes he was to meet Rosemarie at Paradeplatz. They had kept in touch after their first meeting at the airport, gone skiing together several times, once even ... well, anyway, they were both leaving Switzerland next week. She was returning to England and he would be going back to the States.

When he got to Paradeplatz, Rosemarie jumped to her feet from the outdoor table at the Löwenpick Restaurant with a boisterousness that earned her an immediate stare from all surrounding restaurant patrons.

"Guess who's here," she giggled.

Dave gave her a blank stare as well.

"Look there, silly," she said, turning him around.

Carmen was coming up the steps from the pay phones at the nearby tram island. Her green eyes were still vibrant but less determined looking and her dark hair was a little shorter. Rosemarie had bumped into her unexpectedly two days before in Lucerne.

They all kissed cheeks. Carmen looked at Rosemarie and then, as if a crack in the cobblestones had just swallowed up Dave, said *"Du, i han ihn nöd chöne erreiche."*

Dave's stare at Carmen was blanker than ever. Who was she talking about?

"I tried to call Mohamed," Carmen continued as a kind of involuntary afterthought explanation, "in case he could come too." It was as though she had discovered Dave's presence again, not because of the confused look on his face, but more by accident, somehow. "He wasn't in, so I left a message on his machine."

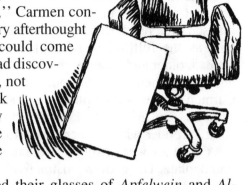

Carmen and Dave clinked their glasses of *Apfelwein* and *Albiswasser* while Rosemarie lifted her cup of coffee-con-gusto.

Carmen had left the Creditvereingesellschaft Bank after a year and started working in her Swiss boyfriend's art gallery. She never realized how classy artists can be until coming to Switzerland and would never think of ever going back to those boring, bureaucratic bankers. Clearly she had become 'swissified' and Dave had a sudden vision of going into Ursprüngli's Coffee Shop next door, looking for an empty table and walking by Carmen without recognizing her amidst the gray-haired great-aunts.

Rosemarie showed prints of her Rhone Valley paintings. "Seems like ages since I looked at these," she said. Two years ago she had discovered computer programming which was much more 'challenging' and lucrative than painting. Now she had just accepted an assignment with Grenzspringer und Co., Computer Consultants, in their new London office.

Dave then told his story: "My mountain-running career lasted only until the first event where I was disqualified for appearing in an outlandish *unerlaubte* costume. The next race was cancelled due to a totally freak blizzard. So, I taught some English, did a little part-time para-sailing and lately I've gotten into doing landscape sketches for postcards and travel posters at the tourist office. It's like, you know, a mellower way of doing the mountain scene.'' His thoughts wandered to next month's 'Bay-to-Breakers' race in San Francisco which he would run in for the first time in five years. ''I'm outta here, man,'' he proclaimed, raising his fist and narrowly missing the waiter's full-sized nose.

He gazed across Paradeplatz with a faraway look in his eyes, ignoring Carmen's rambling commentary on the latest Raeto-Romansch rock band. Rosemarie and he had been drawn to Switzerland as the fulfillment of their dreams and were now leaving instead, older and wiser. Carmen and Mohamed had come to get a leg up and then move on, outside of Switzerland. Instead it was Carmen who was now planning to stay indefinitely. ''Looks like Time has shuffled the deck for us,'' he thought, tweaking his beard, ''but I wonder what happened to Mohamed?''

As if in answer, a figure suddenly appeared at the far end of Paradeplatz. Dave knew, instinctively somehow, that it was Mohamed, even before recognizing the well-groomed looks and broad smile. Only the pocket calculator was missing.

Another round of half-embraces and then they sat down, clinked glasses and reminisced: Dave was the would-be star of mountain sports, now working in the tourist office and about to leave for an unknown future. Carmen was the would-be banker who hated art, now working in an art gallery. Rosemarie was the artist turned computer programmer. Mohamed, it turned out, was the computer programmer turned banker.

After finishing his assignment at Gebrueder Braun, the well-dressed Pakistani had worked for Banque Tigre in their EDP department from where he had then transferred to foreign exchange trading. ''Tough game these days,'' he said, ''but it's the job for me and Zurich is the place.''

''What game is my life in?'' pondered Dave out loud, groping in his pocket to double-check that his Trans Global Airlines ticket was still there. He thought to himself, ''Russian roulette or maybe 52-card-pick-up?''

''Musical chairs,'' chimed Rosemarie, returning from the Ladies Room and swooping into the chair just vacated by Mohamed who had gotten up to wave more fully at Carmen who returned the wave from the window of the nearby departing tram.

AFLOAT TOGETHER

by Ken Becker

The boat is full! So sounds the cry of alarm in certain circles, the simplest extreme when the Swiss discuss how many refugees they should accept, which ones, where from, and why. The emotional picture of the full boat implies starving or thirsting to death or even sinking altogether, the whole country and its fine Swiss population, if even the most needy, most deserving and most desirable refugees were added to the burden. It is a scenario of disaster that needs to be relativized a good deal both through calm reflection and through good humor.

It is a fact of elementary geography that any country can be full, and that if the Swiss don't put their new residents on mountaintops, their more habitable regions can indeed get cramped. Some thought the boat was full already during World War II, when the population of Switzerland was 4.2 million, a bit less than the 6 million it has today. Simple observation, on the other hand, shows that for some Swiss a street car is full when they have to sit right next to each other on a pair of seats.

One must therefore realize carefully what 'full' means to some Swiss (and not only the Swiss, of course). ''The boat is full!'' can mean ''I don't want to be in the same boat with such people'' - an extreme attitude, though unfortunately too often held - or ''I certainly don't want to get too close to them, to sit right next to them on the same bench in that boat.'' The observation in the streetcar may seem dismal to more gregarious people, but it contains a seed of hope as well: Some Swiss uneasiness about the full boat does not necessarily stem from a dislike or fear of foreigners. It may well be a special case of their basic attitudes toward all fellow human beings - even their fellow Swiss. Then the problem is that the Swiss got there first, occupied all the single, isolated seats, and so the threat of doubling up is caused by the newcomers. The fact that they are so strange and non-Swiss does compound the malaise, of course. But perhaps it is a *human* Swiss problem as much as it is in some cases an ugly racist one.

Here is where good humor, more than history and theory, can help overcome these attitudes and make a fuller boat more liveable.

After all, at a *"Fäscht"* (a festival of any sort, where at least *Bratwurst*, beer and wine and perhaps more elegant refreshments are served), where good humor and bonhomie are the purpose and order of the day, the Swiss do sit close together for hours at a time. Insight into the festival of life, as foreigners and Swiss get mixed and fermented together, may help keep up the hope and the effort to build a bigger, better boat together.

With that idea in mind I went to talk with a refugee we know, to get his experiences and impressions from living three years with the Swiss. The first time that my Swiss wife had night duty at the transition home for refugees where she works, George, a Tamil from Sri Lanka, told her, "If you have any trouble in the night, just come and knock on my door, and I'll help you." The seventy refugees, most of them young men, caused no trouble (indeed, she says they are probably better behaved than seventy Swiss young men in a home like that would be); but George became our friend. A good man to talk to, I thought - I hardly expected the interview I got!

I visited him in the small room that is his world most of the time when he is not making tasty pizzas at a pizzeria in Zurich. Once we had settled with a cup of coffee, I asked him how his life in Switzerland had been: his relationship with his boss, his customers, and other Swiss people, his experiences with the system and ways of the country.

Almost all that I got was pain. Not pain from living in Switzerland, from the way the Swiss are or how they have treated him. No, pain from what was happening at home in Sri Lanka and his longing to go back there. He poured out his grief over the relatives who have been killed, and his fear for those still alive. He told me about the fighting between the various Tamil factions, and the violence committed by Tamil organizations, the Indian occupying forces, the Sri Lankan army, and the Sinhalese People's Liberation Front; about young people who have fled into the jungle and have been hunted down and caught there, forced to join the armed groups or else killed; about how their families are harassed, beaten or even killed if the children don't serve. His family, his friends are in that situation where there is so much terror from every side, and so little hope of peace.

But how was life here in Switzerland, I asked him again. Many Swiss, especially older people, have showed concerned interest in

Sri Lanka and its troubles, he answered, and off he went again about his homeland, the torture destroying his land and his people and the torment in his heart. Even ordinary schooling is almost impossible in Tamil areas, and Sinhala is the enforced official language; hardly any Tamils are admitted to higher studies or better jobs; students and most of the professional people have fled the country; the great Tamil library has been burned. Sure, he's met people who cussed him out as a foreigner and asked him why he came here.

"Just look at the news and you'll see why! We don't want to live here, or to die here! Money doesn't make us happy - to be happy we need our life: with family, friends, our land, our language." He has a TV and a video so that he can get more news and see Asian films, but also to distract his mind from his constant concern about his people in Sri Lanka. That and sleep take up most of his free time - the long hours at the pizza oven are very hot and exhausting.

I tried again. "Haven't you had any interesting or difficult experiences with the Swiss here?"

"It's hard finding time to get to know them," he answered. "When they have time free, I am always working, almost all evenings and weekends."

The one hard encounter he narrates didn't happen to him at all - he just observed it in a streetcar. A couple of Spanish children were rather lively. "Quiet you little ...!" an older Swiss man commanded roughly. Their mother protested that he shouldn't talk to her children that way, whereupon the man said something quite vulgar to her regarding foreigners in general and her and her children in particular, and she began to cry. A Swiss woman who had observed all this came and sat next to the Spanish mother. Turning angrily to the man, she snapped, "All children are alike!"

Problems with the Swiss are just not a major topic at all for George the refugee. His biggest problem here right now is that work at the pizza oven is too hot, as it is for most Swiss.

My session with George led me to reflect both on the preoccupation of foreigners in Switzerland with the peculiarities of their life there, and on the image of the boat. For the Swiss their country is a luxury liner that they want to keep as a luxury liner, not too crowded, with Swiss officers, not too many unpleasant passengers, and just the right-sized crew. For us who choose to live in Switzerland, whatever our reasons may be, it is also a luxury liner, but a rather problematic one because it is a Swiss liner, with Swiss officers and mostly Swiss passengers. We write articles about the difficulties of adapting to life on this luxury liner and learning to enjoy it. For those who are forced by fear to live here, however, Switzerland is a lifeboat which they are thankful to have but long to leave, not because they don't like the lifeboat, but because they yearn with all the pain in their hearts to get back in peace to their native shore again.

WE CAN WORK IT OUT

by Chris Corbett

One of the first impressions visitors to Switzerland have is of a perfect sense of order and the feeling of reliability like you would expect from a fine Swiss watch. This is evident in the manicured lawns and fields, perfectly punctual trains and relatively spotless streets. There are also efficient systems for dealing with such things as traffic, parking and, yes, even foreigners. For such a well-arranged existence, the natives uphold certain traditional ways of behaviour. They seem to follow every law and rule as if nothing else mattered, in spite of what the conflicting circumstances might be or what common sense would suggest.

The Swiss hold onto their four languages with great determination for stability and security. This also helps to reinforce authority when dealing with foreigners. I experienced this once with a customs inspector at the airport. He had stopped only me out of a plane-load of people. I told him I had recently moved to Zurich and didn't understand what he was saying in German. My excuse was supported by my British passport. He ignored my comment and went on in German telling me I must learn that language to live in this country. Perhaps he was having a hard day. We were all tanned, returning from vacation. A little more than an hour's drive from the airport, it was snowing on that August eve of the Swiss National Holiday.

As a non-German-speaking resident of Switzerland, the first words I learned here were what I call 'Survival German.' The first or second phrases after *Was kostet das?* (How much does that cost?) and *Danke* (Thanks!) were for fulfilling the need to eat. These expressions helped in my first routine contacts.

I quickly figured out from listening and watching that all the waiters and waitresses have the same name. Whether I was in an outdoor café or a quality restaurant, they would all answer when personally called. Once I wanted to impress my friends with my quick grasp of Swiss society and social customs by explaining this remarkable phenomenon. None of them were aware of this situation. They had either lived here too long or not long enough. Most of my friends didn't believe me but I thought a simple demonstration would convince them.

77

I told them, ''Watch this ....*Entschuldigung!''*
Sure enough the waiter or waitress addressed arrived.

The other common name I observed was *Zahlen bitte* which worked equally well. I wondered if perhaps it was *Herr Entschuldigung* or maybe even *Entschuldigung Zahlenbitte*. My more knowledgeable friends soon explained the subtleties of correct social manners and I learned that I had only been saying ''excuse me'' and ''the check please.''

The Swiss do like to take their laws seriously. For example, one day I was driving home from work. After exiting the highway, I encountered a police road-block with an officer, gun ready, waving down all cars containing young men. His co-worker sat in the police car monitoring the radio. I was told that there had been a recent armed bank robbery and asked if I could please produce my driver's permit and car registration to verify my identity. After checking these documents, the officer noticed that the green sticker on my car for the annual smog inspection had recently expired. I decided to play the role of the unknowing foreigner. This was not too hard since it was so close to the truth. I feigned ignorance of German which was not too difficult either. He went to a lot of effort to try to explain as well as he could in English about the law and how each car had to be inspected annually for emissions. I just kept nodding at him and tried to hide my amusement. While an armed and dangerous criminal was loose in the area and possibly driving by this very second, here I was getting a legal lesson. This officer didn't seem to care about a real criminal. I thought that if I kept talking to him long enough, perhaps the real criminal would drive by and divert the officer from writing the inevitable ticket. Sure enough, my strategy paid off. Suddenly the other policeman turned on his siren. My license and registration were tossed back in my window as the policeman ran quickly back to his car and raced off down the road.

Not all situations with the working public can be handled by appearing ignorant of the language. Sometimes trying to speak in the native tongue can get you into difficulties too.

Soon after my arrival in Switzerland I was having lunch in a neighbourhood restaurant in a not-so-elegant part of Geneva. I had asked the waitress (Ms S'il-vous-plait of course!) for a beer and the menu. She promptly brought my glass of cold beer and a few minutes later a man in a chef outfit appeared and put down a plate of hot food. I gently protested in my tourist French saying something like "No, no" and waving my hands appropriately. He looked slightly bewildered, picked up the plate. In my best French I said *"Je désire un menu."* He looked at me knowingly and put the plate back down. This was repeated a couple of times like a scene in a bad comedy until the waitress noticed and came over to help. She explained in her best English how the daily special was always called 'the menu'. I apologised for the misunderstanding and she brought me the card to select my meal. Of course, the only word written on the front was MENU. Later I learned from friends that I was lucky there hadn't been a brawl, considering the reputation of this restaurant.

A similar incident occurred in St. Moritz. My infant son had to be briefly hospitalized there due to an unexpected illness while on vacation. As he was so young, my wife and I took turns sleeping nights in an extra bed in his private room. On my night of duty he was particularly restless. I had to hold him on my shoulder to get him to sleep. I was walking around with him in the hall outside his room. There was nobody around and it was late at night so I didn't feel conspicuous wearing only my undershorts. All of a sudden, a nurse approached. After her hasty official glance at my appearance, she began to chat quickly some small talk about the hospital. After a minute my son was asleep so I excused myself saying, "I'm going to bed now."

Something must have been lost in the translation because she blushed and said, "I'm sorry but I must go to the third floor now," and walked away quickly.

She must have figured me to be one of those forward Americans you're always hearing about. I counted my blessings that it wasn't a 350-pound matron saying, "Yes, my dear," while grabbing me in a wrestling hold before I could explain.

I really feel my taxes are well spent when I see the types of work it provides. Observe some workers in this country that boasts less than one percent unemployment and you will understand why. I saw a worker in a full bright-orange jumpsuit armed with only a tin can and a screwdriver quietly removing old staples from bulletin boards in a train station. I recognized immediately the extreme importance of this work.

Quite a few Swiss feel it is beneath them to do common labour. This explains all the foreign waiters, gardeners and construction workers. Funny thing though, the foreigners don't seem to mind their work. They actually take pride in it, almost enjoy it. They are not chained to a belief of living to work but rather to one of working to live. Yes, work is serious business here. Not so many years ago a referendum to shorten the customary 42-1/2-hour-work-week was soundly voted down. Actually, Swiss workers take their rest just as seriously. My neighbour was subjected to a police visit because he was weeding his garden on a Sunday that happened to be National Prayer Day. Try to wash your car or hang out laundry on a Sunday - there is bound to be law against it.

You have to admit though that the many employed by our tax money do keep this country spotless. I once saw a road crew of 3 men in a tanker truck carefully washing each highway marker alongside a stretch of country road. They could probably do a couple of kilometres of markers before having to drive back to the public works yard for a refill of water. Then they would drive back to where they left off and resume the whole procedure. Nice low pressure work in the countryside. No one appeared to notice that the proliferation of rain did a pretty good job of washing the markers already.

Another time I watched a man dressed in orange quietly sweeping off the line in the middle of a two-lane road. It didn't seem to matter that the breeze from passing autos would blow the leaves away eventually.

I enjoy my daily interactions with fellow workers whether they are Swiss or foreign. Together we can influence the quality of life here. With more efforts to understand and accept each other, foreigners and natives alike can help make Switzerland continue to be a wonderful place to live and work.

THE PRINCESS

by Kate Mühlethaler

Carnival - this was what she liked most about living in Switzerland. Strange, she couldn't exactly explain why it fascinated her so. Maybe it was the shimmering colours of the exotic costumes and decorations, contrasting with the chilling unfriendliness of the February fog. Or it may have been the expectant atmosphere all around her.

She decided to wade in gradually. That first year she just changed her appearance by wearing a mask. How warm and uncomfortable she felt behind that mask! But it opened up a new world for her - she wasn't a stranger anywhere, and people greeted her like an old friend. However, when the men began to flirt with her shamelessly, she found herself bristling automatically with indignation, completely forgetting that she was disguised. No, this carnival thing wasn't for her after all, she decided and slipped quietly back into the staid conformity of everyday life.

A couple of years later, to please her child, she tried again. They borrowed costumes from a friend and became two grey doves, a mother and baby, with soft blue feathers and grey beak masks. They would go to the masked ball in town to which Daddy always went unmasked. People went to the balls separately or with a friend or two of the same sex, the whole point being to surprise their own partners when the masks were taken off at midnight.

Saturday came and the whole day the six year old child was bursting with excitement. At last it was bedtime and mother heaved a sigh of relief, hoping the child would not fall asleep. When, oh when, would he make a move to go, so that they could get the carefully hidden costumes out?

"There's no hurry," he told his wife, "there's no point going before about nine. The group's always late starting."

"Yes," she replied, her heart beginning to thump painfully with nervousness. The child's excitement was infecting her too.

Finally he left. Waiting a few minutes to make sure he'd gone, she crept into her daughter's room. "It's OK, Mummy, I'm not asleep," said a voice which sounded more than wide-awake. With trembling fingers they got themselves ready. It seemed to take ages.

Eventually the car was driven out of the garage and the two grey doves were on their way. Parking proved to be quite a problem, but at last they were walking briskly along the road. They looked around. Everywhere there seemed to be music and costumed people. Oh, how wonderful to be part of it all! If excitement had been high before, it now seemed almost unbearable as they entered the restaurant where the dance was being held. They made straight for the toilet, where masks and feathers were hastily adjusted with shaking hands. It was hard to tell who was more agitated - the big dove or the little dove.

They were hustled up the stairs, squashed together by various clowns, witches, kings and queens, frogs and even a lonely 'Popeye'. They paid their money, and went into the room, both feeling suddenly extremely shy. The mother made straight for a table in the corner. The music was pounding, and all types of weird creatures and figures were swaying to it. At last they spotted father. Mother sat back with a sigh, and after all the rush, began to look forward to an interesting evening. ''We'll sit here for a while, have a drink, watch the people, maybe have a dance and then, before we go home, we'll surprise Daddy.'' She had it all planned. But the child had a strange look on her face. She couldn't take her eyes off that familiar figure at the other side of the room. Like a magnet she seemed to be drawn to him, and before her mother could stop her, the child had raced over to where her father was sitting. He glanced in amazement at this vibrant bundle of feathers.

''What are you gaping at?'' the child demanded, and pulling off her beak impatiently, she plonked herself down on his lap and promptly began to suck her thumb. He started to laugh, and his laughter increased as he saw the big grey dove come over and sit down beside the little one. ''What an anti-climax, after all that work!'' thought mother, and was determined to repeat the whole performance another year with a different disguise, and, of course, on her own.

Two years passed quickly, and February came round again. This time there was no fog, just a snow blizzard. They lived in Canton Berne, only a few kilometres from the borders of Canton Solothurn where the carnival is a big event, it being a Catholic canton. This time she dressed as a fairy princess, with a half mask, plenty of make-up and glitter all the colours of the rainbow sprinkled on her hair. She felt like a child again, going to her first birthday party. The village where she lived was high up, and renowned for snow drifts, so she decided to take the local bus down to the valley where she would catch the train into Solothurn. She would drive back with her husband after she'd demasked at the stroke of midnight.

She stood shivering at the bus stop, clutching her bus fare tightly. She had to take the last bus down, which unfortunately left at seven pm already. Her spouse was out. He had said, when she had tentatively inquired about his plans for the evening, that he'd go out in the afternoon to fetch something from his father, and planned to go straight on to the masked ball from there. Her daughter was staying with a friend.

At last she caught sight of the familiar headlights sweeping along the road. The snow made everything seem very bright, but she still flashed her torch at the driver to make sure he'd see her. The enormous wheels crunched to a halt on the snowy road. She clambered clumsily up the steps in her romantic attire, paid her fare, and sat down, forgetting that her appearance was anything else than usual. She was soon brought back to reality with a jolt, as she became aware of the nudges and smiles of her fellow passengers. The driver made a few remarks. Soon she began to feel very embarrassed and to long for the distance to be swallowed up which still lay between her and Canton Solothurn. There she would surely be among her own kind. As the bus stopped at the station, she distinctly heard the stifled giggles of two school-boys at the back. "Thank goodness that's over," she sighed as she waited, trying to hide herself in the dimly-lit waiting room. Ten minutes later she was in the train, being whisked nearer to the carnival with every turn of its wheels.

Finally she arrived at the same restaurant as before. There were very few people (it was still early). She decided to get a drink to ease herself into the carnival mood and to pass away the time. Strange, wonderful figures were starting to arrive. Each costume seemed more beautiful, even more fantastic, than the last. She began to feel at home. She recognised several faces, and, plucking up courage, she went up to different people she knew, giving them a hearty thump on the back, but not daring to utter a word, knowing that her English accent would give her straight away. She started to dance. It was ten o'clock. Suddenly something struck her - where was HE?

Perhaps he'd been held up somewhere. It was early yet, wasn't it? Feeling a bit dejected, she decided to go outside for some fresh air. Opening the door, she was greeted with a flurry of snow. Goodness, if it was like this down here, what would it be like at home? She began to feel anxious. If he didn't appear, how on earth would she get home?

At twelve o'clock she felt she must do something. Some people had begun to take off their masks, and she recognised a good friend of her husband's. She wrenched off her own mask and approaching him, brushed off his exclamation of surprise, and explained her plight. He at once had a solution. "You can have my old banger," he said. "I'm in no state to drive myself home anyway, and I can sleep at Robert's." Robert looked as if he could hardly understand what was going on, but, as he only lived a couple of streets away, it didn't seem to matter. They would arrive home somehow. Clutching Beat's car keys, she set off in search of the car. She walked quickly through the cold night among the groups of musicians and masked home-goers. At least it had stopped snowing. Catching sight of the car, she understood all those caustic remarks that had been made about it. It certainly did deserve them - it was just a rusty heap!

After a few tries, it started. Feeling quite confident again, she drove off homewards. She reached the town where she had caught the train, and began the ascent. Luckily the snow plough had been through recently, so the road was pretty clear. Suddenly, as she reached the loneliest part of the journey, some kind of animal shot out in front of the car. She jammed on the brakes to avoid it. The car stalled and wouldn't start again, no matter how many times she tried. She even attempted pleading with it. She got out. She understood nothing about cars. It had started to snow again and the flakes were coming down in great swirls. After a few freezing minutes trying to blow hot breath into her blue hands, she heard the noise of a car's engine. A joyous sound! She hurriedly pulled her torch out of her handbag and flashed it desperately at the approaching vehicle.

The driver was a rather nervous doctor who had been called out to a patient in a nearby village. He was already very late because of the snow. But he helped the forlorn fairy princess push the old car to the side of the road and suggested phoning for a taxi from his patient's house. It would take too long, she thought, and in this weather, it was doubtful if even the most determined taxi driver would ever reach her. It would cost a lot too.

The doctor kindly offered to look out for her on his way back. She started her expedition home, miserable, fed-up and very cold, snowflakes sparkling with the rainbow glitter in her hair. She looked down at her flimsy silver slippers and felt near to tears. Then she recalled with a touch of amusement that the doctor hadn't shown the slightest surprise at her appearance. Oh well, doctors must see all kinds of odd people, she decided. Marching bravely on, she was glad of the posts at the side to mark the edge of the road. She mustn't panic, she told herself. Of course she'd make it! A car passed her cautiously, and about five youths started to jeer derisively, waving at her gaily. She became angry with everything, the youths, the carnival, the weather, the car, herself, but most of all with HIM! Why hadn't he been there? None of this would have happened if he had. Seldom had she felt so completely alone.

She limped on slowly, finally arriving near to collapse. She staggered into the garage to see if his car was there. It was, safe and sound. Entering the house, she flung open the bedroom door. Her startled husband shot upright in his warm, snug bed, expecting an attack, or, at the very least, a burglary. He hardly recognized the wan, bedraggled, snow-covered figure as it sobbed out its dismal story, the mask dangling around its neck, and pools of icy water dripping onto the carpet. "No," he said, he'd decided at the last minute not to go to that dance. He'd heard that the band wasn't good and had gone somewhere else. And no, he hadn't really wondered where she was. He was feeling very tired and could never remember her arrangements anyway.

The fairy princess, sinking down onto the bed, put her head into her hands and howled. The silver and gold make-up, mingling with all the other colours, trickled down her cheeks in a salty stream. "That's the end of the bloody carnival for me," she wailed dramatically.

The next year she went as a rabbit.

A MORNING RIDE

by Janet Rüsch

It was a crisp, sunny autumn morning, my spirits were high, a perfect day for a ride. I set out with the feeling I very often have when on horseback that the world is at my feet. But one mustn't forget, it's a Swiss world, and very often I am rudely brought down to earth or toppled off my high horse, as you might say!

The first person I saw was a woman behind her kitchen window. I nodded and smiled, my lips forming a friendly greeting, but she stared right through me, no smile, no lips moved, not even a twitch of an eye. I continued on my way undeterred as this had happened many times before.

I headed for open country and the next person I saw was an elderly man coming towards me with his dog. I dutifully reined in my horse to one side letting the man pass unimpeded. *"Morge,"* I said, smiling cheerfully. ''Mumble,'' he replied not letting his eyes stray from the point on the path some distance ahead of him. His lips had barely moved so there was no indication of a smile even. My former feelings of elation were somewhat dampened by this time, and I was beginning to feel slightly irritated. I thought of my earlier years in Lancashire and the almost forgotten voices calling, '' 'ello luv, beautiful mornin', in't it?'' as I rode by, ''I 'ave an apple 'ere for yer horse.'' A lump appeared in my throat and the sunny autumn day was slowly taking on a rather dull aspect, and the crispness was turning to coldness.

I plodded on, however, eventually entering the forest. The sun rays slanting through the trees formed a fairy-tale tunnel where one expected to see elves and pixies hopping from one toadstool to another. Ahead of me I saw a figure sitting on a newly-felled tree trunk, no pixie, alas, but a lone forester solemnly eating his lunch. He scowled at me as I approached. Should I speak or should I not? I did, and I wished him, *"En Guete."* He muttered something inaudible. After a short time, I found that the path was completely blocked by a smouldering fire of dead-wood and a red and white plastic ribbon had been strung across the width of the path. It was impossible to pass on horseback on either side as the forest sloped steeply down to the left and up to the right at this point. I had no choice but to make my way back in order to take another path. I was furious! Why hadn't the forester told me about this? He must have been the one to make the fire! He was still munching his lunch when I reached him and, by this time, I was hoping it would choke him!

*****

Luckily, not all encounters with the Swiss are as negative or unproductive as those I experienced on that particular day. I am also quite sure that how one interprets the actions or reactions of others sometimes depends on one's own mood.

As I am of a very friendly nature myself, this was one of the most difficult problems for me to overcome. I realised, however, that, in most cases, the reluctance to communicate was not due to downright unfriendliness, but a certain shyness. Sometimes an inferiority complex seemed to be the reason.

I have tried one or two remedies for breaking down the barriers, whatever the reason for them may be, and in lots of cases they seem to work.

One is 'persistence'. I just don't give up. I smile and greet and wave and nod until they melt. This has worked well in many cases. The woman behind the kitchen window for example, she never fails to give me a wave and a smile these days.

Another tactic I use is 'flattery'; this seems to work very well with both sexes. Take the woman at the local Post Office; she used to be very curt and off-hand, *Grüezi* and *Aufwiedersehen* being the limit of her conversation. So, one day I said to her, ''That's a lovely pullover you are wearing. Did you knit it yourself?'' - This is one of the highest compliments you can pay to a Swiss woman. She was delighted, although she hadn't knit it herself. Since then it's "Good morning Mrs. Rüsch" and "Goodbye Mrs. Rüsch" accompanied by little smiles of understanding or even a bit of small talk if she has time.

It isn't advisable, however, to use this example with men. How many knit their own pullovers after all? But dogs and cars are two subjects which seem to be quite close to many men's hearts. If it's a dog, try commenting on or praising it. No matter how ugly you yourself may find it, tell him how lovely it is. You may or may not have noticed that a lot of dogs resemble their owners anyway, so this could even turn out to be a personal compliment!

If I have a choice, I choose the dog because, apart from driving a car, knowing it has four wheels and whether I like the colour or not, I know precious little about this subject. So, in this case, my conversation is drastically limited.

When travelling in a bus or a train, I usually try the good old English conversation opener - the weather. But this isn't always as successful as in England because it doesn't seem to rain enough here. Snow, of course, is a 'Swissy' subject - conversation being limited to the winter months, naturally, depending on where you live. Buses and trains even leave and arrive on time here but if one has been delayed for any reason or other, this should give you something to talk about for at least half an hour!

If, however, none of these remedies work or seem appropriate at the time, one of the best ice-breakers of all is 'Make 'em Laugh'. How you do this is, of course, entirely up to you.

MEETING MEPHISTO

by Stanley Mason

Most people will tell you that the German Swiss, though hard-working, reliable and level-headed, are stolid folk with a marked lack of imagination. Their country is so well-organized, punctual and hygienic that nothing crazy and irrational can happen in it. Some people seem in fact to surmise that even should there be occult goings-on under way in Switzerland, the local inhabitants would not notice them, being too engrossed in their prosaic concentration on material goods, not excluding money. In any case, while in Britain, for instance, every second stately home has a ghost as a kind of permanent appointment, even the most hoary old castles in Switzerland are quite devoid of such spectral denizens. And though three-metre-high strangers from outer space may at a pinch even appear to the perestroika-dazed citizens of Voronezh, there is simply no chance of that happening in Derendingen.

Such generalizations are always dangerous. After all, the Bernese have had a haunted house in the middle of town for centuries, and the old Swiss peasants used to leave holes in their chalets for spirits to escape through. My own experience also suggests that there are some dark and uncanny corners even in the Swiss psyche, and perhaps the following true story will go a little way to demonstrating that this generalization, like so many others, will not stand up to critical scrutiny.

It was during the Second World War. As a teacher in a Swiss private school, I had been trapped with some of my pupils by the sudden fall of France. Cut off from my family and friends in Britain, and not sure that I should ever see them again, I was filled with vague forebodings. To make matters worse, I had just fallen in love. The stage was therefore set for the direst developments. And when the school holidays came round with the threat of empty days and lonely nights, I jumped at the invitation of a Dutch colleague to join him on a trip to Pontresina.

This Dutchman was not averse to the minor pleasures of life. He liked an aperitif before lunch and dinner, and would not say no to a liqueur afterwards. Since our train journey to Pontresina was long, we spent a good part of it in the dining-car. The result was that, from our first Pernod onwards, we were in slightly elevated spirits. This was not altogether inexcusable; the stresses of term had been heavy, the multiple menaces of war had oppressed us for too long; we were due for some comic relief. We even laughed at our own mediocre jokes.

It was at this point that I glanced back down the dining-car and saw, not without a genuine shock of surprise, a dark, handsome and somehow remotely familiar face. Not many tables from our own sat a character with a glinting eye, a sardonic smile under a neat, black, waxed moustache, and a raised wineglass in his hand. It seemed quite impossible that anything not risen from the bottomless pit could look quite so Mephistophelean. I screwed up my face in a look of alarm as I turned back to the Dutchman.

''Watch your step, now,'' I said, ''we have some very illustrious company. Just take a look. His Satanic Majesty in person.''

The Dutchman looked and whistled. ''I think you can be right,'' he said.

As we gleefully spooned our soup, I pointed out to my colleague that the Devil never travels without a purpose. There must be somebody in the dining-car who was the particular object of his solicitous attention.

The Dutchman peered down the carriage. ''He's looking at you,'' he said.

I turned at once, and met a nonchalant gaze without an atom of deference in it. There was Old Clootie, if you like, staring me straight in the eye.

The incident provided us with conversational material for the rest of the meal. We speculated on what diabolical schemes might be taking the Tempter to the mountains. Occasionally we looked his way and saw his teeth flash as he treated his neighbourhood to a burst of pyrotechnical laughter. His dark eyes darted hither and thither, taking in the mortals around him with a mixture of amusement and contempt. His hand swept over them in an elegant, cynical gesture, rather like a benediction with a minus sign in front of it, dispelling our very last doubts about his identity.

By the time we reached Pontresina, we had lost the Devil from sight. As we had not booked rooms in advance, we left our luggage at the station and began a tour of the hotels. Some of them were full, others looked too palatial for our purses. Finally we found rooms in a medium-class hotel that suited our tastes and our finances.

We just had time to wash and spruce ourselves up before going down to dinner, or perhaps I should say, before going down. For the Dutchman found that the occasion demanded a Campari. By the time we were seated at table, therefore, we were already in a state of faint elation which was no doubt conducive to supernatural experiences.

And in fact we had hardly raised our soup spoons to our mouths when the door opened and our friend from the dining-car, the Old Gent in person, was ushered in. This time our bewilderment was not simulated.

"It's no joke," I whispered to the Dutchman. "He really has his eye on us."

In the next few days, however, the Devil - as we already familiarly referred to him - gave no hint of evil designs as far as we were concerned. His general behaviour, admittedly, was as devilworthy as one could have wished. The waitresses willingly lingered beside his table, and not infrequently were observed to hurry away with cheeks glowing pink when he had whispered something in their ear. He laughed a good deal, and when he laughed his teeth scintillated wickedly. When he went walking, he carried a silver-handled cane. And at night he would put a record on the gramophone in the lounge, always the same record: "*Gold und Brillanten hat sie nicht...*Gold and jewels has she none, rich relations has she none; she can kiss just how I like it, like no other girl on earth..."

Bemused by a plethora of aperitifs and liqueurs, we sat and admired the lord of the underworld of an evening, cautiously watching for any move that might betray his intent. But in the daytime he was far from our thoughts, for we were up and away into the mountains. Neither of us had ever been in the Upper Engadine before. We marvelled at its pure, crystal light, we climbed its rocky pathways, feeling no fatigue. The long approach to the snowy giants up the Rosegg Valley seemed to us an experience without parallel until we climbed the Fuorcla Surlej from Silvaplana - there was no cableway in those days - and had the mountain world suddenly unfurl before us with all the immense majesty of a revelation. We were caught by a brief, violent storm on the summit of Piz Languard, we paid homage to the memory of Nietzsche in Sils

Maria, and walking between Silvaplana and Maloja we asked each other whether this was not perhaps the most beautiful vale on earth.

Then one day, as the week approached its end, the Devil's table was suddenly deserted. He had left. We breathed a sigh of relief, not altogether unmixed with disappointment. This was plain proof that he had not had his eye on us after all.

The next day I too left Pontresina. The Dutchman stayed, but I was to go to Locarno to meet the girl I had fallen in love with. The journey was not one that even the seasoned tourist undertook every day: from Pontresina back to Thusis, by postal coach over the Via Mala and the San Bernardino to Mesocco, and thence via Bellinzona to Locarno. It was a romantic and impressive journey. The Via Mala in those days still lived up to its name. Crags from which water dripped beetled over the road. The gorge dropped, only a few feet from the road's edge, into seemingly umplumbable depths. Then came the dizzy hairpins of the pass, and finally a landscape I had never seen before: the opulent vegetation, the lambent warmth, the Italianate houses, the chestnuts and palms of the Ticino.

At first I felt on my guard in these new surroundings. There was something southern about Locarno that, to a puritanical Northerner, was too seductive to be good. I took up the room I had booked in the Hotel Metropole and, having an hour to spare before dinner, decided to take a walk around the town. Under the arcades the crowds still eddied unhurriedly, most of them holiday-makers promenading in all forms of summer attire. The restaurant tables overflowed on to the pavements, and here the elegant and the bohemian sat in relaxed or vociferous groups, enjoying the cool of the early evening over a coffee or an ice.

I walked on, feeling very remote and a trifle lonely. Yet my five senses were on the alert, and when a sudden voice was raised behind me it stopped me in my tracks. For although it pronounced no name, the voice was strangely familiar, and I knew that it was calling me. I turned and looked. Sitting at a café table on the pavement, beckoning me to a seat, was the Devil.

I put up no resistance at all. Although I had never spoken to him directly before, he was in a way an old friend. I moved to the chair beside him. Fate, I said to myself, is fate.

''Have a beer,'' the Devil said, smiling as though he knew every detail of my thoughts. I had a beer. So I was, after all, part of his plan. It was an idea that to a reasoning person going about his everyday activities must appear utterly absurd. Possibly it would have seemed less absurd a hundred or more years ago, when Old Nick is reported to have spent much of his time distracting chaste maidens from their prayers or whispering in the hairy ears of sadistic factory owners. But today? Well, I wasn't going about my everyday activities; and the idea in fact began to appear natural and convincing to a stranger who had come down from the unbelievable mountains into the leisurely, palm-studded summer of the improbable south.

The beer tasted good, and the Devil proved to be a smart conversationalist. With a glib and witty disdain, he promptly began taking conventional morality to pieces. He smiled and raised an artful eyebrow. He asked me questions about my private life without the slightest sign of diffidence, then nodded as though he knew it all anyway. He leaned forward and told me with a sort of amused, debonair cunning why he would never marry, and for that matter why I should never marry. His arguments were hard to fault; and when exposed to the charm of his polished delivery, you hardly noticed the absence of a moral law.

When we had finished the beer, he volunteered to walk a few paces with me. It was an honour I could not decline. We strolled together back to the Metropole. "I shall have to leave you here," I said. "This is my hotel." His eyes widened politely in a kind of well-rehearsed surprise. "What a coincidence!" he cried. "I happen to be staying here too." When I came down to dinner twenty minutes later, the Devil was just arranging with the head waiter that the lonely Englishman should share his table.

He had a way with waiters that was almost as impressive as his way with waitresses. And in a sense I was not averse to being in such eminently reliable hands.

In the next few days I spent a lot of time with the Devil and got to know a great deal about him. His advice about handling money or handling women - he contrived to make the two problems seem pretty much the same thing - came in sentences that tumbled from his lips like cut gems, glittering with a suave cynicism. He told me things with a sly warmth yet with an undertone of instruction, as though I were his chosen disciple. To recount all his wisdom here would lead too far afield, and anyway, discretion forbids. One thing, however, I can betray about him: his favourite liqueur is Chartreuse.

On the second evening we were not alone at dinner. A dark, handsome young woman had come to join him. I never saw her luggage, so I cannot say whether there was a broom-end sticking out of it. He told me with a rather long, steady look that it was his cousin.

The unreality of these days was heightened by one or two meetings with the girl I had really come to see, and who lived across the lake. They were clandestine meetings, for her family would hear nothing of me, and had any acquaintance seen us he would no doubt have reported the outrageous news. We met in a meadow on the Maggia delta, where the wild bees tumbled among the meadowsweet. We met in the vineyards above her home village, since she could not escape to Locarno, and her father had threatened to shoot me on sight. And after the meetings I returned meekly to the table of His Infernal Highness.

By this time I had come to take the Devil for granted. He was a man of great *savoir faire,* a man whose company was a pleasure and whose friendship - especially to such a mere mortal as myself - was flattering. Was I perhaps wronging him in thinking of him as the father of all evil? I had hardly had the thought - it was at dinner one evening - when he leaned over to me, looked me straight in the eye and asked in a penetrating whisper: "Would you like to go to hell?"

I confess that my legs suddenly felt like jelly. Here, if you like, was the answer to my doubts. I put up no fight at all. I felt resigned, utterly resigned. "Whatever you say," I said.

After dinner the Devil led the dark lady and his new apprentice out into the streets of Locarno. Because it was wartime, there was a blackout, and the night was dark as sin. But he led us unerringly through the obscurity. Finally he bade us hold hands. We held hands, and thus linked we advanced through what seemed to be some narrow passage. Arriving at what he apparently knew, by some sort of unholy extrasensory perception, to be our destination, he halted us and struck a match. The flaring, unsteady light revealed a skull painted in ghostly white on a heavy wooden door.

We entered a dimly lit cavern, a labyrinth of red-walled vaults. The Prince of Darkness in person was ushering us into his domain. From all around us came voices, the laughter of young girls, a twitter of lost souls. We caught a glimpse of lovers in shadowy alcoves, bathed in an eerie, Dantean light. The master of the ceremonies led us to a small table, and a lackey of his - admittedly disguised as a waiter - came to hover beside us. The Devil allowed his cynical glance to rest on us for a moment before he ordered wine: Lacrimae Christi, the tears of Christ.

For myself, I had no strength to demur or even to pass a comment. The events all had a dimension of unreality. They might have come straight out of Faust. The power to differentiate between concrete and imaginary worlds had deserted me. When the wine came, I was willing to let it percolate slowly into the vacuum of my bewildered soul.

The next day the Devil stood with his dark companion and waved me off as my train left Locarno. Had it all been a protracted hallucination? The red vaults of hell, I now realized, were really wine cellars that had been converted into a tavern. The Devil had also given me a name, a reassuringly common-or-garden Swiss name, that might be real enough. He came - need I add? - from Basle. Yet in the many years that have elapsed since that encounter I have never tried to contact him or to pry into the hard facts at the heart of the mystery. Why not? Perhaps because I have been loath to break the spell. Perhaps because, although I am a staunch rationalist, I never forget the words of old Will Shakespeare put into the mouth of his creature Hamlet: ''There are more things in heaven and earth, Horatio, than are dreamt of in your philosophy.'' Heaven and earth, I would say, must here be interpreted as including Switzerland.

HAIRPIN BENDS

by Susan Stafford

Driving up the Grimsel pass a few
years ago, we almost came to a halt
behind a car with British number plates.
The occupants, a couple in their fifties, were taking things very cautiously. Since the series of bends
made overtaking impossible, we hung
on behind, collecting other cars behind
us like ants in a line. When we finally
reached the car park by the hospice, the
driver of the British car stopped and got
out, shaking. "If I'd known what Swiss
mountain passes are like," he said, "we'd
have come by train."
For lowland foreigners who actually
live in Switzerland, on the other hand, it soon
becomes necessary to learn to cope with mountain passes and hairpin bends, even in the Jura. A
hairpin bend is an ingenious invention. It's the
only situation in life where you make progress
by going back on yourself. On a downhill
run, the forces of gravity, logic and your
stomach muscles all tell you that you
should go straight on, but somehow
you manage to get round the corner.
An Englishwoman who used
to live here once told me that she
felt the mountains "hemmed her
in." Others seem to feel that high
ground is just there to help them
get closer to the open sky. Such is
the relationship of the Swiss towards their hills. In fact, they may
even choose to go up them instead of

round them. A Swiss friend of ours recently took us on a hike. We trudged uphill, downhill all day. Only afterwards did I discover that another path around the foot of the hills would have brought us to the same destination much less tired, although admittedly with little sense of achievement. Caught up in this fascination for the mountain roads and hairpin bends, I would now prefer to take, for example, the much slower road over the Gotthard pass than to travel through the tunnel.

As for the Swiss national sport of skiing, it is, of course, just a way of descending a snow-covered hill in a series of elegant hairpin bends. For beginners like us, the art of mastering traverses and turns is a slow process, demanding full concentration. Our small daughter, watching us on one occasion from the foot of a slope, commented: ''You look like caterpillars.''

It may be faster to go up or downhill by the *direttissima,* but most Swiss prefer to tackle slopes slowly and carefully. So it is with social contacts - no instant camaraderie in the American style. Getting to know the people here takes time. The process, in fact, is in many ways like the tortuous drive up a mountain pass.

AN INCONVENIENCE OFF BAHNHOFSTRASSE

by Mari Mueller

After spending four weeks in Zurich on a student exchange program, I was asked to report on a 'cultural experience'. Many possibilities were open to me when I thought about which experience to analyse. But the experience which is most vivid in my mind happened in a fast-food restaurant just off the luxurious Bahnhofstrasse.

We had decided to go there for a taste of America. But that isn't exactly what we got. Our first surprise was when we had to pay an extra 20 *Rappen* for ketchup. The food was good, but it wasn't the same as back home. Yet, the experience for me really began in the ladies room.

Restrooms in Switzerland have posed more problems or challenges to me than I ever could have imagined.

First I tried the handle on the door to the toilet to no avail. Then I noticed a slot for coins, but I couldn't read the sign directly above the slot. So I proceeded to put in a 20-*Rappen* coin. Nothing happened. I put in another 20-*Rappen* coin and still nothing happened. At this point I decided to just observe. Soon a lady came in, placed a token in the slot and entered. So simple. But because of the language barrier I wasn't aware that the sign must have said "get a token from cashier."

After I was finally inside with the toilet, I thought everything would basically function as expected. I was incorrect in that assumption. I presumed the box-like device on the wall contained toilet seat covers which are very much utilized in the States. I pulled and nothing happened. I pushed and was startled by the toilet flushing. There were apparently no seat covers but at least I had learned how to flush the toilet, which is not necessarily easy to figure out in many restrooms in Switzerland.

This particular Swiss restroom added another new dimension to the simple habit of washing my hands. There were some other ladies in the room so I wanted to be sure I didn't make a fool of myself. In some Swiss restrooms I had noticed that to turn the water on, I had to step on a button on the floor. While trying to be nonchalant about it, I searched ardently for this button with my foot. Not a drop came from the faucet.

I realized at this point that I was being watched. I had to do something so I put my hands in the sink and was surprised when the water suddenly turned on. I didn't know how - but it worked. It went off again while I was getting soap from the soap dispenser. Then I tried to turn the water back on with my hands covered in soap. Nothing. I pushed, pulled, turned, stepped all over the floor. Still nothing. I realized I had made a mess with the soap all around the sink. Finally I turned in despair to the lady. She laughed and merely placed her hands under the faucet and automatically the water turned on.

Then I tried the drier. Instead of turning it on, I turned the lights in the restroom off. By this time everybody in the restroom was aware of me. Eventually I realized that the hand-drier also turned on automatically when my hands were under it.

Although I had to laugh at myself, this cultural experience was also very frustrating. The language barrier is definitely a cause for misinterpretation that every traveller learns to accept as part of the adventure in travelling to other countries. But even without a word being said, it's those little differences in simple everyday matters like going to a restroom that made me feel like I must be from another planet.

After thinking a bit more about some of these day-to-day cultural challenges, I was able to gain some valuable insights about the Swiss. The restrooms here are actually ahead of those in the States and very sterile. The water doesn't run longer than necessary nor does the drier. Swiss wash their hands often and these appliances allow them to do so without touching where everyone else has. It made me aware of just how clean most public areas in Switzerland are kept and that there is still a strong tradition here of not being extravagant and wasteful.

I went into that fast-food restaurant in Zurich to get a taste of America. It backfired. I left with an important taste of Switzerland.

THE NIGHT OF MY UNCLE

by Roger Bonner

There are many stories I could tell about my uncle. Some are hearsay, bandied about by relatives, others I witnessed myself. My aunt plays an equally important part in these tales. Had it not been for her indomitable will, my uncle would have lacked the catalytic stimulus that drove him to extremes. But they are both gone now, sleeping side by side (peacefully at last) up on the hill behind the church of that small Swiss village called - let us say - Brodelsdorf, an apt name for the setting of so much 'seething' domestic life. That is where Uncle Karl battled with his wife Gertrude for nearly forty years.

They lived off the main road in an old, rambling farmhouse, half-timbered, with a sloping roof and crooked barn door that once opened to my grandfather's roaring forge: he was the village blacksmith and saddler. In his youth my uncle helped his father by slapping the horses on their quivering haunches and yanking up their legs for the glowing horseshoes to singe into hooves. Later my uncle dropped the profession of blacksmith, but continued making saddles, branching out into upholstery, and finally even starting a furniture shop. The smithy was transformed into a showroom and the barn door replaced with a large display window.

When the shop first opened, it was the talk of the village. The farmers would come lumbering up to it in their heavy shoes and scratch their necks. Wives would poke their husbands and huddle together with other wives, buzzing at the sight of all that finery: pink curtains and red drapes with tassels, silk pillows, eiderdown quilts, white and fluffy as snowbanks, and amidst that splendor an inordinately (almost obscenely) wide French bed. It was enveloped in a glossy crimson bedspread that spilled resplendently down onto the floor in broad ruffles. Everyone agreed that Aunt Gertrude was behind it all. Uncle Karl was too simple a man ever to let such a notion of flagrant, almost sinful luxury cross his mind.

But the times were changing, and prosperity came creeping even as far as Brodelsdorf, tucked away in the foothills of the Jura mountains. The farmers, influenced by television, hankered for a change; their wives were keen to redecorate the old houses, and business flourished for Uncle Karl. Aunt Gertrude, with her nose for money, had seen that coming, and smiled to herself as the bank account grew fatter and fatter. Except for refurbishing their house, she had hardly ever withdrawn any money to spend on herself. She came from a poor farmer's family and was raised with seven other brothers and sisters, all known for their sullen fierceness. The father, an alcoholic who never spared the rod, instilled the fear of God into them at an early age. At seventeen she ran away to work as a waitress in the many taverns that dotted the valley. It was in one of these that she met my uncle. He was a quiet man with a dry sense of humor who always ordered a bottle of beer and guzzled straight from it.

In those days people said he was handsome, but when I recall the long ears and that sagging face, accentuated by a nose red as an overripe strawberry, and the bushy eyebrows shading forlorn, watery eyes, I find that hard to believe. Perhaps it was his curly hair, making him somewhat cuddly like a sheep, that gave him the reputation for being good-looking.

My Aunt was an austere beauty with high, ruddy cheekbones and large eyes that narrowed cunningly in later years. She was the no-nonsense type, wiry and agile, who could work like a horse and handle any drunk. She never minced her words and went to church regularly; everyone respected, and some even feared her. Men lusted after her virginity, sealed tight as a nut beneath the simple clothes she wore so well on that taut body.

My uncle also took notice and came regularly to the Restaurant Storchen. At the time he was more than usually sad because his fiancee had died of tuberculosis a year before. He would brood and drink bottle after bottle of beer. My aunt would sit next to him late in the evening, placing her hand on his shoulder, and when the time came to leave, she would gently help him out.

He returned every evening and would stare at her rushing back and forth across the rough wooden floor with tray after tray of beer. One winter night, as snowflakes batted at the window, and cigar smoke hung in the air like a thick haze, Uncle Karl lingered about until he was the last customer. Outside it was freezing; he had a long way home. Aunt Gertrude, bending down close to him, whispered: "Come and stay. It's warm in my bed."

A year later they were married, and she moved into the rambling farmhouse where a hoary, widowed father sat ramrod straight at the kitchen table and banged for his food. His spinster sister ruled the household with venomous rigor. Aunt Gertrude was inured to such conditions and could hold her own. The strain, however, showed on her marriage. Rows with Uncle Karl would last late into the night, accompanied by shouts and stomping feet on creaking boards. On one culminating Saturday the sound of a shattering chamber pot barely missing its target made grandfather go up to lay down the law. Afterwards the situation remained somewhat calm, only to flare up occasionally.

Then Aunt Gertrude gave birth to a lusty son, and two years later to another even lustier one. They bellowed for their milk. As they grew older they became the delight of grandfather, who softened in his dotage, and let them clamber up on his lap to tweak his handlebar mustache, a sight which must have filled Uncle Karl with wonder when thinking back of the belt lashes he had received as a boy.

When they were a boisterous ten and twelve, grandfather took ill. Aunt Gertrude had to nurse him for many months until he died. Now Uncle Karl banged on the table when the meals were not served on time, and the old battles ensued once more with untold vehemence. It is these scenes I remember from my visits to them as a boy during school vacations: Aunt Gertrude scurrying about the kitchen, firing up the ancient wood stove to cook steaming pots of beans and bacon, while engaging in verbal thrusts and parries with Uncle Karl. Next to the sink where she clattered the dishes there was a shaft dropping straight to a pigpen in the barn below. After rinsing the plates in a bucket of water and mixing in the kitchen refuse, she would slide back the hatch and dump the swill down onto the pigs. So there was always this muffled grunting and squealing as a sort of rustic background music to our meals. The kitchen was dark and sooty and from the low beams slabs of curing bacon and sausages dangled like bats.

As old Martha, grandfather's sister, grew more and more enfeebled, Aunt Gertrude usurped power over the house. Uncle Karl had his workshop, she had the household. And when Martha died after being bed-ridden for a year, there was no one left to dispute Aunt Gertrude's rule.

Now Uncle Karl had always liked to hit the bottle, and many are the stories about my aunt's attempts to reform him: the pots of peppermint tea she forced on him in later years when he had kidney trouble, how old cronies smuggled beer into the workshop while she was away shopping, how she checked his breath, so he started sucking peppermint candy.

Drinking had a long tradition in Brodelsdorf; it was so to speak institutionalized. On Saturday night it was a custom to raise hell with the boys. Not even Aunt Gertrude could break that habit. But usually Uncle Karl would return early, as most of the men did, just to avoid trouble. On one balmy summer night, however, when he was about 60, there had been a party to celebrate the opening of the first village branch bank. Uncle Karl had laid the carpets and delivered the furniture, so he was one of the guests of honor. The wine flowed freely, and when it was time to go home, he and a couple of other dauntless spirits struck out for the hills to drink the outlying taverns dry.

"To hell with her!" he shouted several times, raising yet another bottle in a toast when it was already past midnight.

Getting home was an arduous task. Uncle Karl liked to sing when drunk, and on that Saturday, or rather very early Sunday morning, he was particularly spry. Two friends had to brace him and hold his mouth to prevent him from serenading the entire village. At one point he almost staggered into a water trough for cows. The sky glittered with stars; he wanted to climb a tree to pick them. When they finally reached his farmhouse, a friend decided to accompany him to make sure he got there in one piece. The two crept stealthily round to the back of the house. Uncle Karl fumbled for the key. His friend had to steady his hand so he could stick the key in the lock. He turned it once, twice... nothing budged. He shoved his shoulder against the door; it was as unyielding as a boulder. His friend tried with the same result.

"The bitch has locked me out!" Uncle Karl cursed.

They reeled to the front door, but it too was locked tight as a dungeon.

"So she thinks she can keep me out of my own house," Uncle Karl slurred as he raised a fist toward the bedroom window. He wanted to pick up a stone to fling at her, but his friend dragged him to the side of the house.

"Listen, come home with me," he said, trying to hold him up.

"I'm sleeping in my house...in my bed!" Uncle Karl boomed.

He straightened himself and headed for the workshop. He rattled and kicked the door, then tried the window. When it too refused to give, he poked his elbow through the glass and undid the latch.

"Help me climb in," he mumbled.

His friend, a worker in a nearby foundry, had accumulated as much paunch as Uncle Karl, and so they both labored to haul themselves over the sill, grunting and sweating all the while. Once inside they flopped down on the floor like sacks of flour.

"You're not leaving," Uncle Karl yanked his friend back. "I stashed away some beer ... we've got to celebrate this..."

He reached inside a Louis XV sofa he was re-upholstering and pulled out two gleaming bottles.

"The one place she never looks," he chuckled, raising the bottle to his mouth.

The two must have laughed and guzzled their beer until dawn. The workshop was separated from the main house by a thick wall, so Aunt Gertrude probably heard nothing. But she did wake up earlier than usual on Sunday morning, not because of the church bells pealing throughout the valley, but because of the sound of laughter. At first she dismissed it as coming from some villagers, joking after returning from early mass. The laughter, however, grew more voluble from titters to outright guffaws, and the number of people seemed to increase. She tore open the window and stuck out her head. Down below in front of the display window a small crowd of people had gathered.

"It's Gertrude," one farmer said, nudging his wife.

The others looked up and slowly moved away, trying to suppress sporadic bursts of laughter as they trailed down the road.

Aunt Gertrude hastily pulled on her bathrobe and rushed down the stairs. When she got to the display window, she stopped dead in her tracks and gasped, then covered her face in an attempt to hide the fits of laughter which began to shake her body. There on that huge, sumptuous French bed lay Uncle Karl and his friend, flat on their backs, mouths gaping wide open, their chests heaving alternately in steady, blissful snoring. Between them on the ruffles of the glossy crimson bedspread, now sullied and wrinkled, were two very empty bottles of beer.

LIVING WITH MOUNTAINS

by Irene Ritter

It took me many years of living in Switzerland before I understood the role played by the mountains in the Swiss way of life. Mountains were at first, for me, natural decorative elements with an attractive choice of Alpine scenery. Then, bit by bit, I became aware that they were far more significant.

These Alps have shaped the course of Swiss history, the tourist industry and the mentality of the people themselves. Mountains create physical and mental confines for those who inhabit the valleys between them. Although the lowlands may be more open, the stress of the Swiss way of work in overcrowded cities imposes its own constraints. But up above the air is pure and, in the stillness of the heights, vistas widen and human horizons expand.

It has never ceased to impress me how relaxed and spontaneous the Swiss become when they go up mountains. Released from the bondage of social codes, it is as if they cast off status in the valley below to climb into a sphere of kindred spirits. Mountains have their own special aura. They affect people. Differently.

It is in the winter that the mountains hold the greatest fascination for me, when snow-fields sparkle with a myriad of diamonds in the sunshine beneath a deep-blue cobalt sky... it has a touch of Fairyland.

*****

Leaving our Swiss husbands to earn our bread in the city, my Swiss friend and I used to spend a few weeks skiing in Grindelwald each winter. She was an expert skier. Following her down the ski-trails, I used to feel like Dopey, the seventh dwarf, behind Snow White: the one always tripping over himself a long way behind. She was a very patient Snow White.

Coming down the Scheidegg run late one afternoon, I somehow lost track of her and found myself skiing alone down a slope leading into some woods. All of a sudden I plunged straight into the snow. At first I was too stunned to know what to do. I seemed to have no pain anywhere. Behind me, my skis were sticking out of a snow bank like a pair of open scissors and were so firmly embedded that I could not move them. The more I struggled the less I was able to extricate myself. Then I felt someone click my bindings loose. My skis slipped off and I was grabbed under the armpits and hauled upright. Abashed, I looked into a pair of dark sunglasses over a well-tanned face whose owner was talking rapid Swiss German to me. I realized he was asking me if I was hurt.

"Thank you very much. I'm all right, I think," I stuttered in my best *Schwizerdütsch.*

"You had a bad fall," he said, peering at me anxiously.

"No, nothing hurts, thank you. It happened so fast I ... I don't know what I did," I ended lamely.

"You were lucky. You could easily have broken a leg." He bent down to pick up my skis.

I smiled wanly and proceeded to brush the snow off my hair and my clothes. My rescuer was dressed in a white blouse-like anorak over grey ski pants and, taking off his sunglasses, he pushed back a battered greenish-grey peaked cap, rubbing his forehead as he watched me. He still wore a frown of concern.

"Are you sure you are all right? Shall I help you with your skis?"

"Yes, please ... oh my goodness," I cried, suddenly realizing he was not alone. About a dozen men, all wearing the same outfits, were standing around grinning at me. I found myself in the midst of a Swiss Army alpine unit! Highly embarrassed, hoping and praying I was not going to make a fool of myself, I bent over my skis to hide my confusion and made ready to start off.

"Thank you again for helping me, you were most kind. I must find my friend now, she will be wondering what has happened to me."

"Good luck and be careful."

I just saw him wave his hand as I fixed my gaze ahead, intent on making a dignified departure. The trail led through the woods. Never having skied alone, I tried not to panic by concentrating on keeping control of my feet so that they would not part company. The snow was packed hard under the trees, the narrow tracks like icy tram-lines. My heart was in my mouth as my skis accelerated and I sensed my ever-increasing speed. I shot out of the woods, rigid with fear at my reckless pace. But to my intense relief the trail widened and rose gently onto fields of softer snow. Bending my knees into the snowplough position, I managed to ease myself onto the crest and come to a standstill without falling.

"Oh Lord," I cried to myself. At the foot of what was still a steep enough slope, I saw Snow White waiting for me. She waved her pole and yelled something I couldn't hear. Gathering what remained of my courage, I braced myself for the last descent, grimly setting my feet once more in the snowplough position. I arrived upright but feeling like jelly, my knees wobbling under the strain. Expecting commiseration or at least concern, I was quite put out to find my friend highly amused and obviously enjoying herself.

"Have you joined the Swiss Army?" she asked me.

"Me? No, why?" I replied, my nerves still on edge.

"Look behind you" she said mischievously.

I turned round. There had I, unwittingly, been leading the group of white-bloused men, now weaving swiftly past us in single file, some of them raising their sticks and shouting good-bye to me.

"What have you been up to?" asked my friend, by now wide-eyed with curiosity. "Where did you pick them up?"

"They picked me up," I answered ruefully.

"What, all of them?"

We burst out laughing.

"Just one."

*****

There is no denying that the *Putz-Geist* (the cleaning spirit) rules paramount among Swiss virtues. Cleaning is a way of life in Switzerland. The conscientious Swiss *Hausfrau* spring-cleans her home every year. Not to be outdone, the men of Lucerne and Kriens spring-clean 'their' mountain, Mount Pilatus, on the third Saturday of every June.

Invited to witness the *Pilatus Putzete* in order to write up the story, I joined some 150 men at 6 am at the Kriens cable-car station. A couple of women came along as team cooks. The men, armed with picks and shovels, electric saws, ropes and other gear were allocated in crews to different parts of the mountain. We all took off in cable-cars to the summit.

I didn't have the right boots on. Having scuffed my heel a few days before, I wore a pair of soft, comfortable brogues. They did, however, provide a bonus. I was given a guide all to myself to show me around and make sure I didn't fall off the mountain. He was the Head Ranger, an ex-policeman, very charming, but most disappointed that my footwear prevented him from roping me down

some sheer rock-face to give me a bird's-eye view of the crews at work. Frankly, I was quite relieved. I was not really all that mad about dangling on a rope at high altitudes! We concentrated on the Alpine flora instead. "I always go and check the narcissi when they bloom," he said, showing me these delicate flowers and white anemones that looked like fine bone china, and so many floral treasures that most people walk past and never see. That was fascinating. So were the marmots we spied in the distance.

"The eagles," he said, "are like us - mountain patrolmen. Whilst they clean the mountain picking up the wildlife debris, we remove the winter debris, checking and repairing the trails." The men do it all on a voluntary basis - for the love of the mountain. He took me to see the Kriens Fire Brigade in (cleaning) action. The meadows were not vacuum-cleaned, neither were the forests shampooed nor the rocks mopped down! Fallen trees and loose stones were removed from the paths, rough steps cut into a cliff, with short railings affixed for easier access, and fresh paint added to the trail markings.

With an ex-policeman in front and the chief of the Fire Brigade behind me, what possible harm could I come to, whatever I had on my feet? I was led on a tour of inspection up the mountain paths they had just cleared. There was still too much snow on the trails higher up the mountain and this crew had decided to call it a day. They would come back a few weeks later to finish the job. Meanwhile, leaving me in the safekeeping of the Kriens Fire Brigade - fourteen men strong - my guide went off to check other crews at work.

The fireman-cook had a campfire going with an enticing smell of coffee brewing in a cauldron. Liberally laced with *Schnaps*, the *Kafi-Buffet* (hot sweet coffee with brandy) was handed round in paper cups. I have never imbibed so much *Kafi-Buffet* in all my life! Strangely, it had no inebriating effect on me whatsoever. Maybe I was so hungry that it fed me. I did not even bother with the lunch bag we had all been given and, being neither a sausage nor a beer fan, I farmed most of it out to the Fire Brigade. When the cauldron was empty, down the mountain we all went - to more *Kafi-Buffet* at the restaurant below! When they invited me to join them at the next stop for the evening meal cooked by the wives, I deemed it better to head for home before the sun set, in preference to walking down the mountain in the middle of the night. So, waving the Fire Brigade good-bye, I made my way to the cable-car station.

This also happened to be the day the Pope visited Lucerne. Suspended between heaven and earth in my little cable-cabin, I watched the congregation at open-air Mass on the city common below me. Did the spirits inside me create this feeling of serenity or had the Papal blessing reached me ...?

HEADACHES 403 - 408

by Claire Bonney

Not too long ago I called up the local officials in Zihlschlacht. (No, there was never a battle way out there in Thurgau. I once read that the *Schlacht* part is some Alemannic bastardization of the Latin word for 'long hedge rows of berry bushes.') I was interested in getting back the name I was born with, have always used for business and have never wanted to part with.

Before January 1, 1988, a Swiss woman legally had to use her husband's name. She was, however, allowed to hyphenate, which made my name Brüllmann-Bonney. Today, two hundred francs worth of forms, a new identity card, a new passport and a new driver's license later, my official name is Bonney (no hyphen) Brüllmann. Now that's progress! I shouldn't complain though. It's much worse for my boss. She had a double name like 'Smith Jones' before she was married. She has had to drag around 'von der Mühll-Smith Jones' with her for the past thirteen years in penance for her connubial bliss. A name like that doesn't even fit on all the forms you have to sign.

"Hello," I said. "This is Claire Bonney and I am married to Matthias Brüllmann who is a citizen of your village. (In Switzerland, you are a citizen of the village in which your father was a citizen, even if you yourself - or he for that matter - have never been there. Having married before January 1, 1985, I am also a citizen of the village in which my husband's father was a citizen. Knowing that the village bears the responsibility of housing me in its old-age home when I am indigent and infirm and no one else will take me, I was tempted to ask about the facilities since I had the man on the line anyway. Quick thinking, however, told me that I'd better stick to one thing at a time.)

"I want to have my name changed back to Bonney now that the new marriage laws are in effect."

"What did you say his name was?" he queried, "Buulmann? We don't have anyone here registered by that name."

I pursed my unwilling American lips and tried again.

"BbbRrrüüülllmann," I said, crisply enunciating the 'B', vibrating the 'r' on the roof of my mouth and giving him a fine *Umlaut* working into a long and luscious 'l'.

110

"Wie bitte?" (I beg your pardon?)

I sighed, "Berta, Robert, Ueli, Lotti, Lotti, Marta, Anton..." I trailed off, racking my brain for a Swiss name that begins with 'N' (Yes, I do know that the official name-spelling list of names is printed in every Swiss phone book, but the cat was lying on it sunning herself and I didn't want to get scratched.)

"I see," he said, "Which Brüllmann did you say you had married?" (I hear him going quickly through papers and stamping my husband's file with some sort of 'House Committee for Un-Swiss Activities' stamp.)

"Yes, we can do that," he said brightly. "But we'll need your *Familien-Büchli"* (Family Book).

"I don't think we have one." I am sweating now. The cat stretches lazily.

"What? But you've been married for three years!"

"I know," I said "But I don't think we have one. What is it anyway?" (Muffled sound of ink pad being furiously pounded.)

Patiently he explained that the *Familien-Büchli* is something every Swiss family must have to enter the birth dates of each child.

"But we don't have any children."

"Also," he replied, "In that case, it will be twenty-five francs for the *Familien-Büchli* and forty francs for the name change. We'll send you the Certificate of Name Change in two months, but you must then have it entered in the Basle Registry."

"Thank you very much," I said. What a relief!

"Wiederhören Frau Brüllmann." (Be hearing from you again, Mrs. Brüllmann.) The phone clicked off.

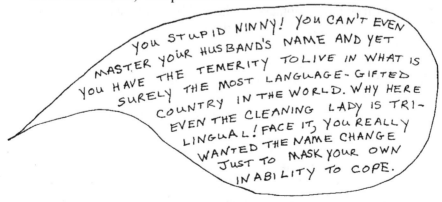

*****

111

About two weeks after we had moved to Basle, a woman called up ostensibly to welcome us in Swiss German as newcomers. She also wanted to know if we wanted to subscribe to Basle's leading newspaper. I answered in Swiss German that I guessed that if we had wanted to, we probably would have. She replied, "But you CAN read German, can't you?"

*****

In a streetcar going across the Bellevue in Zurich sat an American family in one of the four-person compartments. Man, wife, son, daughter. Across the way, in the 'singles' seats was an old man in a beret. The girl, about eight years old, stretched her little tourist's feet tiredly out toward her Daddy. That was it.

QUIT BEING SO DIFFICULT! YOU SHOULD BE GRATEFUL THAT THE PHONE RINGS EVERY ONCE IN AWHILE. THERE ARE LOTS OF LONELY PEOPLE OUT THERE WHO WOULD GIVE THEIR EYETEETH FOR A FRIENDLY TELEPHONE CHAT.

The old man leapt to his feet, feeling called upon to deliver the following sermon in English:

"I know you are Americans and you don't raise your children properly, but here in Switzerland we do not put our feet on streetcar cushions."

At that, he got out his white handkerchief and vigorously wiped the plastic seat cover where the now drop-mouthed child's feet had rested for one-tenth of a second. She said, "Gee, I'm sorry."

The old man was then moved to give a short outline of European history with special emphasis on the subtleties of Swiss-American diplomatic relations. It went like this:

A. Shoes are for walking on.
B. Seats are for sitting on.
C. The Swiss support and are proud of their public transport
   system.
   1. Everyone knows how dangerous it is to ride the subway in
      New York.
   2. Americans have no sense of culture.
D. Europeans do not like to get their coats dirty.

The girl's father stood up to the full 6'5" that he was and stated in no uncertain terms that his daughter had already apologized and that enough was enough.

Sitting in the back of the '8' and tempered by years of re-education in the laws of Swiss reserve, I overcame the impulse to rush over to the father, knock off his Texan cowboy hat and kiss him on both cheeks.

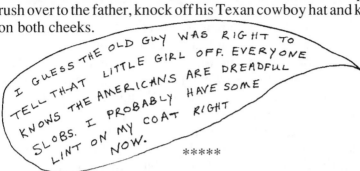

I GUESS THE OLD GUY WAS RIGHT TO TELL THAT LITTLE GIRL OFF. EVERYONE KNOWS THE AMERICANS ARE DREADFUL SLOBS. I PROBABLY HAVE SOME LINT ON MY COAT RIGHT NOW.

*****

After eleven years in Switzerland, one little thing still really bothers me. The phone rings. I pick it up. Now I know that I could infinitely simplify my life merely by announcing "Bonney," but the ingrained habits of my early training, plus an innate sense of self-protection left over from a five-year stint living as a student in Zurich's infamous Langstrasse being what they are, I say, "Hello."

"Who's there?" an unnerved voice cracks back.

"Well, who are YOU?" I answer icily.

"I must have the wrong number."

I weaken. I KNOW I am not supposed to be this rude. "Well maybe you do and maybe you don't," I say. "My name is Bonney."

"But I looked under Brüllmann and found this number!" the caller exclaims.

"That is my husband's name," I explain. But by this time they have usually hung up.

RELAX, RELAX, RELAX, RELAX! IF YOU WERE LIVING IN THE STATES, YOU WOULD BE GETTING TEN TIMES AS MANY OF THESE CALLS. IF YOU HATE TELEPHONE SALES PITCHES SO MUCH, WHY DON'T YOU FINALLY FORK OUT THE MONEY FOR AN ANSWERING MACHINE?

*****

I came to a museum in Basle where I now work with a lot of optimism and a German not only heavily accented by my loud-mouth American mother tongue, but now with an Ikat stripe of a dialect bearing witness to a ten-year stay in Zurich. It costs three francs to get into the museum and taking tickets is part of my job.

"Three francs please," I would say. The Baslers would stare, blankly aghast. *"Drew Franke bitte,"* was actually how it sounded.

Now people in Basle who manage nicely when they hear *zwei, zwo, zwee* and all the other infinite variations on the word two, somehow cannot comprehend the 'three' spoken as *drew* of their rival Zurchers. They cannot even fathom what I might possibly be getting at as I sit there behind my desk holding a ticket in one hand and the other hand open-palm-up. After the phrase *Drew Franke bitte* is repeated three times with the formerly open palm now closed, and thumb, index and middle fingers (No, not index, middle and fourth fingers - they wouldn't get that either), pointing up to heaven, I switch my tactics.

"DRY" I screech.

Ooh, they look relieved. They are pleased. They understand me.

"Ooh, you're American aren't you? My son (my cousin, my brother-in-law, the next door neighbor's kid) lives in New York. He's a film-maker (stockbroker, graphic designer, acting student)."

To remedy the annoyance of this constant dialogue which takes place at least three times a day, five days a week making me figure that after five years at the museum, I have now heard of every Swiss who has ever visited my home turf, my painter friend Gaby made a great museum uniform for me. A black guerilla turtleneck with "It costs three francs. Yes, I am American" painted neatly white in German across its chest. I wore this turtleneck proudly to work and asked my good friend Peter, who happened to come into the museum that morning, if it wasn't a marvelous antidote to the problem I had been having.

"I don't know," he said, "I was too embarrassed to look at you there long enough to read it."

NOW YOU'VE REALLY LOST IT! HERE THEY ARE TRYING TO ESTABLISH NORMAL HUMAN CONTACT WITH YOU AND YOU GO AND BLOW IT. IF YOU HEARD A SWISS ACCENT FROM THE TICKET-TAKER AT MOMA, WOULDN'T YOU JUST <u>HAVE</u> TO WOW HIM WITH A "<u>GRÜEZI</u>"?

FAMILIAR DISTANCE

by John Bendix

I watch Switzerland but only infrequently belong to it, for I have become an insider while remaining an outsider. I speak dialect, have Swiss in-laws and have returned for 25 years to familiar places there which are as much a home as I shall ever have. But I always leave again, escaping my responsibilities to the country and remaining a distanced observer. It is not comfortable to feel at home in a place you do not belong.

By profession I am an analytic spectator. My experiences with Switzerland have been colored by an interest in how social and political life is organized. Some of my earliest attempts to come to grips with Swiss life were through such distanced lenses. My earliest challenge was to learn the impossible Swiss-German dialect.

It is not, in fact, impossible to learn dialect. In my case, it took ten years. I was not helped by living on the Hasliberg. Postman Huggler insisted upon speaking *Haslitiitsch*, which meant the number ten was always *zächen* and never *zäni* or even *zehn*. This was hard on those of us who were struggling to master High German. He was making a point about preserving his dialect, but it was not one I was in a position to appreciate at age 8. My sporadic visits to friends later meant I was sometimes in the Aargau, sometimes in Basle, sometimes in Lucerne. I dutifully imitated what I heard, despite the hilarity this produced because of the mixture of different dialects I was speaking. For years I could not hear the difference between dialects and was mystified by how Swiss could identify where people came just by their dialect.

My speaking dialect proved to be very useful for a project I started during my third extended stay in the country. It was about the history, culture, politics and economics of the Haslital. Versions of this project were to preoccupy me for many years thereafter. When I began the project, I had to go out into the community to collect information. Relations had been uneasy between the school I attended and the community where it was located. We were a community of transitory strangers while they were a community of perennial residents.

I began to encounter Haslitalers, as the people in that region are called. Rather than meeting only taciturn farmers, I found many thoughtful people who were happy to discuss the region they lived in, even with a naive foreigner like me who needed to be set straight at times. No matter how imperfect my dialect, using it opened many doors. I remember one of these interviews particularly well. I had been trying without success to reach a certain community official. Through his brother I was finally able to locate him out in the fields, haying. I walked up to him, relieved to have found him, and explained who I was and what I wanted to know. He looked at me for a moment - we were literally in the middle of nowhere - and said, yes, he'd be happy to talk about my topic, but could we first discuss the disgraceful state of American foreign policy? I learned from that encounter never to underestimate how well-informed the Swiss can be, even when you meet them in out-of-the-way places.

One conclusion from my research was that social change in such communities was much more deliberate than in the America I came from. I began to think of Swiss conservatism less as a world view or ideology than as a response to the constraints of eking out a living on very poor soil. Every resource had to be husbanded for there was little good land but many natural disasters and so little to go around but so many people. The Haslital, like many mountain valleys, resolved some of its problems through emigration. Communities resolved many issues by deciding that the good of the whole came before the desires of the individual. Prohibitions to prevent the overgrazing by cattle, to prevent the precious topsoil from washing away or to prevent any one individual from becoming wealthy at the expense of others were jointly decided upon. Village life was not easy and often not even particularly pleasant. But it did support, protect and provide for the inhabitants.

When each village reacts in this fashion, a strong sense of identity is created. Villagers develop a powerful determination to resolve their own problems without outside help. I believe the origin of the strong independent streak in Swiss communities, a tendency which still lingers on in many places today, has a great deal to do with the past natural constraints under which natives lived. But going it alone is a sentiment at complete odds with the economic and political centralization every industrialized country has experienced in the twentieth century. Berne politicians must bend over backwards to accommodate recalcitrant communities who refuse to act in accordance with Berne's wishes. Sometimes such communities balk at cooperating with Berne or with other communities even when it is in their economic interest. This stubbornness can only be blamed on their attitudes from the past and their pride in an independent existence even when they literally cannot afford independence.

Switzerland works better as an idea than it does as a nation. The picture of the nation presented for outsiders, and tirelessly promoted by the Swiss National Tourist Office, is that of a unified, peaceful, neutral, wealthy land filled with bucolic cowherds on spectacular Alps. Insiders know a different picture. There are bitter inter-community squabbles over resources, restive young folk who feel constrained, widespread misgivings about certain categories of foreigners and many poor farmers dependent on heavy subsidies.

Nineteenth century Swiss leaders were far too successful in selling the idea of the *Eidgenossenschaft* (Swiss Confederation) to its members. The plans for the 700th anniversary celebration in 1991 have made it quite evident how artificial the idea of Switzerland is. The country is centralizing but remains very decentralized. *Gemeinde* (community) and *Kanton* (canton) autonomy confronts *Bund* (Confederation) power. Maintaining viable agriculture is to some people only the heavily subsidized gardening of the landscape for the enjoyment of tourists. Developers continually fight preservationists who argue that it is only unspoiled nature which will continue to attract tourists. Swiss moods vary from apathy to participation, from love of their own self-righteousness to the distaste for foreigners. At heart, Switzerland has an ideology of unity and a practice of disunity.

I am only mildly consoled to think that my discomfort at being an inside outsider is so neatly paralleled by the contradictions of Switzerland. But perhaps these very paradoxes - also the paradoxes of my own uprootedness - are what keep pulling me back.

STILL SMILING

by Muthana Kubba

No matter what they say about the Swiss, one thing is beyond any doubt: they are human after all, even if they try hard to hide the fact.

It was on one of those unforgettable, beautiful summer evenings when it stays light well into the evening that I had my very first real encounter with Swiss authority. I had just enjoyed a good swim in a friend's lovely garden pool and was cheerfully pedalling my bicycle uphill on my way home. Everything looked so pleasant and peaceful.

Out of the blue, a police car whizzed past. When it was a couple of hundred yards ahead of me, it squealed to a stop and two mean-looking policemen jumped out and headed towards me with grim, determined faces. Then one of them ran back to the car to get his cap, as if authority could only be imposed when he had his cap on.

Perplexed, but in a happy and careless mood, I stopped and waited until they stood in front of me.

"But I didn't rob a bank today," I said putting on a blank face to hide my reckless humour.

"Offending a policeman on duty is a punishable offence," one of them replied very angrily.

"So is robbing a bank," I added daringly.

"Your bicycle licence plate expired two days ago."

I realized it was June 2nd and one is supposed to pay eight francs to renew a third-party compulsory insurance on all bikes by May 31st. The Swiss, I may add, are the most highly insured nation per capita on earth.

Now really amused, I ventured, "If I were in your shoes, I would go about this differently. It is obvious, even to you, that I am a middle-aged man cycling home after a hard, long day. Why can't you just say like any other policeman everywhere else would 'Would you please renew your bike's license plate, it ran out two days ago?' Don't you think this is more effective than your approach?"

"Do you want to pay the twenty-franc fine now or shall we send it to you?" they retorted without even pretending to have listened to me.

"You could have added, 'We are very sorry, Sir, but we must charge you the fine prescribed by law. How do you want to pay it?'" I replied with deep intonations making my point very clear.

The next day I mentioned this incident to my best friend in this part of the world who always has good explanations about local attitudes. He told me, "Here people attach great importance to appearing to comply with the law. Riding a bike with an expired licence plate is a violation of the law, inviting immediate action, almost as serious as parking a car on someone else's parking lot. Less obvious offenses are usually tolerated provided no one gets hurt."

I never received that twenty-franc fine. Maybe they were listening after all.

A NEW COMMANDMENT
by Richard J. Bloomfield

In the course of my theological studies in the United States I thought I had been well prepared in the field of biblical content. However, when I moved to Switzerland in 1981 I learned otherwise. I don't know in which book the folks in the small village of S-chanf in Engadine had found it, but they had evidently stumbled onto a commandment that was unknown to my professors in North America.

I stumbled onto the existence of this new commandment quite by accident. It happened during one of my first worship services in the Reformed Church in S-chanf. The church was full of earnest-faced mountain folk. I was standing with a young couple at the baptismal font holding their child in my arm. Next to me were the godparents.

For some reason or other the child to be baptized had something against me, or, at least, against the sound of my voice. When I began the baptismal liturgy, the little boy in my arm began to cry. I spoke more loudly. The child intensified his crying. I raised my voice a few more decibels and continued. At the same time I tried to communicate with my eyes that the parents should do something to comfort the squalling child. But it was too late. The contest between the iron will of the crying child and the iron will of the baptizing pastor had already reached hopeless proportions.

At that moment I realized just how silly the whole scene was. One little child and one grown pastor both screaming at the top of their lungs was really a ridiculous situation. At least I thought it was ridiculous and began to laugh. The hopeless struggle to outdo the screaming infant, the helpless parents and the earnest-faced congregation were just too much for me and I couldn't stop laughing. It also seemed to be too much for the people in the congregation and they, too, started to laugh. In the midst of all this laughter I baptized the child. The joy of baptism seemed to be reflected in the laughter of the congregation. I felt we had overcome a possibly embarrassing situation with laughter and was pleased with the result.

As I shook hands with the people after the service, however, no one was laughing anymore. In fact, each person apologized to me as he left the church. ''Excuse me for laughing out loud during the service." The earnest-faced mountain people meant it! One doesn't laugh in church.

"Thou shalt not laugh" is the commandment that the people felt they had broken. It was at the door of the church that Sunday morning that I learned that these people had at least eleven commandments. "Thou shalt not laugh" definitely belonged in their list of forbidden activities.

This prohibition surprised me at first. I had gotten to know the villagers as folk who can laugh and party. In fact, you would have to go a long way to find wedding parties that can top the parties in the Engadine. There seems to be no end to the jokes and skits that these people can produce at a party. It seemed, then, that the commandment "Thou shalt not laugh" applied only to church.

I received a confirmation of this assumption when I found an old book on etiquette. In the section on behavior in church was the clear admonition to remain "serious" during church services. "Laughing," the book warned, "shows lack of respect for God himself and for the pastor as well. People who laugh take neither the Christian religion nor divine worship seriously." There it was in black and white: the commandment that accounted for the earnest faces of the churchgoers and their apologies for laughing. It was an old and well-learned lesson: "Thou shalt not laugh."

Traditions awaken a great deal of respect in my soul. Traditions and historical settings are two of the reasons that I moved from California to Switzerland. However, this tradition of the eleventh commandment was one that I could not respect. For six years I tried to demonstrate that you can be serious with a smile on your face. "A God who can laugh" became one of the recurring themes of my sermons.

The earnest-faced mountain folk proved to be good learners in this regard. When I left S-chanf after six years, no one apologized at the door for having laughed during church. I think it was the only tradition that I managed to change, however.

ON FITTING IN

by Kate Mühlethaler

I first set eyes on my future Swiss husband through teeming Scottish rain and swirling mist outside Loch Lomond Youth Hostel. Some months later I received an invitation to visit him at Christmas, which I gladly accepted.

I was met in Zurich by his parents as he was away at work. They couldn't speak a word of English, nor I German, but they managed to meet the right girl. It was about 4 am. I was whisked off into the back of their car and was wrapped up in a blanket. A salami sandwich was thrust into my hand.

Too excited to fall asleep, I lay in bed feeling as if I were in a coffin. No beam of light could penetrate those solid Swiss shutters. After a while I heard cocks crowing, accompanied by a strange sound - the sound of guns! I was aghast, surely Switzerland was a neutral, peace-loving country? I was expecting to hear the sound of an alphorn or someone yodelling. But shooting, definitely not! When my friend arrived later, he explained it was only shooting practice. I was surprised to learn that although cleaning the car, hanging out washing etc. were considered a disturbance and not permitted on Sundays, shooting was. This was just the first of many puzzles I was to encounter.

One day we decided to go skiing. Not knowing how to brake, I just sat down, much to the amusement of several onlookers. Things got worse as we progressed to the T-bar lift. Glad to have a rest, I sat down gratefully. My friend, beginning to lose his balance (and temper!) shouted frantic directions to me in his then limited English. A couple of hours later, still finding it difficult to brake, I unwillingly crossed the path of the ski-lift, causing two angry people to fall off.

After numerous letters, I set off happily for a second Swiss holiday, certain that Switzerland would be plain sailing in summer. My friend didn't have as long holidays as I, which meant I was often alone with mother-in-law-to-be. We got along well, speaking French. It had been my main subject at college and she'd completed her *Welschlandjahr* many years previously. While Ulrich was working, she and I always went for a walk between noon and 2 pm.

I began to feel a bit like a dog! The silence everywhere during those two hours really hit me. On the stroke of 12 the streets of their small town emptied dramatically. Nothing stirred as we walked past the sleepy houses with their tidy, model gardens. After London, this was a real culture shock for me. I doubted whether I could live in Switzerland. Whatever would I do during this enforced 'quiet time'? We always walked the same route, right out into the countryside.

Many years later I learned by chance from my sister-in-law that my mother-in-law had been ashamed of being seen with me in my mini-skirt, but had been too polite to ask me to change into something more modest. The mini hadn't yet hit Gerlafingen, and mine were extremely scanty.

One day Ueli suggested going on a short mountain hike. For him, the 'hike' may have been short before, but after dragging my poor, untrained body up and down mountain slopes and over glacier cracks, I began to dislike him, the mountains, and anything vaguely to do with Switzerland. Our path ended at the side of a mountain where there was a long, forbidding ladder down a sheer drop, over which I didn't even dare to look. I refused to budge another foot. He advised me to "treat it like an ordinary ladder, just don't look down, and when you get to the bar in the middle, swing yourself along it to the top of the next ladder." My protests became even stronger and my legs turned to jelly. I asked myself how a respectable city-bred girl like me could have got involved with this Swiss dare-devil. Just then a party of solid BRITISH climbers arrived at the scene. Sensing my panic, they offered to tie a rope around me. Apparently I sang "Onward Christian Soldiers" all the way down without realising it, to the amusement of my rescuers above. We finally arrived at the mountain hut where we were to spend the night in tense silence.

The atmosphere improved the next day until we took a chairlift which would save hours of strenuous walking. Ueli was on the chair in front of mine and I watched him 'take off'. I got into my chair and enjoyed the feeling of floating along in the clouds (well, almost). Suddenly I noticed that Ueli was on firm ground again and both he and the chairlift attendant were gesticulating wildly. I thought there must be some danger. They kept shouting something about my rucksack. So I hurled it to the ground. At this, they seemed to go completely berserk, hopping around and waving madly. When finally off the lift, I found they had only been trying to warn me that the chair would not come to a complete stop and that I should be ready to jump off at the landing. The atmosphere became frosty again as my poor partner had to climb down a steep embankment to retrieve the forlorn rucksack. Since then I've learned that many Swiss men get heated about things they soon completely forget.

In due course we decided to get married. After all, my parents were beginning to show signs of being able to pronounce his first name correctly. The surname's STILL not right. We spent a few years in the USA before returning to live in Switzerland for good.

I applied for a secretarial job and had to take French and German tests. My interviewer, a kind man, did practically the whole German test himself and I was accepted. Swiss working hours were difficult for me to get used to. I woke up only after *Znüni*, the 9 o'clock break, that sensible hour when most of the English-speaking world starts work. I remember one particular day when the efficient and dynamic Sales Manager swept into our office with the post. He gave a crisp running commentary on what I was to do with each letter. After I'd heard the new, interesting-sounding word *dringend* several times, I asked innocently, "What does 'dringend' mean?" A terrible *faux pas!* He probably never recovered.

Once I had to accompany some Brits from our agency in England to dinner. We were soon on first name terms. This became awkward for my boss, but after a while he suggested we also try first names. The next day in the sober atmosphere of the office, I began to have second thoughts. The only other boss-secretary pair who used the *Du* form were having an affair. My office colleague couldn't wait to hear me call him *Du*. When he appeared I started every sentence with *"Wollen wir...?"* to avoid the use of *Du* or *Sie*. I became a real expert at this. Was I becoming more Swiss at last?

I also tried to be a good housewife, but I refused to hang up the washing with all the socks together and colours MATCHING like the good Swiss housewife is taught. I considered my higgledy-piggledy array much more interesting. My husband once invited a school friend and his old-fashioned wife for a meal. I set aside two days to get the house straight before they came, as I'd heard she was a real *Putzteufel*. They duly arrived and the customary packet of biscuits was pressed into my hand. But I immediately noticed a troubled look on Sylvia's face. She cornered my husband a few minutes later whispering "she'll have to get a cleaning lady." Then she asked where I kept my cleaning utensils. Dumbfounded and with my mouth wide open, I pointed weakly. She went straight into action, bustling about with a no-nonsense, resolute look on her face. With grim determination, and a bucket of hot, soapy water, she proceeded to "get the worst off" to "help me out." I didn't know whether to laugh or cry. Her husband acted like it was the most natural thing in the world to see his beloved cleaning wherever they happened to be. We haven't invited them again, although several friends have asked for her address! When I related the incident to my mother-in-law, she felt the whole family had been disgraced.

Fitting in turned out to be even more difficult with motherhood. Before our baby was born I enrolled in an infant care class. I was soon out of my depth. I'd always thought you had a baby and that was it (more or less). However, I was drawn into long discussions about the merits of various baby powders and the disadvantages of certain nappy materials of which I'd never even heard. It seemed so very complicated. One evening I arrived home near to tears, convinced that I could never cope with it all and that we'd have to give the baby away. The highlight of the course was when we were let loose on 'Baby', a hard, plastic doll with glaring, watery-blue eyes. When my turn came to change its nappy, there were just 5 minutes to go till the lesson ended. I'd seen it done ten times already. I was startled out of my boredom when someone pointed in horror at 'Baby'. In my haste, I'd stood the baby on its head and was ramming its plastic pants over its behind with all my might. No-one was amused, and I hung my head in shame. Nevertheless, my daughter has managed to survive.

I found it difficult to make friends with Swiss women. I'm sure it's no fault of theirs. They seem to have a different idea of what a friend is, or maybe I do something wrong. It seemed one couldn't just 'drop in' or phone to chat without a reason. I hoped I would make a few friends through my daughter with play groups, mother and toddler clubs, etc. But when we built a sandpit in our garden hoping neighbourhood children would come to play, our nearest neighbour promptly built one too, only a much bigger one. There were many children around, but they were rarely seen and never heard. They stayed at home and only came to play (of course, never on Sundays) if they were formally invited.

Some enterprising mother actually had the marvellous idea of starting a play group. I could hardly wait. When the day finally came, six kids turned up accompanied by six mothers. I waited for the first mother to leave so that I could also retreat. But the afternoon wore on, six children playing, with six mothers watching them. At about the third meeting, one mother brought along her offspring and then actually left. Poor woman! She would never have gone had she known she was to become the main topic of the afternoon's conversation. Nobody dared to be absent after that and the playgroup was short-lived.

Other kids here seemed like wound-up clockwork soldiers in comparison with our lively daughter. Mothers sorted out any 'disagreements' with a soothing voice and endless patience. I recall plane journeys when Eva flatly refused to fasten her seat belt please. She ran up and down the aisle and finally disappeared under the skirt of a long-suffering airhostess, or begged the other passengers for sweets. I remember the sinking feeling as rows of heads turned to look back for ''that little pest's mother.'' I would have loved to look back too but I was, unfortunately, in the last seat!

Eva had a particularly loud tantrum once in a crowded department store. A well-meaning Swiss matron commented, ''What that poor child needs now is an ice-cream.'' This cry was eagerly echoed by my daughter. When I didn't comply, her rage increased and with it a flood of the worst swear words, in English, paralysed the whole of the ground floor. I'll never forget the profound relief I felt when I heard an English friend describe her own beloved child as ''a horrid little devil!''

One incident started a process of re-thinking. We were celebrating the birthday of an English friend's son in the traditional 'Guy Fawkes' manner on November 5th, with fireworks saved from the Swiss National Holiday in August. We were sitting by the fire eating baked potatoes and sausages while the children carried 'Guy', stuffed with rags and straw and nailed to a cross, in a solemn little procession. When hoisted onto the top of the bonfire, the pathetic figure was illuminated by the flames. Suddenly a familiar thought came to mind. ''What do the neighbours think about THIS? It must make people think we all belong to some kind of weird sect.''

Well, maybe we do! We can never REALLY fit in. We're different. So I made up my mind to keep my strange customs and my 'foreign' friends, run my household as well as I could and concentrate on just being me. I can't help myself or anyone else by trying too hard to fit in, and losing part of myself in the process. Since that day when I stopped trying to fit in, I have found that, at last, I AM fitting in, in my own, unique way.

WHAT HAVE WE DONE TO THE SWISS?

- AND VICE VERSA

by George Blythe

Many reading this will claim English as first language and enjoy its advantages. Yet if we shelter under the umbrella term 'English speaker' we share not only glory but also guilt for the less wholesome side of our culture. Some of us left our home country to escape the very dangers that are slowly but surely creeping into Switzerland.

We are not so conspicuous as other groups: We needed no warning notices in our own language as did some of the ethnic communities forming new roots in Switzerland. We have few problems. In fact, the Swiss seem to like us and use English for trade names and advertising.

Yet real problems, for which 'we' were responsible, have been fermenting below the surface: side effects from by-products of our world-wide culture are undermining the Swiss without their realising it.

Our shadier influences could be summarised under three Vs - vandalism, violence, and video-brutalos. Even the first two were almost non-existent in Switzerland some twenty years ago. At that time, vandals in England were avid writers on walls, particularly lavatory walls. In North America the situation was not so bad, though slogans were frequently smeared on walls in the poorer areas. This problem was unknown in Switzerland, as were vandalised public telephones. It is not clear what brought the 'English' illnesses to this and other countries on the European continent - junkies? pop festivals? football hooligans? One thing is certain: The paint spray business has profited from graffiti-type vandalism. Helvetia's robes are soiled.

I once overheard two Americans chatting in the lift of the Heuwaage parking garage in Basle. They looked at the schizoid spraywork on the walls, then at each other, till one said, ''Well! Just like New York!'' ''Maybe,'' said the other, ''but at least there's no mugging here.''

This brings us to V for violence. It has been reported that you can walk safely at night anywhere in Swiss cities without fear of mugging. This is no longer true since the major Swiss towns have problems with drug addicts and the social consequences. 'Foreigners' have been blamed for the violence, but the greatest danger comes from a small element of radical youths, including Swiss, who vent their aggression on foreigners, the elderly, and defenceless people alike.

It is true that the world has become less chivalrous of late. Yet twenty years ago, when the Mafia in Italy was strong, when student unrest and riots peaked in neighbouring France, Switzerland remained an island of calm. During the sixties I remember seeing a heap of small, rounded paving stones left by roadworkers near the main doors of Basle University. A notice appeared on them with the legend: ''The students thank the local council for their generous gift, but have at present no use for it!'' Such stones were then the favourite ammunition of the Paris rioters.

It might seem from this that the Swiss could look upon violence along the lines of their French neighbours with amused detachment. But over the years, beginning towards the end of the sixties, riots did occur, increasing in frequency and severity.

Although the British and Americans were by no means immediate neighbours, there were initially surprising interfaces of interest. As far back as 1902 Sir Henry Lunn had pioneered the first winter-sports 'package' trip in Adelboden. His son Arnold Lunn also promoted skiing, formulated the modern slalom, and organised competitive events. Environmentalists might contend this was a mixed blessing. The English had become fashion moulders in matters of sport and travel. 'Tea Room' and 'Cake' appeared in their wake like camp-followers. (Alas! The drink served is usually less English than the name.)

The British built the first Swiss railways and advised on setting them up. Now the pupil has overtaken the teacher in efficiency.

Despite the long-standing Swiss admiration for things English (such as stage and film productions, flexibility, British humour and American 'playfulness'), these are primarily appreciated by Swiss who have lived abroad or had close contact with us over the years.

Electronic gadgetry gave us the most leverage. For the ordinary, peaceful, if retiring Swiss, unarmed by higher education or a critical attitude, it must have been tempting to believe that everything 'English' was 'in'. Were not the basic commands for computers, television and videos all in English (though the hardware may be Dutch or Japanese)? The ground had thus long been prepared among the young, when a new mind-killer appeared - the video-horror cassette, known locally as a *Brutalo*. The final 'o' makes it a slang parallel to 'Porno'.

The obsession of English-speaking people with 'thrillers', plus media efforts to escape censorship and responsibility, formed an ideal matrix for diseased minds. When asked by the Basle police why they had committed a brutal crime, some youngsters admitted they just did not know. There was no motive. They had seen a *Brutalo*, perhaps drunk some alcohol, and decided on action.

All cantons have now outlawed this type of video, but let's think of our other 'gifts' to the Swiss - Rambos, skinheads, football rowdies, punks and bashers. All this must have had an effect on Swiss youth. Aren't we trend-setters? Now Switzerland has canned music in supermarkets, louder versions in the second-rate boutiques, and ghetto-blasters on the kerbstone.

Health impaired by abuse of fast-food and other bad habits will not be offset by going to what are now called 'fitness studios', even if the American name is thought to have more magic than plain gymnastics. There is almost a growing 'dependence' on English words, causing the Swiss to neglect their own languages and commit cultural suicide.

These unwanted effects of Anglo-American culture are not alone in ringing the changes - the Swiss still have a word to say - but our influence has 'hardened' attitudes in the young, may have encouraged hostility, and in some cases even indifference towards any idea or person outside the group they 'support', whether this be 'heavy-metal', 'acid music', or some sort of drug or electronic cult.

This process is not peculiar to Switzerland. But one is more aware of it in a country so oft praised for peace and tranquillity. Neutrality and mediation have become Swiss watchwords, and all this has had an effect on its people, old and young, for half a century; for long they have believed violence and crime hardly existed; some even left doors unlocked. This image is changing. Small countries, like small children, are very impressionable and the big brothers have not set very good examples.

*****

And what have the Swiss done to us?

Outside in the big wide world the Swiss are known for hard currency, bitter chocolate mergers, high-quality watches, and the chemical giants. A few scandals, disastrous accidents occasioned by the latter, may have caused anger abroad, but this is directed largely at the companies - which are usually multinational anyway. For the same reason the Swiss get little credit or blame for producing antibiotics, antidepressants, vaccines, or herbicides and insecticides since their resident research teams are often 'multinational' too.

Some of Helvetia's men of learning may have caused a stir in the world and acquired some following - for example Jean-Jacques Rousseau and Carl Gustav Jung - but this was mostly at an academic level. They had little influence on most people.

It was a different matter with the religious reformers. Zwingli caused many of the English clergy to embrace Protestantism. Calvin, especially through John Knox, exerted a strong influence not only on the Church but also on Scottish ways of life. Common people became less submissive - good in some aspects as long as they did not become more arrogant in others? I am thinking of 'holier-than-thou' attitudes. Most of this early influence during the sixteenth and seventeenth centuries stemmed from Geneva, a republic in its own right. By 1620 an English translation of the Geneva Bible was already in America. The Swiss influence through pen or preacher was mightier than the sword. Some facets of this teaching are not popular among English-speaking people. Yet even in Scotland attitudes have mellowed, and a steady wind of change is blowing through the glens.

Several Swiss banking families and other entrepreneurs established themselves in London and indeed throughout the world, but their influence was not felt. Few people - even those who drank Ovaltine - were aware of it. Naturally, the Savoy and the Ritz were held in awe throughout the English-speaking world, but few associated them with César Ritz from the village of Niederwald in Switzerland. Yet to this day, training by Swiss cooks and hoteliers is regarded as non plus ultra in the catering trade.

Oscar Wilde said: "I don't like Switzerland, it has produced nothing but theologians and waiters." The film version of "The Third Man" introduced an even more limited opinion that all

Switzerland had ever produced were cuckoo clocks! Even then, the true home of these clocks is the German Black Forest, though the mechanisms may have been Swiss made. Another, less common, fallacy is that the Russian word for pencil *Karandash* stems from a Swiss firm, Caran d'Ache, who manufacture them. The reverse is the case! Moscow-born artist Emmanuel Poiré signed his caricatures in Paris 'Caran d'Ache', his own invention of a French name sounding like the Russian for pencil. The Swiss firm later adopted this pen name in honour of the artist. Facetious comments, from Voltaire to Lord Arran, may lend a little colour but they shed little light on what the Swiss have done TO us, unless it has been to make some of us cynical or envious.

The question of what the Swiss have done FOR us would be easier to answer: The International Red Cross Organisation and unfailing diplomatic intervention, both of which have saved lives, property, and tears. Since Henri Dunant conceived the idea of the Red Cross during the Solferino slaughter, other international organisations have sprung up. This may have influenced our lives more than we give credit for.

There are of course thousands of Swiss living in English-speaking countries, some in influential positions, but no need to worry! Apart from Swiss Centres - such as the one in London proudly flying the White Cross - it would be hard to detect one flicker of national presence. People outside the Helvetian Confederation are quite 'safe' from any Swiss influence.

This cannot be said for those of us who came from abroad to live here; even the most dyed-in-the-wool British, case-hardened Americans, temperamental Italians or fiery Spaniards have suffered sea change over the years. It is sometimes a slow, subtle process, first noticeable on leaving Switzerland. For my part, it became apparent on returning 'home' after many years' absence, seeing my country through what at first were taken to be more realistic lenses, but which had of course acquired a 'Swiss finish'.

I was determined not to criticise in England, but some things went against the grain. For example, separate collection of waste was a joke; glass, paper, potential compost, aluminium all went into the common 'dustbin'. Months later I read in the SUNDAY TIMES about the 'litter lout' and a 'Save the Children' campaign for recycling old newspapers. At least they have reached a stage where paper can be TAKEN to a collecting point. In Switzerland we are thoroughly spoilt with there being COLLECTIONS of kitchen and garden compost, paper and old clothes. We just put them into the right sack (provided free), on the right day (announced in the local paper), and they are collected from our door-step. In even the small-est Swiss com-munities there are collection areas for tins, used batteries, vegetable and motor oils.

Bigger countries have bigger prob-lems, but is it natu-ral that trains and telephones are vandal-ised, violence is ac-cepted, strikes are rou-tine, discipline dismissed, sloppiness 'in'? More sadden-ing is the persisting ignorance about neighbouring countries and cultures. Charter flights and package tours have done nothing for a generation used to getting a lot for a little.

I feel isolated; my perspectives have changed *malgré moi* and others sense it, sometimes sympathise. *Un cri de coeur:* is it possible to be Swiss without being a voting citizen in a community? This is part of what the Swiss have done to me. No doubt I am not the only immigrant to Switzerland caught between two cultures, two fires.

ABSEILING DOWN THE GARDEN

by Brian Fairman

I never considered abseiling as a skill associated with gardening. Not, that is, until I had a house built in Switzerland.

The story begins nine years ago in England where I had just had a house built. It had been beset with all sorts of problems for, in spite of unemployment, we had a lack of craftsmen, there were late deliveries and the whole project was six months overdue. "Never again," I said, but then I took a holiday in Sardinia and met Brigitte, a Swiss, who was eventually to become my wife. A visit to Switzerland followed. As I had not been there before, I acquainted myself with a few facts. It was landlocked, had four languages, no natural resources, no political party with a majority, major issues are put to referendum, it has one of the highest living standards and its inhabitants have the longest life expectancy. It shouldn't exist!

My first visit was like a time-warp as I rediscovered qualities which we used to enjoy in England, but had somehow lost. Cleanliness, politeness, skilled workers, tea rooms, a low crime rate, an efficient postal service and those trains! Everything worked! No wonder they were so wealthy. They had education, skill and they worked hard to produce quality.

Many more visits followed before we married and settled in England, but with the intention of eventually moving to the Riviera Vaudoise. In spite of my vow 'never again', Switzerland had given me new hope and we decided to build a house. I'd heard comments about property being expensive but this is only relative to what you are used to. Americans seem to find property prices high but, coming from the south east of England, just outside London, I found the prices for property in Switzerland very reasonable.

An agent found a plot of land on a hillside above a picturesque village with a magnificent view of Lac Léman and the Alps. But when we came to see it and I saw how STEEP it was I said, "I want a house, not a ski jump!" The agent explained that the top could be cut out and the earth moved to form a terrace and the garage could be under the house and ... It all sounded very alien to me, but not to Brigitte, who was used to seeing houses in 'impossible' places. We received a dossier with detailed house-building regulations for that community telling us what could and could not be built. We decided to buy.

Buying was a pleasant surprise as I was used to the English system where both parties have a solicitor using mysterious long words and much paperwork which takes a long time and of course a long bill! In Switzerland a notary acts for both parties. A meeting was held where a simple contract was signed and the deal completed before retiring to a bistro to celebrate. All very civilised, quick and simple.

Stage one completed, we then had to find a builder, or rather an entrepreneur, who would organise the design and construction as we proposed to stay in England until the house was completed. We were given the name of the entrepreneur and on our next visit we met and viewed examples of his work. A tall, bearded and jovial man, he enthusiastically showed us the features of his Swiss-styled houses which were technically and quality-wise well beyond anything I had seen before. Although I had been studying my 'French in a Week' (!) course for some time, my ability to communicate was virtually non-existent but the gut feeling was right - he was the man for the job.

Via the post the plans were finalised, a contract prepared, and building finance arranged. The latter was again a revelation to me as a Swiss bank was prepared to finance the project without actually requiring me to deposit my blood as security!

Work started in the spring and regular reports were sent to us. We visited the site in the summer and, arriving in the evening, we found our garage and basement set in a massive hole with the walls of the ground floor ready for the concrete ceiling to be formed. Next morning we got up early and hurried to the site to watch the floor being made. We arrived at 9 but the job had already been done. The Swiss do like to make an early start! Only one young labourer remained and, unlike most of the labour force who were Portuguese seasonal workers, he was a Swiss who would one day be an architect but, as part of his training, he had to start at the bottom and gain practical experience.

A frantic week followed when we met all the craftsmen and made our final choice of fittings. Back in England, we continued to receive regular reports. It was uncanny, schedules were kept, deliveries on time, no delays. It was almost boring! On our next visit the main shell was complete and work had started on the interior.

Everything was tidy, organised and clean. By now I should have expected as much but I still found myself marvelling over their work standards.

The great day came and we finally made the move and arrived to see our house finished, on schedule, of course. The house had been cleaned (need I say how clean?), the heating was on and the entrepreneur and the landscapers called with flowers - a very nice greeting to our new home.

Our 'ski jump' had been transformed into a wonderful terrace with retaining walls, flower beds and a lawn. The 'front garden' is a very steep slope 15 meters high, so the ability to abseil when planting would be a distinct advantage! But we have to take some precautions on the terrace, like no sun-lounge chairs with wheels, as sooner or later somebody would surely depart down the garden at great speed and disappear into the village below. I can just imagine it, "Go and get Auntie Anna back. She's on the way to Vevey on a sun lounger!"

It is said that the Swiss learned many of their standards from the British. Perhaps it's time we asked them to return the favour.

LEARNING THE ROPES IN HEIDI'S PLAYGROUND

by David Speicher

Switzerland runs like, well, what else, a Swiss clock. Simply everything and everybody is organized. This is true for everybody here, for housewives and mailmen and particularly for business people. They, of course, have their day completely planned out. They start the day by being early for work. Arriving late is something respectable business people just wouldn't do here. Appointments are set up in advance. You want to see your boss about something? Better call him (rarely her in Switzerland) and fix a time later that day or week. This is the famous concept of *abgemacht* (agreed). Of course, once something is *abgemacht* let neither God nor beast cancel or change it for any reason barring death.

It's not that the Swiss really work harder than others do. It's just that they think they do and everybody else assumes they do. Part of their mystique is that the Swiss take the time to think things out before acting. They try to understand the whys and whats of a situation before taking a decision. This saves going back later and wasting time to try to patch things back together after something went awry. They are geared to long-term planning and solutions and do not get bogged down in short-term management and short-sighted goals like so many Americans do. Whatever the Swiss build, it's meant to last a long time, if possible, forever.

As a foreigner here, it took some time for me to get used to working day-to-day with the Swiss. At first I tried to dive in and become one of the team. That is difficult here and outsiders are not especially welcomed with open arms. The Swiss need time to get to know you and sometimes they might make you think making friends is like pulling teeth. I was consoled to realize that Swiss people are just as reluctant to make friends with other Swiss, sometimes even more so, than they are with foreigners like me. My Swiss-French wife was treated like a foreigner by some people when we first moved into the German-speaking region. She took a job with an American company that had a heavy Swiss-German atmosphere. Being new, Christine tried to get to know her co-workers better. Two of her Swiss-German colleagues then bluntly informed her that they didn't think it would be worth it to get to know her too well as others had left that job after a year or two.

After a while here, I learned not to force myself into adapting too quickly and to just go with the flow of things. Switzerland and the Swiss work-force (made up of Swiss and various foreigners who inevitably become more Swiss than the actual Swiss) have their own unique ways of working and outsiders cannot change this. People are accustomed to having a stable job at a good salary. Job security is never a question if a person is a capable employee. The supply of labor here is extremely tight and unemployment rarely goes over 1 percent.

The Swiss have a remarkable attitude about work. Work is something you do to pay your bills but above all, it is what justifies your existence. Therefore, it is not necessarily a pleasure-producing activity. In fact, if you are perceived as enjoying your work too much, and having too much fun at it, you risk not being taken seriously by your colleagues or your boss. They probably presume you cannot be doing a good job if you seem to be having fun at it.

These attitudes towards work and always being organized have a definite influence on the stress level here. This may explain why Swiss people are very serious and rarely have time for socializing at work, or after work for that matter. It is not customary to ask someone spontaneously to go out for a drink after work, unless, of course, you have *abgemacht* it earlier in the day, week or month for that day. I often recall many wonderful and impromptu American 'Happy Hours' and find myself wanting to tell the Swiss how much fun and camaraderie they are missing.

For someone like me who was accustomed to having lots of social contacts with working colleagues, this came as a shock. Eventually I realized that good contacts can be met and friends made with a little patience and good fortune. To find out who is a potential candidate for being friend-material, I try to tell a few jokes, preferably not about the Swiss, of course. Something like: "Why did the elephant paint his toenails red?" Answer: "So that he could be seen climbing the north face of the Eiger." It's not important if someone laughs at this type of joke, but it has sometimes produced a genuine Swiss smile accompanied by another joke or a playful comment. When I get a cool "Hrruumph" and that prospective friend walks away, I'm now aware I'll see him again at the

Company Christmas Party at Year-End where I've heard such jokes being told by the most earnest Swiss.

By using humor or other techniques and a sorting-out process, I've made some good friendships with Swiss people. One of my good friends from my American university days, who at age 32 is head of a leading USA sports conglomerate, told me that "having fun is the key to making good business deals." He would have trouble in Switzerland - until he learned that this key doesn't necessarily fit into Swiss locks.

After eight years of living in various places in Switzerland, I am convinced that a big part of the lack of personal warmth attributed to the Swiss is inherent in their upbringing and way-of-life. People who live and work in Switzerland are under a lot of pressure. Shops are closed over lunch-time and at 6:30 pm weekdays. On Saturdays, they are open only till 4 pm and closed all day Sundays and holidays. This means that all stores are jammed after work and on Saturdays, as everyone who holds down a job goes shopping then. I wasn't expecting so much traffic on the roads during school and family vacations or that it would be so difficult to find a non-crowded ski lift on weekends. It seems like everyone wants to pay bills at the same time at the local PTT. I get around most of this hassle by planning and taking the time to learn how the Swiss cope with these inconveniences.

Finding an apartment is like looking for a gold nugget in a river bed. It's hard to find, especially one large enough. Families rarely have their own washing machine or dryer and usually have a weekly washday in their apartment building's communal washroom. In addition, in the German-speaking region you normally have to wash the stairway to your apartment twice monthly as part of your rental contract. After meeting with high-powered customers all week and discussing big money contracts, I find it a rather humbling experience to have to come home and wash my landlord's steps!

It is this sobering day-to-day reality of Swiss living that puts a lot of stress on the work-force. I may now live in the most modern country in the world, but because of time and space limitations, I sometimes feel I am governed by rules that were designed for an elementary school. After a short time in this country, I realized that some parts of Swiss culture cannot be changed. Those who are used to Swiss ways of doing things find them ideal. Of course, those who have a non-working spouse at home to take care of everything outside the work-place are at a distinct advantage. But feeling at home here may take a long period of adjustment for outsiders.

I have lived for a while in Belgium and Italy and know there is a big, wide and wonderful European world out there. In my job and in my private time, I travel frequently outside of Switzerland. This has made my challenge with Switzerland much easier since I can interact regularly with people of different nationalities. In the end, it has also broadened my perspectives about the Swiss since I meet a lot of Swiss businessmen *en route*. These Swiss seem a lot more objective and open when they are outside their country. In fact, when returning to Switzerland on airplanes with them I have sensed a change coming over them upon arrival on Swiss soil. Is it their getting organized again?

Becoming involved in some local groups has helped to make me feel at home. I became coach of the local basketball team and also joined a few international social clubs. This gave me a way to meet people, make friends and learn more about Swiss society in an open, easy way. It also gave me an avenue to meet other foreigners who were experiencing the same 'adjustment pains'.

I know many English-speaking foreigners living in Switzerland who want to assimilate but who never take the time to learn the local languages just because so many Swiss speak English. That is a big mistake. French, German and Italian may not be the easiest languages in the world, but they are certainly far from being the most difficult. It is very challenging to learn a new language and I have found that the Swiss respect someone who is trying to learn. There is an additional language to learn, the Swiss-German dialect, but that comes along very nicely as you improve your High German.

Switzerland may be a difficult nut to crack. However, after a period of adjustment, I have found that life Swiss-style is a pleasure, even though the day-to-day struggle can be tough. At first I thought the Swiss were sometimes difficult to work and get along with. But after I understood more about them and their way-of-life, it struck me that they have a lot of things figured out well. Sometimes the short-term decisions don't make any sense, but later, the long-term benefits are crystal clear. That has been the key to Switzerland's political and economic survival in the past and will certainly serve her and her inhabitants well in the future. Somehow that's been *abgemacht*.

KANTONSSCHULE ROMANCE

by Kris Jenson

Our eyes meet across an empty room. My heart halts, his mouth falls agape. An eternal moment passes before I gather composure and courage enough to rasp, "Is this the math room?" Our moment is consummated, and unrestrained passion leaps forward in the form of a - OH NO! a handshake!! - with my hands spurting out sweat like a geyser!! I try in vain to wipe them on my Levis which immediately resemble a drowned towel.

But before he can ponder as to what species of slug has just slithered and dripped across his hand, it is announced that an enthralling report on antidifferentiation and general discombobulation is about to begin, a subject which tends to sedate even the most rampant, rabid, raging and ravenous hormones. His eyes clutch mine and he whispers, "You must sit by me. I'm alone in the front." Without exorbitant reluctance, I seize the neighboring chair.

As to the content of the presentation that followed, I couldn't tell you a thing. But I did notice his name written neatly on his folder, Markus, and was struck by his purple and green Argyle socks which actually matched his whole attire. And I meditated upon the concept of love. To say whether or not I loved, lusted or liked him was simply, at this point, impossible - primarily because of my incapability to breathe in his presence.

This is how it began. I was only aware of the bait, an astoundingly gorgeous and charismatic creature whose Toblerone eyes melted my logical existence.

After class, the questions began. First the inevitable: "Where do you come from?"

Having already been informed of the patented Swiss fact that all American girls are free and easy sex machines, I was put into a catch-22. Not quite fitting this description, but not wanting to offend any Swiss by questioning their vast cultural knowledge, I took a third alternative. "England," was my calculated response.

I was soon to see the lack of wisdom in this choice by his rebound: "Which region?" "Which city?" "What do you think of Shakespeare?" "Does our English tea please you?" "What do you

141

think should be done about the Thames River pollution?'' And finally, the topper, ''Do you find the American dialect repulsive?''

That was it for me. Utterly flabbergasted, I couldn't help asking with a strained voice where he had amassed such trifles.

''Standard curriculum in English, geography and history classes,'' was his matter-of-fact response.

Luckily, inspiration came amidst this interrogation and, without further delay, I declared: ''I was born in the Theatre of the Round.''

Word about me circulated. I had not anticipated the efficiency with which Swiss youth spread gossip to one another.

''I thought she was American!''

''She wears Reebok tennis shoes in gym glass - naturally she's American!''

''Why did she lie, then?''

''You know Americans - they do what they want.''

This was the typical conversation, in different words and dialects, but all ended with the same result: ''She lied, the wench.''

In the next math class, they all sat smug and silent, either tired of the subject from so extensively discussing it amongst themselves, or considerately sparing me such rot. Except Markus. He mournfully cooed, ''Why did you betray me so, Mousie?'' (In French they say 'cauliflower' or 'steak' as terms of affection, not to mention some of the things we say in English, so who am I to quibble over being called a creature that feeds off rubbish, spreads disease and is heavily used in scientific experimentation?) I told him everything with pleading eyes. He nodded compassionately, the playful love once again gleaming in his eyes, plummeting to my own love abyss, causing it to surge upward with my soul and climactically splash together with his. I was slightly on the brink of being overjoyed, spasmodic, in unrestrained ecstasy - but not quite - as that would have been fairly obscene in the classroom.

The ten o'clock break came, the time in which couples are permitted and encouraged to walk together, firmly clasping clammy hands. We willingly joined in. The students observing us began new gossip, causing the scandal over my nationality to quickly blow over, thus saving me much time, money and grief in pursuing a name change or plastic surgery.

The next stop - the cinema. He asks me to choose the movie, so I do. He clarifies its badness and invites me to choose again. I do, and he patiently recounts bad reviews before inviting me to choose again. This cycle is repeated until every last possibility is ruled out. He patiently explains to me that according to Swiss etiquette the man gives the woman the opportunity to choose and the woman graciously defers this privilege.

Thinking it a bit superfluous and tedious, but too tired to squabble, I graciously submit to 'Herr Markus' who promptly chooses my first choice - "That is, if it's all right by you."

Normally I like to go Dutch but under these circumstances I graciously let him pay.

He leads me to a seat, in the middle! The seats have little walls between them, their version of armrests! It looks like we're actually here to SEE the movie!! This is a big change from sitting inconspicuously in the back, waiting for the lights to go out with stiff anticipation to spring on one another.

We discuss philosophy and religion for ten minutes before the movie begins. We watch intently as the Hollywood magic unwinds its tale, forgetting each other's existence. Suddenly, in the movie's most suspenseful moment, lights flicker on. Dazed, we dutifully trudge to the ice-cream stand to fulfill intermission tradition. No one, including us, mentions the movie, daring only random, inconsequential chatter lest we forget where the movie left off. In a jiffy we're back and the movie ends. We stretch and look at each other in foggy remembrance, then wander into a nearby café to have a brilliant discussion over steaming cappuccino until my last bus and his curfew are due.

Hand-holding ceremony and movie ritual complete, the time is ripe for second thoughts. To a girl raised in a guys' neighborhood, the idea of friendship with a guy outside of romance comes naturally. However, in the Kantonsschule, talking to a guy with any frequency is flirting, and some people's imagination is limited as to what a guy and a girl could be doing with each other outside of school. I keep on talking to my male friends, although I realize this only confirms that American girls behave like sluts. Markus finds my behavior dubious and asks for a log of each minute spent away from him. Furthermore, he is actually offended by my healthy lack of such paranoia! He interprets my trust as disinterest.

This comes to a dramatic halt one night at 11 o'clock when I am walking home alone. I hear muffled footsteps behind me. At first

only a casual observation, my apprehension rises with every passing hair salon (the percentage of those here is equal to that of Circle
K's, 7-11's and gas stations combined in Phoenix, Arizona). Not
much traffic and no pedestrians, I nervously check over my shoulder to see only vague shadows scurrying behind bushes and bus-
stop signs. I begin to walk faster. It too. I begin to run. It too.
Infuriated by this intolerable infringement upon my safety HERE in
this peaceful, neutral and secure country, I whip around and belt
him one, pounding him with my school briefcase. His protests hold
no weight in my ears, as my understanding of high-pitched, panting
Swiss-German between cries of profanities is limited. Snatching
his wallet, I rift through it until I discover his identity - a private
detective - and my boyfriend's name and number amidst his list of
clientele. I apologize to the mute ears of this unfortunate, uncon-
scious man, and think of a certain jealous neck I'd like to wring.

Finally, I meet his family. There I am, an American planning to
attend a feminist women's college, major in Physics and Art and
write books, now being primed for marriage. His father is smoking
a pipe somewhere, so I am stranded with his well-meaning mother,
receiving vital instructions about cooking, baking, shopping, raising children, the importance of ironing socks, underwear and
dishtowels (to kill harmful bacteria), the best shape for toilet
scrubbers, products that protect the ozone layer, the different sorts
of trash to be sorted, and, of course, the father as the center of the
family to be revered and obeyed. Markus looks on with an amused
smile and twinkling eyes.

That night, I had a very peculiar dream. Markus and I had married,
I a physicist and he an environmentalist. We had moved to Spain,
where neither of us knew the language or culture. We both had set
up on-line workstations in our home and were taking turns feeding,
changing, or playing with the baby, often taking care of her
together. He cooked, I cleaned and financed the household and HE
ironed MY underwear. His self-esteem was strong enough to accept
my talents and higher income. I, in turn, felt secure enough in
myself to play to his male ego a bit, letting him feel obeyed and
revered (while in fact he was only treasured).

Suddenly a hook-shaped toilet scrubber wrenched me from our
love and happiness together, and I was handcuffed to a well-
dressed, shrieking two-year-old and a washing machine, with an

ironing board chained around my ankle. Screaming amidst the swirling flush of non-toxic toilet cleaner in my eyes and the seething hot dishwater singeing my suddenly pregnant belly and my bare feet stepping on a shattered plate and mushy Bratwurst, my ears swarming with the pugnacious chain-saw hum of my mother-in-law's whining voice, drooling and yelping incomprehensibly...

I woke up, realizing that I've been in Switzerland too long.

THE LANGUAGE OF PLAY

by Angela Ashton

Just a few months into our new life in Switzerland, the transformation of our English-speaking child into a bi-lingual seven-year-old was well under way. It all happened so quickly we hardly noticed, but visitors did. "She's talking to herself in German!" my brother announced in surprise as he watched his niece, Melanie, playing in the communal garden of our Swiss apartment home.

The speed with which she picked up a second language makes me feel both proud and envious. For an adult, the innate ability of a child to gain such fluency through play highlights the tedium of trying to 'learn it from a book.'

A neighbour, whose children were born in France, and who spoke only French when they moved to the German-speaking region of Switzerland, assured me that Melanie would soon be speaking a second language. "One summer playing on the streets with the other children will do it," she said.

I can now see that she was right. Within a matter of months, Melanie, who was almost four when we moved here, was able to participate in most of the children's games without problems. After a few years, we were frequently told it was impossible to distinguish her acquired guttural Bernese tones from those of the other children.

Of course, there were the occasional tears, tantrums, and anguished cries of "They won't play with me." But I'm sure this was just a phase which would have happened with or without the language barrier.

Her integration into a new culture and her first faltering steps to learn the language began as soon as we arrived at our new home just a few miles outside Berne. The originality of her bright red Raleigh bike - at least to the Swiss - made it a popular asset. It helped to put her on the road to fluency in Swiss German which her parents could never match.

Her fluency in the language came faster than her ability to translate and when her little friends got up to the sort of mischief four and five-year-olds excel in, I would yell, "Tell them not to do that."

Melanie was very helpful. She turned to them and said in English, "Don't do that." She had about as much effect as I did. For a while my only method of communication with these children was the 'shout louder and they'll soon get the message' approach.

A few months later, however, Melanie suddenly realised she could turn German words into English and vice versa. Today, she has it down to such a fine art she should really be charging me a fee for her interpreting services.

Initially, the fact that she could not speak Swiss-German seemed to be of little importance. A neighbour's little girl confidently told her mother just a few days after our arrival, "Melanie speaks our language. I say come and she comes." A simple response to a simple request was all she needed at first. But child's play is often more complex and language oriented. The language of play was *Schwizerdütsch*, the Swiss dialect. To survive, Melanie had to learn it.

The power of language through play cannot be underestimated. Melanie listened to and repeated almost everything her friends said and did. If they said they were going to put a jacket on their baby doll then Melanie copied them in both word and action. If they said they were going to jump in the sandpit, she said and did the same.

When a young child is undergoing the natural process of learning its mother tongue, it can - given the opportunity - learn several other languages at the same time without difficulty. This process, unfortunately, doesn't work for adults, but explaining that to a child is rather difficult. "Why don't you speak German," Melanie once asked. "I didn't speak it when we first came here. Come out and play with me and my friends and you'll learn."

The 'play and speak' method was certainly enough to help Melanie reach an acceptable level for both kindergarten and school without the necessity of formal German lessons. The thought of how their offspring will cope with school work in a foreign language is, of course, always a worry for parents from abroad. If they are only here for a few years many decide - finances permitting - to send their child to a school where it will be taught in its mother tongue.

This could be a 'lost opportunity' as the support for such children in Swiss schools is very good and it's far easier for them to integrate into their immediate environment if they go to the local school. I'm sure Melanie has gained immeasurably from the experience. Although by nature a little reserved, she always seems open to new experiences, has no fear of speaking a second language and is now determined to learn French!

Not everyone relishes the thought of bringing up a child bilingually. If you're not fluent in both languages then you're not going to be the best person in the world to check homework, but with a good dictionary you can usually get by. A worried friend once asked me, "Aren't you afraid Melanie will give up speaking English?" As we always speak English together as a family, I don't think there is any possibility of this happening. English at home, German or the Swiss dialect outside. This absolute division seems to help Melanie keep the languages separate in her mind and she hardly ever mixes the two but can go from one to the other without hesitation.

One thing is sure. A bilingual child in Switzerland is not an oddity. As the country has four official languages, school teachers are well used to dealing with bilingual children and from kindergarten up, extra language lessons are available for those who need it. In Melanie's class alone there are children who speak German-French, German-Italian, German-Greek, and even one other German-English speaker. But the language of play is *Schwizerdütsch!*

ECHOES

by Susan Tiberghien

This morning I'm alone in the house, listening to the echoes of children. For twenty years, my life has been tuned to the Swiss school day. There's always been a child coming or going, there's always been a child home for lunch. Now for the first time the youngest has left for the full day. I walk on tip-toe through the quiet house.

I hear echoes from when we first arrived and tried to make room for everyone - a French father, an American mother, and five small children. We quickly learned that large families were not Swiss. The real estate agents looked at us and shook their heads in dismay. Finally we found a small house for sale. The Swiss owners, with just two children, were looking for something larger. We said we'd manage and moved the furniture and all the beds around until we found a corner for each of us.

We settled in and the children went off to school. The front door of solid oak opened and closed heavily. I worked against the clock each morning getting ready for the two and a half hour lunch break. Come 11:00 I began to listen for the bicycles. Then the heavy door was pushed back and forth - with one thud after another - until the five children were all home. The door stays shut today. I open the window nearby to let in the sunshine.

I hear other early echoes from when we made still more room for number six. We bought double deck beds, turned the garage into a playroom, and transformed the wine cellar into a bedroom. Daniel came from Vietnam. He was two years old. The walls rang from his nightmares. Each night I went and held him in my arms until he slept in peace.

There were eight of us then and some of the Swiss habits of discipline and order were helping. The kids didn't seem to bump into one another, they didn't push, they didn't shove. Even on the staircase, they'd wait their turn. The stairs were wooden. If I listened carefully to the steps, I could tell who it was.

They took turns playing the piano. Six practice periods every day. Bach, Mozart, Schumann ... Schumann, Mozart, Bach. The sounds came from the hall in the cellar where we put the upright piano.

Once, four of our children were to play at the same recital. A Swiss mother took an interest in our family and asked why each child didn't play a different instrument. It was hard to explain that they seemed to like doing the same thing, one after the other. I remember instead telling her we had four pianos at home.

And the sounds of birthday parties. Our children loved birthday parties - Pin the Tail on the Donkey, Musical Chairs, Potato Races, all those games that I, the American mother, organized six times each year for their Swiss schoolmates. The whole house was turned topsy-turvy, with a donkey on the wall in the kitchen, chairs lined up in the hall, and potatoes rolled under the couch in the living room. We sang "Happy Birthday to you," or rather "*Bonne Anniversaire a toi*", which sounded almost the same. When the mothers came, they smiled at so many children all together in the same house.

There are echoes also of Christmas, when we decorated the tree in the middle of the front hall and the children's excitement ran up and down the staircase. And echoes of Thanksgiving, with the table set for family and friends. Each year we invited Swiss neighbors to share our feast and to listen to the story of the first harvest in the New World read out loud by the oldest child.

Soon came the noise of mopeds in the driveway, of Beatles records giving way to rock music, of teenagers voices filling the house. I remember the first "boom" (teenage party), in the play-room down in the cellar, planned by our oldest son for his fifteenth birthday, from 6 to 10 pm. The "booms" gradually moved upstairs to the living room. The furniture was moved out, sometimes the parents too. The curfew hovered around midnight. The house was noisy during those years, the sounds collided.

Then one by one the children moved on. When the oldest boy went away to the university, the voices in the house shifted. The next two were girls. The father was traveling a great deal. The echoes of those years are feminine. We drank tea in the kitchen and talked about literature and love.

After the two older girls went on to university, it was the turn of number four who played jazz on the piano and brought in his musician friends with drums and a base fiddle. Late at night they played Risk or Monopoly on the dining room table, the sounds of dice and muffled whispers.

Upstairs number five was preparing her baccalaureate exams through correspondence courses, while she danced each afternoon at the Conservatory. Quiet was established, at least in the morning. I see her sitting at her desk and calling to me. "Mom, do latitudes go up and down or do they go sideways?" I didn't remember. I looked it up in the encyclopedia and called back the answer.

Our pianist went on to school in the States, our dancer to school in Paris. Just our youngest was left at home. The echoes were muted. Solitary television, radio, records, cassettes. Then the sounds grew louder with "House Music". The lights went on and off as the playroom became a disco.

This morning he went for his first day as an apprentice in radio and hi-fi. The house is empty. I pick up left-behind trophies, discarded sneakers, forgotten books. There is silence. It's like an accordion closing in on itself, getting ready to open out still wider.

Our two oldest children are married and there are two grandchildren. They come to visit. I recently pulled down the carton of toys from the attic. Will the echoes sound the same?

MY FARMER

by Heidrun West

Everybody should have a farmer. I have one, and how I'd hate
to lose him. Particularly now that we have become friends.
The parking area in front of our garage is one of the few points
where tractors can stop and allow cars to pass. It was during one of
these enforced stops that the farmer and I got to talking - or
nattering, as my husband calls this intellectual activity. I still
remember being pleasantly surprised by the farmer's friendly
directness. It was such a balm on my newcomer's wounds.

With not enough land close to his farm, he rents bits and pieces all
over the nearby hills. Mountain farming is labour intensive at the
best of times. But this ferrying of grass and hay from the fields to
the barn, and carrying manure back to the fields makes this farming
family's day even longer. Sometimes I hear them drive down the
hill before the bells 'ring the day in' at 5 am. In summer their tractor
tuckers home as I fall into bed at 11 pm. One endless marathon.

I soon learned to recognize the sound of their tractor, and even if
I hadn't, their laughter and singing - or the occasional exuberant
yodel - would draw me to the edge of the road. We got into the habit
of exchanging a cheery wave and a shouted hello. And no matter
how frosty and hard the ground, whenever they pass by, a soft warm
wind blows through my garden.

This family is in the unusual situation of owning farm land that
has not been in the same family for generations. They were moved
here from the Waegital, a beautiful mountain valley, not more than
ten miles away. Its location and topography made it the perfect site
for a dam. In 1923 the valley was flooded - and with it the church
and the cemetery, the school, the farmhouses and pastures. Where
cows once grazed peacefully, trout and perch feed, cruising past
roof tops and chimneys and the church spire. The farmers were
compensated for the loss of their ancestral lands with farms else-
where, and so this family came to live here.

Their new land, however, did not come with membership in the
Genossame - an association of farmers that I believe is peculiar to
Switzerland. Hundreds of years ago, when farmers first settled
here, they decided that the rivers, the woods and pastures would

152

need to be common property as these valuable resources could only be successfully worked with the help of all. Co-ownership was limited to the founding families of the *Genossame*. With farms being passed from father to sons, and all sons becoming members of the *Genossame* at birth, it is almost a natural law that a farmer is by definition also a *Genosse*. Over the years, however, some of the pastures have been turned into pricey building land which is made available at very low cost to the male members of the *Genossame* or sold at current market prices to outsiders. The *Genossame* may even build houses and apartments which they then sell or rent at a profit. No longer are all of the *Genossen* farmers, yet the rights and prestige continue to be passed on to sons and their sons. This sense of continuity and pride in possession makes the *Genossen* the aristocrats of the village. A farmer who is not a member of this decision-making and profit-sharing forum is, therefore, at a marked disadvantage. No matter how many of my farmer's future generations live here, they will never 'belong' - no more than those of us who came here from another country. I often wonder whether our sharing this fringe status is what made 'my farmer' accept us so readily, without the usual cautionary period.

But let me introduce 'my farmer' to you. Even though this term represents a whole family, when we speak of 'the farmer' we really mean the Grandfather as the head of the clan. He must be around 70, a thinnish man of medium height, a little stooped perhaps, but still with dark and curly hair, a tiny golden cow in his left earlobe. In the early years it was Grandfather driving the tractor with Grandmother standing behind him and their daughter, Ottilia, sitting on the flat-bed truck. Sometimes, when he was alone, he would stop for a rest and treat me to a bit of his life. "I'm happy at home," he told me, breaking into a contented smile. "I don't go anywhere, not even to the *Beiz*. Once a year I go to the farmer's market in Uznach, about 15 kilometres away, and that's enough." But once, he wanted me to know, he had even been to Zurich, not to discover city life, mind you, but to change trains on his way to the Aargau area where he was serving his military duty. And yet he does enjoy my birthday cards with pictures of the New York skyline or the harbour in Shanghai. "As long as I don't have to go there," he keeps saying, a mischievous glint in his eyes.

Gradually Grandfather's place on the tractor has been taken over by Ottilia or one of his grandsons. But since his accident in June, he has hardly been able to leave the farm at all. I visited him in hospital and brought him his favourite *Stumpen*, a Swiss cigar. He sat on the edge of the bed, looking smaller and thinner. While we were talking, he kept looking out the window to the hill where the others were working harder than ever to make up for his share of the workload. "We were lucky," he said, cradling his left arm in a heavy bandage from fingertips to elbow. His eldest grandson had been driving the tractor as they were picking up freshly cut grass on a very steep slope. He had been walking alongside and pushing the tractor with his right arm. "All of a sudden there was a *Chlöpf*, a terrific noise, the tractor overturned, pinning my left arm underneath it. It caught the dog too. Poor little Senn bit me in my right hand in his final pain."

Fortunately, some other farmers had seen the tractor suddenly disappear from sight and came to investigate. His grandson had hit his head badly on the cabin frame, "blood was running all over him" and he had also injured his knee. "He needs treatment, too," Grandfather reported. "But he can't go to hospital now, not while I am here. That will have to wait until I can work again." Out of the window he looked, longingly, sadly. "We have learnt a lot, you know, we just went on to steeper and steeper ground, a little further each time. No telling what would have happened if the tractor had turned over once more." He cried when I left, and I felt like crying, too. It was more than the crushed arm. It was his dignity that had been broken along with the bones - the dignity to do his share of the work.

Grandmother's hair is streaked with grey. Wearing a dark skirt, dark woolen stockings and high leather boots - irrespective of the weather - she looks more robust than Grandfather. But she, too, is rarely on the tractor these days. "My legs hurt too much to work in the fields," she says. Yet, almost seventy years old, she still does all the cooking, washing and mending for a household of seven - without the help of an automatic washing machine, a dishwasher, an electric sewing machine. She hates to admit that it is almost too much for her now.

But Grandmother does enjoy talking, on the phone and otherwise. I can never call up to order eggs without being given the exact status of her health, plus an in-depth record of her neighbour's ailments. Then I am informed about farm life. At one time, it was the cows that were giving less and less milk and would have to be moved to another barn. A 'diviner' had discovered a deep water vein beneath their barn which had affected the cows' well-being. "Maybe if you moved your bed," Grandmother advised me, "your backache would go away too."

Another time it was the hens that were not laying and would have to be killed because someone had given them the evil look. "You won't understand this," she said, "you're not a Catholic, are you?" Not that I saw any correlation between poultry and religion, but I have learnt that it is no good interrupting her train of thought. "Anyway," she went on, "it's a punishment not going to Church regularly and having failed the Church in some other way. Even though," she indignantly pointed out, "my youngest grandson serves as altar boy. So these poor hens will have to leave this lovely earth; there is nothing else we can do with them."

Fortunately she knew just what to do about the evil eye. They would get new hens and as soon as they were laying, she would send some eggs down to me. True to her word, some months later I found the usual bag at the front door, containing not only eggs but the healthy smell of twenty cows and their calves in a warm and humid barn. Each egg was painstakingly wrapped in newspaper carefully torn into squares. Egg boxes wouldn't help much, as those hens have never heard of uniform, standardized, neutralized production methods. The eggs not only vary in size, shape, texture and colour, but they also bear traces of earth and grass; occasionally a feather sticks to the shell. Lacking the efficiency of pre-programmed supermarket hens - who undoubtedly lay their eggs directly into boxes - these hens hide their eggs all over the farm and it is up to the youngest grandson to find them. Their taste? Incomparable.

I only hope the fox does not discover this generation of hens. Or else he will go the way his cousin went: shot down and roasted. "He didn't even taste so bad," Grandmother assured me.

Strange as some of her tales sound, there may be an underlying truth that escapes our scientific analysis. Dependent on the weather, on the quality of the soil, absorbed by caring for their animals and their fields, these farmers have retained a link to nature we have lost. Maybe this link enables them to detect influences we cannot even imagine to exist. Producing food, after all, is a matter of survival to them. Many of us fool ourselves that it is the responsibility of the supermarket.

Unlike her mother, Ottilia never talks for the sake of talking. But her words have punch. If I look sick, she will let me know it immediately. If something troubles her, she'll come right out with it, expecting me to do the same. When I came back after two years abroad, she welcomed me, ''Hey, you really have turned grey! Did you have problems?'' The warm concern in her question more than made up for my injured vanity. By nature jolly, she accepts the hardships of her life, and she certainly has her ample share of those, with a shrug and a laugh - like bad weather one cannot change.

Built like a rotund pillar of strength, she handles the tractor with the certainty of a sleepwalker. Ottilia lives in trousers and never seems bothered by wet and cold weather, rarely wearing more than a dark sweater or a blue cotton jacket. Rain has to fall in sheets, the wind cut your skin with a knife of ice before she dons one of her three hats - the brown woolen one, the olive felt hat like the baddies wear in films, or the wide-brimmed black one. Ottilia wears her hats on the back of her head, giving her an air of jauntiness, the me-against-the-world look. And why not? A woman who does the work of at least one man, if not two, has the right to wear a man's hat any way she pleases. Right? Right.

Her sons take after her, big and husky, yet good-natured and soft-hearted like puppies. The oldest two, hardly twenty, drive and smoke as if they had been doing so all their lives - Sepp with pipe and a jeep, Toni with a cigar and a tractor. They are strong. Once, I had already broken several tools trying to remove a bush - without even budging it. I called Sepp as he was driving past. Very coolly, the unlit pipe in mouth, he pulled, once, maybe twice, and out it was - roots and all. Not a word, no effort and no further tools were wasted - a shy smile betrayed the careful economy of action. The youngest, Heiri, still rides past us on his moped four times a day to and from school. Slimmer than his older brothers, with his grand-father's curly dark hair, his gold-rimmed glasses, he delivers the eggs with the courtesy of an English butler.

Our friendship has reaped many treats, though I never really know what I do to deserve such generosity. In June I found a crate of glossy black cherries at the front door which I know took hours to pick. Even if they had allowed me to pay for them, cherries of that perfection would still have been a rare gift. The cherries were followed by plums in September, apples in October.

But the real treat is not for me but for my garden. I believe that we should be as good to the earth as it has been to us. So when autumn comes, I need to cover the ground with compost or manure. Compost I use as fast as I can produce, and manure is difficult to get - unless you are lucky to have a farmer as a real friend who is willing to risk his reputation. A farmer, you see, runs the risk of being considered a 'lazy farmer' if he gives some of his manure away. Not only does 'my farmer' share it with me, but what I get is true gold: well-rotted, beautifully crumbly stuff. If you appreciate its value, you must be asking "How come SHE is so lucky?" Well, Grandfather likes to see me gardening in my bikini; and when I recently asked Grandmother for my yearly supply, she told me not to worry, Grandfather had already given instructions to have the nice old stuff set aside for me. "With a *Poschtuerli,* a figure like that, she deserves it," he said. So if you see me swimming lap after lap or puffing my way through the fitness exercises at the local gym, do not accuse me of vanity. I am simply earning my manure.

PRATFALLS ON THE LANGUAGE FRONTIER

by Stanley Mason

Anyone who moves from one linguistic region to another is sure to run up against difficulties. These are obviously greatest for those who have no inkling of the language spoken in their new surroundings, but they are still considerable even for those with a rudimentary to respectable grasp of the new lingo.

I had not been in Switzerland long when I wanted to buy some nylon stockings for a girl friend. I couldn't think of the German word for stockings, but the English word 'hose' immediately suggested itself, so I went into a shop selling ladies' lingerie and asked for *Damenhosen*. The girl behind the counter seemed slightly taken aback, and when she came and dangled some lacy panties before my eyes - she perhaps thought I was a transvestite or something and had to be humoured - I was taken aback too. In fact, I was seriously embarrassed, as I was still young enough to have a sense of shame.

On another occasion I was in town with two young Englishmen, neither of whom knew a word of German. We began to feel peckish in mid-afternoon, so we went into a restaurant, and the waitress, who spoke a little English, persuaded us to try a seasonal speciality that she said she could recommend. It turned out to be a paste made from sweet chestnuts which looked rather like a dish of worms. We were somewhat intimidated by the sight, and ate the stuff without enthusiasm. An hour later we still felt peckish, so we tried another establishment. We were agreed that what we wanted was not a sweet, but a somewhat more substantial snack. This time I consulted the menu, and my eye fell on an item that we could just about afford and that was designated *vermicelles*. I explained to my companions that this must be pasta, a kind of continental macaroni (in those days macaroni was about the only kind of pasta you ever saw in England, if we mercifully forget the incredible invention of spaghetti on toast), and they at once approved. Five minutes later we got our snack: it was that chestnut paste again, looking more like worms than ever. I checked the menu: *vermicelles de châtaignes*. We felt that we had been tricked by a malicious fate. We sat there, unable to start on the stuff, wishing that we were in Timbuktoo, where we could at least have had camels' eyes.

Another true story will exemplify the same dilemma operating in the opposite direction. An Austrian lady I know was interned in Yorkshire during the war. One day she and her companions were given leave to go to the cinema in a nearby country town. When they came out they all wanted to go to the toilet, so they began to look around for a public convenience. Their search was soon successful: they had hardly got into the main street when they found a sign that said 'Closed'. That was surely what they were looking for, as it could only be the English word for *Klosett*. But they were disappointed - there was no means of getting in. It must have been a Thursday afternoon, for all down the street there were signs saying 'Closed'; yet none of the doors were open. They began to suspect that the townspeople were playing a mean practical joke on them. They were by now nearly bursting - with indignation, of course - but there was nothing for it: they had to wait till they got back to their internment quarters. Continence, after all, is a virtue, or so say those who don't have it imposed on them.

Misunderstandings of this kind may of course occur in far more everyday circumstances. English people in German-speaking parts may well be nonplussed when they hear the locals saying *Servus* to each other as they part, but there is no need to succumb to the same misconception as Hemingway did and to think that the Swiss, to whom service is the highest of all principles, even use the word as a kind of morale-raiser when they quit each other's company. The word *Servus* is simply Latin for 'slave', or 'servant', and it was probably students who first used it, meaning 'I am your slave', just as Anglo-Saxons used to end letters with ''I am, Sir, your most obedient servant''. In any case, it isn't the Swiss who say it, but the Austrians.

The Englishman or American who first sits down to eat with the Swiss and is wished a ''good appetite'' from all sides may also be at a loss as to what to say in reply. The fact is that you either have a good appetite or you don't, and no amount of pious wishing is likely to alter the status quo. The English in any case are much more reserved in their attitude to food and feel it rather infra dig to be wished a good appetite, almost as though someone were standing there ready to drop a flag so as to let them loose on their victuals, or to say: ''One - two - three - they're off!'' In point of fact, the only thing I've ever heard an Englishman say to another about to address himself to his food is ''I hope it chokes you!''

This brings us - through the word 'choke' - to a quite different chapter of Swiss-English linguistic relations. Just as the English can never learn to say *Chuchichäschtli*, the German Swiss hardly ever manage to pronounce certain English consonants. The English 'th', for instance, often defies them to the end of their days, and I think now that I must have had a sadistic streak when in my youth I used to make my pupils repeat the sentence: ''Sigfrith the Fifth had thirty-six sick thanes, and the thirty-sixth thane was the sickest since thirteen-sixty.'' Mrs Thatcher has been a strain on German pronunciatory faculties for years, and perhaps if only for this reason it will be a blessing when she makes way for a successor, though for heaven's sake not a Jones or a Jackson - German speakers are constitutionally unable to pronounce the English 'j', and we suffered enough in the days of the man they always referred to as President Chonson. This is, of course, also the place where 'choke' comes in. If a German Swiss tells you he enjoys a good 'choke', there's no need to panic and begin looking round for a way of escape. What he means is only a good 'joke', though when you've heard one of his jokes, you may decide that 'choke' is not a bad description after all. I once knew a Swiss who had an English girl friend by the name of Joyce, and, as you've guessed, he called her Choice. But in reality, of course, he didn't have any choice at all.

The situation is no better with the English 'w'. From long listening to reports on German television of the major British tennis tournament, I now know that it takes place in 'Vimbledon'. You can't find this place on the map, but the frequency with which German sports commentators name it would be sufficient, one would think, to bring it into existence. The same dichotomy, or rather absence of dichotomy, extends to 'wine' and 'vine'. You may always have believed that 'wine' is the product of the 'vine', but if you listen to German speakers long enough you will realize that they are really one and the same thing.

The catches of the spoken languages may be seriously aggravated in written applications. When I took my first office job in Switzerland, I had a secretary who hardly knew a word of French or English, so I had to write out my letters by hand for her to type. In one of the first of them which happened to be to a French VIP, she opened with full diapason: *"Nous avons l' horreur d' accuser réception de votre lettre..."* The distance between honour and horror in France is evidently only a very short step. On another occasion I had to write to a colleague by the name of Robert who had been criticizing me, and I wanted to do so in a firm but studiedly polite tone. Once again, the catastrophe came at the very outset: "Dead Bob..."

A SWISS PATRIARCH

by Karla Noell

Weathering like old trees, some people withstand all the storms of life, molding their characters around their difficulties. Peter Gubler was one of these. When I came onto his horizon he was already bent, but not burned out. When he died I was away and missed any indignity he might have suffered. He would have been glad of that.

His shrewd, bright blue eyes peered out from under thick bushy brows and kept track of all that was going on in the community. Solidly built, he had, at well over seventy, a powerful body, which was crowned by a shock of white hair. He often knew about things before they happened and I seldom saw him register surprise. Long after his family had given up hope that he would listen to their admonitions on slowing down and decreasing his work load, he stolidly went through his workday, happy to be left in peace. He tended his fruit trees and raised sheep.

I loved Peter Gubler for his perspicacity. He himself possessed two sorrows which belied, or perhaps were covered by his gruff exterior. The first concerned one of a pair of twin sons. Another was that neither his sons nor his grandson expressed the desire to take up farming. There would be no young Gublers coming along to cultivate and care for the land he loved.

When I came to live in this small farming community in the French-speaking part of Switzerland, I was a curiosity. As I learned later, a German-speaking Swiss falls within the Vaudois prejudice parameters. An American does not. Our family of four could have dropped in from outer space, so far out were we from the local concept of a foreigner. As a Bernese, Peter Gubler was right on target. He'd bought his large land-holding just after the war. He and his wife and children may have gone through years of isolation before grudging acknowledgement was extended by his neighbors. He knew what it was to be a foreigner in his own country. He was sensitive to my own situation and must have expressed the desire to know me, otherwise our meeting wouldn't have happened. Our friendship, which was to last until his death, was formed at that moment and he made me understand that if I ran into trouble, I should come to him.

After some years of casual friendship, Peter invited me to his home for the first time. Haltingly, strangely unsure of himself, he explained that his wife was not well. He informed me that he and his wife had had twin sons. One had become an engineer, while the other had become a cheese-maker. Then the cheese-maker decided to make a trip across Canada. They had received two post cards from him and then nothing. At first they thought that he was staying away in order to avoid his obligation to do military service or that perhaps he dared not call home, for fear of the Swiss learning his whereabouts. His wife's heart had begun to fail at the time the Swiss Embassy had given up hope of finding the missing boy. He was believed dead, but Peter's wife was sure that their son was hiding from his father out of a sense of failure, because Willi had always felt that his father admired and preferred his brother who had become an engineer. Peter explained that he was telling me all this, although his son had been gone then for more than four years, because I was American and might have an idea how to trace Willi. This would help keep his wife's hope alive.

I reasoned that if Willi Gubler were alive, he would be obliged to carry an immigration card. To stay alive he would have to work and probably pay taxes. I promptly wrote to the Canadian immigration officials and the internal revenue office. Neither agency ever replied to my enquiries. However, they did respond and in a most delicate and humane way. Although they gave out no information about Willi Gubler, they contacted the Salvation Army, and there some loving person took the matter in hand. Willi Gubler called his mother once a month until the day she died.

From my place in the line of mourners which comprised the whole village, I finally got a fleeting glimpse of Willi Gubler as he walked next to the coffin of his mother. I don't believe he ever said a word to his father or his brother. He returned to Canada immediately after the funeral and no mention was ever made of his coming or going. At least not to me. But whenever I passed in front of Peter Gubler's house, I was asked in for a glass of wine or a good meal. Buckets of cherries appeared on my front door step the morning of my birthday, year after year.

I had just returned from a visit to my mother in the US when I was informed of Peter Gubler's death. I was stunned. It had simply never occurred to me that he could die. Someone reported that his family had thrown out his possessions when they cleaned out his house. As if dying of hard work and old age were like dying of some kind of communicable disease.

The community functions as it always has, but there is no one who has the stature Peter had. His sheep have disappeared from the hill, an apartment house stands in their place. His house has been sold and I feel an outrage which is difficult to justify. I explained my feelings to a friend and she told me that I was right to feel that way because Peter Gubler had been the 'Doyen' of the community and there wasn't anyone else to take his place.

SWISS HUMOR?

by Alex Porter

An American woman told me
that the Swiss don't have any humor.
She really told me that.
She was even serious about it.
She also said that
nothing can happen to you in Switzerland.
"Oh, really?" I said. "Well, I am Swiss!"

This is not a joke now. I'm Swiss and
I had to get this story translated into English.

This story is actually not really important to me.
And it may not even be important for you
but it was important for the translator.
Otherwise he couldn't survive in Switzerland
if there weren't any translations.
Just think what would happen
if only important things were translated!
Many translators here would hardly survive.

To be honest,
if the Swiss didn't have humor,
we would all die tomorrow.
Their humor and my seriousness
is all that keep people alive here.

This place is too clean
and everything works automatically.
There are no problems at all here.
That's what you think, isn't it?
You say I said that. Well, I was lying.
I was sure that you would believe me.
This is the problem of all
the English-speaking people coming here.
They believe whatever we tell them.
They really do because we act so serious
and it's a serious place.
And no one would ever suspect

that we play this being-serious-game
just to meet the expectations of
English-speaking people.
And when they have left
and closed the door behind them,
we look into each other's faces
and burst into laughter
till tears drop from our eyes
and until our bellies hurt.
Sometimes we laugh for hours,
until the telephone
or the doorbell rings
and a foreigner asks us
something else about Switzerland.

Instantly we are serious again.
Completely serious, kind,
friendly and never ever laugh.
If they make a joke,
we just pretend that
we don't understand it at all
and we look into their faces
just like our cows do.

Sometimes we can't hold our inner smile
and so we turn around and
make one of our cuckoo clocks perform
or we jingle one of our souvenir cow-bells
or even blow into one of our long alphorns.
We make all these sounds.
But the moment these noisy things stop,
we stop too, and say we're sorry,
we have serious things to do.

They believe us.
We sell them cuckoo clocks.
Do you know how funny this is for us?

Alex Porter

We sell them these cuckoo clocks
from the Black Forest
which has nothing really
to do with Switzerland at all.

These souvenirs don't melt or spoil
like Swiss chocolate or cheese.
So the Swiss like to sell cuckoos.
Tourists assume these are Swiss products -
these silly sculptured time pieces
with their fake birds going in and out
saying important things like 'cuckoo'.

A Swiss would never have
one of these tasteless things in his flat
unless he's got a visitor
from a foreign country coming to his place.
These cuckoos and Lederhosen
are just a national joke.
Like the clocks every Swiss
has under his helmet
with his army rifle, just in case.
Don't you know that the next referendum
is about the clocks under Swiss helmets?

Or, take the banks.
Do you really think
that they all have so much money?
Do you really?
Yes, they have.

To be honest, I am an artist.
I live in a cold, damp flat in Lucerne
where all my writings and books
get soaked in winter, spring and fall.
The walls of my flat
are getting grayer and grayer.

Here's a Swiss joke.

I don't have any insurance
which pays me a cent from my last car accident
which I survived by a hair.

There aren't any other flats
available for the next decade
which I can afford to pay.
So everything is getting moldy,
my health and my humor.
Both are in bad shape
because of this cold, damp flat.

And no one believes me at all.
If I tell this to foreigners
they laugh and tell me,
"Yes, the Swiss do have a sense of humor"
and they laugh heartily
the first time since coming to this country.

The sad thing is that not even the Swiss
believe me any more because they've heard
I was born in America.
They think I just make up these jokes
about my flat and my car accident
just for the foreigners.
They really laugh at me.

So if you ever come to Switzerland,
feel free to have a good time
and laugh with all the Swiss.
When you least expect it,
they might just laugh with you.
Then you'll see that the bankers
and all the rest of them
only look so serious because
they always try very hard to hide
all that good chocolate
stuck on their teeth.

SUMMER WITH SWISS SONS

by Lane Anderson

I had never seen such trees.

Immense, magnificent trees in every shade of green, many covered with colorful blossoms.

The river, whirling and rushing towards its demise in Lac Leman, was clear and cold. Standing near it, you could feel its cold and its power. It murmured incessantly of the glaciers and waterfalls of the Alps, where it was born.

It was so different, so foreign from my homeland. I had spent my whole life in America's Southwest, where a spot of green and a trickle of water constituted an 'oasis'. The river Aare had many times more water than our legendary Rio Grande, even in its flood.

Upon my arrival, I was suddenly plunged into two worlds. There was Berne, with its ancient buildings and cobbled streets - and its even more ancient trees and river. And there was the Kinderklinik, with its spotless white and orderly atmosphere - the epitome of what is valued by the Swiss.

There were two emotional worlds as well. There was the joy of seeing and visiting my two sons after eight months of separation. There was also the coming divorce, to be conducted in a language foreign to me, far from my home and friends.

I had come to Switzerland to visit my boys, Christoph and Nicholas. They had been brought there a year before by my Swiss wife, who had changed her mind about living in California and being married to an American at about the same time.

Christoph, age 7, had been struck down by a motorist in the small village where he lives, and was in the Kinderklinik, recovering from two broken legs and tendon damage. Nicholas, age 4, was at home in Vielbringen, a *Dörfli* near Berne.

It was May, and Berne was breathtakingly beautiful. I had traveled to Berne the previous summer to try to convince my wife to come home or include me in her Swiss life. But the trip had been so fraught with emotional turmoil that I had somehow missed the beauty.

I had been studying German and immediately attempted to try it out. The Swiss proved to be very helpful and friendly, and many spoke English in response to my obviously Anglicized butchery of German. It seems that they are very proud of their multi-lingual accomplishment, and pleased with the opportunity to exhibit it.

It was sometimes disturbing, however, that whenever I found myself with a group of Swiss, and tried to join the conversation with my 'High German', they quickly reverted to Swiss German. I've since learned that, for the Swiss, *Hochdeutsch* lends a formality to any situation that makes a truly genial and relaxed conversation impossible.

I was prepared to take lodging in the Youth Hostel, where I had stayed the previous summer. Christoph, however, informed me that parents were welcome and, in fact, encouraged to stay in the Kinderklinik. So I stayed the first week on a small cot beside Christoph. When he went home, I stayed in the hostel.

Soon, the day of the divorce arrived, and I put on my best clothes and marched into court. The courtroom was in the ancient castle of Schlosswil. I imagined that there might be a dungeon reserved for foolish Yankees who had unsuccessfully tried to wed Swiss *Fräuleins*. My wife's family had lived in nearby Vielbringen for several hundred years and her father was a retired lawyer. I had a deep sense of impending doom.

Entering the courthouse, I was relieved to find friendly and helpful faces, rather than the stern faces set in powdered wigs which I had imagined. Judge Burri, accustomed to this sort of proceeding, guided my wife and me to a quick and equitable settlement, ignoring the dreadful documents that the lawyers had crafted. A few hours after I entered the castle, I walked out with it all behind me and only the six weeks of visitation with my sons that the judge had given me were on my mind.

Nicholas had forgotten how to speak English when I arrived, but it was obvious that he understood the English that I spoke to him. Since Christoph had several more weeks of school to finish up, I took Nicky first. Partly because of his English, we went to Youth Hostels, where we encountered a generous portion of English speakers.

Our first stop was Langnau, where we stayed in an authentic Bernese farmhouse that had been converted into a hostel. It was run by a lovely Bernese family, which made it all the more authentic. The family's five-year-old daughter adopted Nicky as a brother and showed him around. After only two days, however, rain drove us out, and we went to the Ticino - the Italian-speaking region in the south.

In the Ticino, we found the warm sunshine that we sought. We also found a hostel near Lugano that was perfect for us. The hostel in Figino was just a hundred meters from the lake, and the staff were incredibly loving toward Nicky.

After two weeks, Nicky's English was coming back to him. It was an incredible experience to have him all to myself. He had changed so much in the months that we were apart. But now school was out and we went to fetch Christoph.

It was still raining north of the Alps, so we returned to the Ticino. This time, we stayed at the hostel in Savosa, a suburb of Lugano. The hostel had its own swimming pool and was well-equipped for children. We spent a leisurely two weeks playing together. I cooked their meals (mostly spaghetti) while they played outside, then we ate by the pool.

Once again, we were delighted with the love and patience lavished on the children by the Ticinese. The boys could be wild and the *Ticinesi* did not seem to mind. We might have spent our whole vacation there, but the hostel was overbooked.

The weather seemed to be getting bad on our side of the Alps so we decided to try Zermatt on the other side. In Zermatt, the hostel was full, so we stayed with the Nature Friends - a non-profit environmental group that runs inexpensive hostels. The Friends were a good find, but Zermatt was too crowded with tourists.

After Zermatt, we tried Nature Friend houses in Meiringen and Grindelwald, but we failed to find the easy-going and tolerant attitude towards the children. The Nature Friend Houses were just Swiss enough so that I always felt like my boys weren't 'under control', or that their behavior was not enough 'in *Ordnung*'.

When we tried Youth Hostels again, it was much better. We stayed in Zug, Meiringen and Basle at Hostels where I didn't have to worry so much about what others thought about my children's behavior. In fact, the young Swiss were much rowdier. Apparently when they get away from their *Ordnung*-laden homes, they like to cut loose a good bit.

My sons met English-speaking folks from Scotland, Ireland, Australia, Canada, America, India and even from England. We compared the sizes of all these countries with Switzerland and Christoph and Nicky resolved to practice their English until next summer.

At that point, Nicky's six weeks were up, and we had to take him home. Christoph is a big boy, and without Nicky, capable of pleasing and charming even the most proper Swiss *Hausfrau* - for we had found that household propriety was enforced by the *Hausfrau*. With this in mind, Christoph and I headed for our favorite Nature Friend House, Naturfreundhaus Gorneren.

Nestled between glaciers and waterfalls, Christoph and I found total peace at last. The wild, awesome ruggedness of the Alps was balanced by the lush, green valleys and the delicate Alpine flowers. The sounds of cow bells and rushing water lulled us to sleep at night.

We prepared our meals alongside our fellow guests on an immense wood-burning stove. Our refrigerator was a cellar down in the permanently frosty subsoil. Every afternoon we walked together to Uli's barn, just a hundred meters away, and returned with a bucket of steaming milk - milk unlike any I had tasted before, so rich and sweet from the Alpine meadows and glacial waters.

Ten days and nights we spent there, communing with one another, with nature and with the other guests. The effect was holistic. The gorgeous natural surroundings brought out the best in all of us. The sparkling sunshine and crisp air cemented the bond between me and my son.

When I finally had to bring him back, the circus was in town, and both boys accompanied me to it. Then I took them to their tiny *Dörfli* in the Bernese Oberland - with its beautiful blossomed trees and its rushing Alpine river - and as we said good-bye until next summer, I thought "What a beautiful land they live in!"

I would have to come here often to see Christoph and Nicholas. Well, it could have been much worse. I could have married a woman from Siberia - or Los Angeles.

HAVEN'T WE PASSED THOSE COWS BEFORE?

by Susie Vereker

I'm not a great athlete but, since mountain walking is obviously a part of Swiss life in which everyone should participate, I bought a hiking guide from the American Women's Club. After weeks of my trying to persuade them, my family agreed to set out on an expedition one sunny Saturday in July.

My husband studied the instructions at the front of the booklet about the need for correct shoes, bad weather gear, emergency drinks and food, but we decided these were probably intended for prospective mountaineers attempting the north face of the Eiger.

"How about a map though? I do think we need a proper map, like they say," I remarked. (My father was a military man who had brought me up on maps.)

"No time for messing about in the shops or we'll never get going," said the man in my life.

Having selected a walk that would be suitable for a five-year-old and an unfit woman - only an hour and a half long, according to the guide - we set off for the Jura. Without much difficulty we found the beginning of the hike, parking our car on the side of an obscure mountain road. It was then three o'clock and still too hot to carry any gear.

At first, we found ourselves struggling up what seemed to me to be a precipice. The three boys raced ahead of us.

"I'd hate to go on one of the American women's 'difficult' hikes if this is meant to be easy," muttered Peter.

At the top of the crest, however, the going became much better and we walked along through fields and pastures which reminded me of the Heidi films on television. We followed the yellow *tourisme pédestre* arrows and the guide book's instructions for an hour and a half, but we still seemed to be moving further and further from the car. Then the arrows petered out and the instructions became much less clear. "Those cows look familiar - haven't we passed them before? Why didn't anyone bring a decent map?"

We returned to the last signpost. All the boys had a different view about the correct route. I decided to retrace my steps back to the car with the youngest, leaving Peter and the teenagers to argue about the quick, 'right way' down. "You keep the car keys," I called, "you're bound to get there first."

Rory and I ambled down, enjoying the scenery. We met a few other walkers on the way and an old farmer who had evidently been sampling the valley wine on a fairly regular basis. We reached the car around six o'clock but there was no sign of the rest of the family.

After an hour's wait I began to run out of ideas about how to entertain a small child on the edge of a Swiss mountain forest. Rory played on a pile of logs. We discussed plants and flowers - there was plenty of nature around. We played a few guessing games. We jumped up and down to keep warm - pity our sweaters were still locked in the car. We sat in a small patch of sunlight but our patch moved away. It was pretty quiet up there. We heard voices but the wrong hikers appeared around the corner. Two cars passed by - one driver stopped to ask the way! We walked down the road a while and watched some young people driving up to an isolated farmhouse, going to some sort of party, perhaps.

Another hour went by. I considered various plans, disguising my anxiety from Rory. Who could I call on a Saturday night and ask to rescue us from wherever we were in the Jura? We hadn't been living in Geneva that long so not many candidates sprang to mind. Peter would be all right as he had money and could stay in a mountain hut or inn...or somewhere. About eight o'clock it became too cold to wait any longer. Remembering my early days as a Girl Scout, I constructed a message with twigs on the bonnet of the car "GONE TO FARM NEAR" with an arrow to indicate the direction of the farm!

It was embarrassing to have to gate-crash a party in slow motion - the guests watched as we trudged up the cart track towards them. Luckily Rory was still full of energy.

When we reached the farm, there was a group of about 20 people staring at us in a not particularly friendly manner. I addressed a middle-aged woman, hoping that she was the hostess in charge: *"Bonsoir, madam, avez-vous un telephone?"* I began nervously.

"Non, pas ici." There was a silence. I tried again. *"J'ai perdu mon mari dans les montagnes."* Some men carrying a pig on a spit remarked that it was careless to lose one's husband but the guests still did not seem too thrilled by our appearance. Suddenly a young woman noticed how cold we were and produced sweaters. Without waiting for a further invitation, I led Rory inside the old farm building and sat by the open fire. I felt extremely irresponsible and foolish explaining in my halting French that I had no money, no food, no keys. The kind young woman offered to drive me down to the village where there was a restaurant; she would give me money for food.

Everyone became much more friendly and a lively debate was taking place about what the crazy foreigner should do, when Peter drove up the track. He explained that he and the boys had been wandering around in confused circles - the little stroll in Jura had taken them five and a half hours.

"If you'd had the car keys, would you still be here?" he asked. I wonder...

Though two years have now passed, any suggestion of another nice little family walk in the mountains has fallen upon distinctly stony ground.

DOES YOUR HUSBAND YODEL?

by Ann Robert

When I was a child I used to play a game called 'Pairs' with my friend next door. We would call out pairs of words like 'Jack and Jill', 'black and white' one after the other. The loser was the one who ran out of ideas first. Here are some more pairs: clean and tidy, spick and span, law and order, cold and reserved, free and easy, open and friendly. With whom does one traditionally associate the first four? With the Swiss. And the last two? With 'us', the friendly foreigners. And yet in my experience these clichés are just about as out of date and hackneyed as the London fog or the idea that every Swiss knows how to yodel.

Who are the Swiss anyway? The Jura separatists or their Bernese opponents? The farmers you see carrying loads of hay on their backs down the mountain slopes or the owners of the five-star hotels in the nearby ski resort? The gnomes of Zurich or the 50,000 spectators at the national wrestling championships? The visitors to the Geneva book fair or the participants in the Engadine ski marathon? In this country, with fewer inhabitants than London or Los Angeles, there are four official languages and a State system that can oblige a lawyer or a theologian to pass new exams if he wants to move to a canton that could be only a few miles from his old home. In countries like the USA or England, which have a huge immigrant population, there is one binding feature - the English language. Not only do Switzerland's four cultures manage to survive, but each of the four has to assimilate part of the rising foreign population. Fitting these six million individuals into one category seems impossible.

I have lived in and out of Switzerland (mostly in) since 1960 when my father first came to work in Berne at the British Embassy. It's a funny way to get to know a country. For the first year I was at boarding school in England. During the holidays in Switzerland, I found that the diplomats lived in a world of their own, regarding the 'natives' as outsiders and having next to no curiosity about them. A few young Bernese men from good families were invited to parties because for some reason there always seemed to be more diplomats' daughters than sons around. These boys all spoke English and

French. I had been told that the Bernese spoke German and was rather put out to find that I couldn't understand a word of what was being said in the shops, in spite of having lived several years in Germany. A year later I set off to study French at Neuchâtel University. Everyone says that the best French is spoken in Neuchâtel, and I thought I would enjoy living at home in Berne and commuting each day. At first it didn't quite work out that way.

I was shy and it took me the best part of a year to dare to enter the University coffee bar. I didn't go to the yearly students' outing, thinking I would know no-one. I couldn't help thinking of the good time all my friends were having at English universities where everything is done to integrate students into three years of closed campus society. Later I realised that most of my new Swiss colleagues knew nearly as few people as I did. They came from different schools all over the canton, and their only advantage over me was that they knew the surroundings and could speak the language, whereas I had to concentrate hard when more than one person was speaking. After a while I too was asked to parties, and was invited to stay overnight with friends when I missed the last train home. I joined a students' club and became a member of the Students' Council. One girl had me to lunch at her home every week for the next four years I spent at the University, right up until I got married.

Life in Switzerland is really not as difficult as many English-speaking immigrants describe it. Of course Americans may be more friendly to newcomers by welcoming them into their churches, their homes and their clubs. The Swiss do take longer, but their friendship is for life. When we went on a sabbatical to California our German Swiss neighbour looked after our mail, opening letters, paying bills and sending on private correspondence. Others looked after our garden and when we came back our house had been dusted and someone had shopped for us. There was a welcome home sign on the door, and a cake and bottles of wine. Is this being cold and reserved? Maybe it is different on the other side of the *Rösti* barrier in the German-speaking part of Switzerland, yet all the German Swiss women I know here are fun to be with and no more *hausfrauisch* than I am. In the village where I live, there are many people of different nationalities, mostly married to Swiss, yet I have never heard myself or any of them criticised for their lack of knowledge of the language or the Swiss way of life.

In shops here and in Neuchâtel the atmosphere seems to be generally open and friendly. In our village when the baker is away, the greengrocer sells bread. When the grocer is on holiday, the baker stocks milk, butter and other basic products.

I remember once when my eldest son was two and I was in a *Confiserie* in town buying bread. He stretched out his hand and grabbed a fistful of *Pralinés* at Sfr. 3.50 (then) per 100 grams. I waited for the skies to fall. "Oh, never mind," said the lady, "children are like that, let him have them." I had hardly stammered out my thanks when he took another handful. There was the same friendly reaction. I ran out of the shop before her patience was tried too far. I've been buying my chocolates there ever since.

Switzerland is a small country and the mountains take up a lot of room. People live close to one another and wide open spaces are not part of the scenery. Even my husband says he feels cramped here compared to America. But in some places I feel more at ease here than abroad. In most places in America there is a certain prudery which doesn't fit in with the image of a 'modern' country and reminds me of the American swimming pool in Plittersdorf, Germany, in the early fifties with its stern notice 'No Bikinis'. Even thirty years later we were stared at in motel pools all across America because my husband and boys were wearing European swimming trunks and not shorts. Getting into a public swimming pool in the States and, to a lesser degree in England, is like trying to break into Fort Knox. When we arrived for the first time and dived in we were whistled at because it was mothers' and toddlers' time and we hadn't noticed that everyone who didn't fit into that category was sitting around looking at the clock. When we did get into the water, every movement was watched and nearly everything was forbidden, with rules such as "You must not jump more than twice on the springboard," or "You must not touch anyone else in the water." You could hardly hear the children's shouts above the tooting of horns and the blowing of whistles. Are there more accidents in Swiss pools? I don't know, but they are much more relaxing and fun.

The same could be said for maternity hospitals. Things may have changed now, but when I had my first child in Princeton, New Jersey, I was glad I could only stay in the hospital five days, because only the father and the grandparents of the new baby were allowed to visit, and only the first of the five was in America. During my whole stay, the baby was only brought to me at feeding time, and my husband took him in his arms for the first time when we left for home. My other two children were born here in Neuchâtel. I felt quite spoiled in the hospital with my newborn right beside me and with as many visitors as I wanted.

Another well-known cliché about Switzerland is that it's so clean and tidy. That's really true if you compare it to England nowadays where the wind wraps newspapers around your legs and you stumble over fast-food containers in the streets. In America the unemployed can be seen picking up cans along the highways and even my husband (who had a good job) picked up around twenty cans each evening on his walk back from the BART station - a profit of $2 a week! In Switzerland the highways and streets are indeed clean and tidy, but this is due to a well-organised refuse collecting system, and not to individual cleanliness. Dog-owners, for example, seem to boycott the little 'doggy corners' that one sees quite frequently, and allow their dogs to soil anywhere, as long as it's not in their own garden. Parking lots are full of little piles of cigarette butts that have been emptied out of car windows. In spite of public rubbish dumps and free incineration plants, dead animals and garbage are constantly being hauled out of holes and crevices. Near our house a small stream runs at the bottom of a wooded gorge. In springtime the ground is covered with primroses, and the trees are home to a host of birds and squirrels. Yet people come out of their way to tip mattresses, electrical appliances and other waste down there when there is a free public waste disposal plant only two miles further. A lot of people in this country, and that includes industrialists, seem to think that it's only wrong to pollute if you're seen doing it!

It also seems unfair to claim that the Swiss are set in their ways and impervious to new ideas. Newcomers want to introduce things they enjoy in their own country and are astonished that their ideas are not welcomed with open arms. But people who have been getting along without car-pools and babysitting groups and coffee parties don't necessarily see why a stranger should come along and tell them how behind they are. My children stay for meals with friends at least as often as I have other children here and we have car-pools for football practice and swimming lessons as the need arises.

A few years ago, I went to Berne with my parents to visit a new member of the Embassy. At lunch the talk got on to 'the Swiss'. I wasn't asked, as I once had been in the United States, if my husband knew how to yodel, but I became quite annoyed at the stream of clichés and hearsay coming from one who had only just arrived in the country. I said suddenly, "I AM Swiss you know." There was a short embarrassed silence, and then, "Oh no, that's not at all the same thing..." But it is; I like being Swiss, I like living here and I find there are a lot of warm and friendly people around.

BUS STOP BLUES

by Gillian Uster

Question: How many men and how many days does it take to construct a bus stop in Switzerland?

Answer: In the case of our bus stop at Hof Himmelrich in Baar, Canton Zug, it took at least ten men and a mere six weeks. Granted, they had to contend with two four-day working weeks.

Where I come from, South Africa to be exact, it would probably take two men and a day to erect a tin construction with a wooden bench AND THAT WOULD BE THE END OF THE STORY.

We were thrilled to hear that the *Gemeinde* of Baar had decided to introduce a new bus route to go right past our apartment block, which is situated on a fairly steep hill and a good walk from the nearest shopping centre. But we were certainly not prepared for the action, noise and dust of the weeks that were to follow. To make matters worse, when they started, I had just completed my annual spring cleaning of all my windows and curtains.

First on the scene were three men armed with tripods, measures and maps. They spent a pleasant day in the sunshine improving their tans while measuring. They consulted each other at regular intervals.

A day or two later the farmer's field on the left side of the road was mowed and the mobile site office-cum-kitchen-cum-toilet was towed into position. It was clearly a case of all systems go.

The right-hand side of the road was totally unsuitable for a bus stop as it took the form of a steep bank ending at a stream some 7 metres below. But the workers were undaunted and transported truckload upon truckload of soil to the spot to build up the entire embankment. This took at least a day and a half. Dust rose in clouds and covered everything in sight with a yellowish red film. Some of my neighbours blamed this on the pollination season, but I knew better, as I saw the whole spectacle from my dining room window.

Meanwhile, construction was going on on the left-hand side of the road. The farmer's field was obviously reclaimed by the powers that be and the bulldozers were happily excavating their way deep into the fertile soil.

The right-hand side of the road was left for a few days (probably to settle) and the construction workers had great fun in directing the steady flow of traffic all day long.

What never ceased to amaze me was that the workers always started promptly at 7 am. Usually by 7:30 am, at peak traffic time, they parked the dozer or grader in the middle of the road so that traffic was only able to flow on one side. By 9 am, when the traffic jam was over, the men and their dozers and graders and dust and noise simply vanished into thin air. Of course it was for their hallowed *Znüni* (nine o'clock snack time).

Next came the steam roller brigade to roll the right-hand side. This was obviously a great success as the workers could then use this useful shoulder to park their private cars on and thus leave the entrance to our apartment block more accessible to us and our visitors. It also meant that the little Baar bus (the whole object of this exercise) was able to make its way up and down Aegeristrasse every half hour without the difficulty it had experienced since its inception.

I also noted with glee that the number of passengers seemed to have increased. On one occasion I even counted 6 people.

The concrete trucks were next to arrive on the scene. This caused at least two days of chaos and traffic jams as the Baar bus and regular traffic made their way up or down the hill. There was much shouting and noise. The trucks queued up all day long with their huge tubs of concrete revolving and clanging while waiting to deposit their precious loads on the left or right-hand side of the road. Fortunately we were blessed with three very hot days in a row and the concrete was able to dry and set beautifully, much to the interest of all the neighbours who daily inspected the progress.

What came next was a surprise to us all. I was rudely awakened one morning at 6:45 by the start of a pneumatic drill which sounded like it was in our bathroom. It wasn't, but just outside our apartment, the pavement was being drilled away. On the right-hand side, where neighbours had always parked their cars, there was also a series of gaping holes. By the end of that day we discovered that a new pavement was being constructed on both sides of the road which stretched a good 200 metres from the proposed bus stop.

We were amazed as our pavement had only been constructed a mere three years ago when our apartments were built. The neighbours across the road were most unhappy to lose their parking spots.

This process took a few days and the whole area was shrouded in plastic sheeting. Next came the paving stones which formed the edge of the pavement. As soon as these were in position, I noticed the neighbours had taken to parking on the pavement, probably in protest.

What followed next was a complete re-surfacing of the road and pavements within 200 metres of either side of each bus stop. This meant that we lost our yellow pedestrian stripes (painted only a couple of months ago) and our white central road markers. But that took only two days to re-do and all was well.

The bus stop signs are now proudly in position with the correct maps and prices, but we still await the automatic ticket dispenser and a bench to sit on. In my opinion, these are the two most important objects that belong to constructing a bus stop. Perhaps some sort of shelter for rain and snow is not a bad idea, but I have my doubts. The site office, cum-kitchen-cum-toilet, was towed away last Friday and now there are only a few strands of red and white striped tape across the newly surfaced areas.

My husband mumbled something about their having an official opening ceremony. I suppose he's telling the truth. The Swiss usually like that sort of occasion. It is a nice bus stop, but sometimes I wonder what the whole lot has cost, surely more than the price of the two busses.

FROM HOUSEWIFE TO *HAUSFRAU*

by Angela Ashton

Your impression about life in Switzerland naturally depends on your own role in society. My status involved a change from housewife to *Hausfrau* but, I wondered, would there really be any difference? My answer, after four years as a Swiss *Hausfrau*, is YES!

The main distinction between a British housewife and a Swiss *Hausfrau* stems from a difference in the education system of each country. The British system dictates that once children reach their fifth year of life they can start school. Once they are at school they stay there for most of the day. In Switzerland children start school almost two years later and full-day schools are few and far between.

Thus, when her children leave the house in the morning in England, Mrs. Smith has approximately seven hours to work as she pleases inside the home or outside. This is not the case for Mrs. Schmid as there are almost no schools in Switzerland with facilities for allowing children to have lunch at school. Swiss schoolchildren have to go home for lunch. Somebody has to cook the lunch and nine times out of ten it will be their mother.

Any Swiss mother who wants to work away from home over lunchtime faces a major stumbling block unknown to her British counterpart. Unless she has helpful relatives or friends, or the money to pay somebody else to cook the children's lunch, she must get home in time to do it herself. This tight timetable does not make it impossible for a mother to work outside, but it's not easy and the majority of women with young children have to be full-time homemakers.

I do, however, know several Swiss mothers who have part-time jobs and still manage to get home to cook lunch! They have a lot of energy and organizational skills and you cannot help admiring their efforts against very difficult odds.

The way of life of a full-time housewife and a full-time *Hausfrau* also follows a different pattern. Something a housewife doesn't have to do, but a *Hausfrau* usually does, is to learn to share cleaning jobs and household facilities. This is because many people live in apartment blocks and each *Haus* has its own set of rules and

184

regulations covering just about every household activity you are likely to come across.

First of all there's the communal cleaning jobs. For me this means mopping the concrete floor of the washing and drying rooms twice a year as well as brushing and mopping down two flights of stairs once a fortnight. Both activities came as a complete surprise to me. If you ask the right questions before you move in then, of course, you will know what is expected of you. But if you don't know the right questions to ask...?

Another household practice which revolves around a communal approach is the laundry. One washing machine and a tumble drier are often shared by six or more families. As a *Hausfrau* you can forget the housewife's approach of washing as and when you please. It's all done strictly by rota. You may be allotted one day a week or you may choose a few hours here and there depending on *Haus* rules.

In our block we are not allowed to wash before 7 am or after 9 pm. Washing on Sunday is also forbidden. You are permitted to wash over the lunch break but it's inadvisable. This is because lunch is such a big thing that in certain areas - especially outside the main cities - the electricity supply cannot cope with the demand and the washing machine is automatically shut off.

If you happen to be unaware of this idiosyncrasy of Swiss life it can have unpleasant consequences. I once opened the washing machine door during a lunch break convinced that the wash was finished. My conviction was somewhat watered down by the deluge which poured out and the only thing I succeeded in washing was the laundry room floor.

These household regulations come as a slight culture shock to the British housewife but they can have their good side. The sharing aspect forces you to take other people into consideration more readily and vice versa. With a little give and take on all sides, this can produce a happy and helpful atmosphere.

For example, after I had my second child I was so busy I was often late getting down to the laundry room to sort out my washing. When I finally got there I would find that my clothes had been taken out of the tumbler, neatly folded and placed in my basket. During this period other little jobs were also done for me by considerate neighbours such as cleaning the sandpit and bringing in my daughter's bike in the evening.

A particularly nice act of neighbourliness once occurred where we live when celebrating the day of Saint Nicholas *(Samichlaus)*. Every child in the block opened their front door to find a packet of nuts, tangerines and chocolates in their snowboots. Such small gestures of kindness can outweigh the disadvantages of sharing a washing machine or having to clean the stairs.

So, housewife or *Hausfrau*? It's neither a better nor a worse situation to be in. At the end of the day housework is housework in any language. It's just the system that's different.

A LETTER TO THE EDITOR

by Steve Courso-Hafner

*E*ditor's note: Of the many letters sent to me in response to the articles in 'Ticking Along with the Swiss', only one letter was received with outright criticism. It came from California from a man who had only read about the book in a review. His letter started, "Just what kind of characters were solicited for their comments on their experiences in Switzerland." He was outraged by a number of quotations made from the stories in the review. I could not help wondering what this irate correspondent would think after reading the whole collection of stories and not just a review of them. I airmailed him a book free-of-charge to California and told him I would be interested in his honest opinion after reading the book. Also, since he was obviously so well-informed about life in Switzerland, I invited him to submit a story. A few weeks later, the following letter was received:

Dear Mrs. Dicks:

Thank you for your book. Reading it certainly changed my views from the ones expressed in my previous letter.

Most of my recollections about Switzerland fit well as captured in your and contributors' articles in 'Ticking Along with the Swiss'! Well done!

I was born in 1909 in Zurich and lived on the Lindenhofstrasse until the age of 14 when my family moved to the U.S.

I returned to Switzerland in 1970 and found that many things had changed, others remained the same! We purchased a house near Rapperswil and, needing a considerable amount of appliances for about Sfr. 1,500.-, we went to a small electrical store in Rapperswil. When we wanted to pay for our purchases, the owner exclaimed to us, two complete strangers to him, ''Don't pay now. Take everything with you and after trying everything, you can come back and pay.''

Many years ago I often walked to school with Olga Schober whose father owned the Konditorei famous for its hot chocolate, *Gugelhopf* and jams. Many years had passed but curiosity, and the desire to taste that hot chocolate again, made me visit the Schobers where I was greeted by a pleasant matronly woman. In my best *Züridütsch* I asked if per chance an Olga was still around as she and I had gone to school together. Shyly and with her head down she replied ''Ja, ich bin Olga.'' - She remembered!

I remember many conversations with our Basler friends who were always saying, ''Yo, Yo'' to everything and I with my *Züridütsch* always answering ''Ja, Ja'' broken with ''*Aber Ebe*''.

At Sprüngli's I became a pastry name expert! Instead of pointing to my selections and saying ''*Eis vo dene*'' ''*Zwei vo da*'' I could order by name, thanks to the salesperson who taught me to know 'my sweets'. I have never found a Patisserie to compare with Sprüngli's in all my travels!

One of my most memorable experiences on returning to Switzerland was being invited by my friend and neighbor, Cedric Dumont (Director of Radio and Television and well known as a conductor) to join in the 125th Anniversary of the Swiss Railway to ride on the famous train, the ''Churchill Arrow'' (Pfeil). We left from the Hauptbahnhof at 9 pm and returned there at 3 am! What an experience to be up front with the engineer at 65 miles an hour, watching lights fly by! In every town we stopped, banners, bands, song, food and drink awaited us! I don't remember how I got home from the Bahnhof!

Early in November, there's the yearly wine display at the end of the Bahnhofstrasse at the lake, 7 excursion boats are tied together, making it possible to taste and order in comfort. Quite a job when you consider there are over 100 merchants there - lots of fun and *Gemütlichkeit*. I haven't heard of anyone falling in the lake so far. Imagine a situation like this here in California. We would certainly all end up in jail!

While shopping at Jelmoli's in my American-made suit, a salesgirl approached me and in her best English said, ''Can I help you Sir?'' I waited a moment, not looking at her, then in my best *Züridütsch* replied, ''*Nei danka ich luege nur uma.*'' Walking away I heard her say in surprise to another salesgirl, ''*Da isch ya kein Amerikaner, er isch an Schwiizer!*''

I remember walking down Bahnhofstrasse in December, when it was covered with snow, trees glistening from thousands of small Christmas lights. Santa Claus riding through the streets in his special tram is an unforgettable sight. Thank you Zurich for bringing this magic to us all!

Two places which dominated the Bellevueplatz for scores of years were the Kronenhalle and the Odeon. Both of them as different as Day and Night. The Kronenhalle was known worldwide for its excellent food and a display of house paintings from many of the world's greatest artists. Those paintings by Renoir, Matisse, Picasso and others had been left there in payment for their bills! The Odeon was quite different. It was the headquarters for all the spies of Europe and the world starting with World War I. This was the famous Mata Hari's favorite watering hole. The place finally gave up its ghost.

Long ago, the Circus Knie performed a 'high wire' act outdoors at the Bellevueplatz in Zurich. A beautiful girl of about 8 was the star attraction. She became the chosen one I dreamed I would someday marry. There wasn't a fence or wall I would not climb, balancing myself with a worn-out broom to become more acceptable as a *Seiltänzer*. Years later, on one of my return trips to Switzerland, I was invited to an After-Opening-Night party for the performers at the Schwanen Hotel in Rapperswil, a yearly tradition established by the Knie family. I was introduced to my 'first love' - no longer a performer, but one of the owners. With a champagne toast I assured her that she would always rate as my first love.

Some things never change, others do!

When I was a young boy, my Grandmother often took me to the Limmatspitz where we had hot chocolate and pastries in the alcohol-free restaurant there and listened to the band playing in the Pavillon. Later, on Saturdays, my friend George Usenbenz and I would deliver pastries to this restaurant in a round container from their well-known Konditorei. Once we dropped the whole works. What a harmless accident that was compared to the horrible drug scenes occurring in that park today! Is there no one left with enough spirit to clean up this beautiful park?

Not all changes have been so bad. During one of my last trips to Zurich, while walking along Bahnhofstrassé, I felt strange amongst the people - Asians, Blacks, Turks, Spaniards, Arabs, Italians, etc. ''But then after all,'' I said to myself, ''isn't the mixture of people and races what has made this country? Everyone should be grateful and thankful for being able to enjoy the freedom of the Swiss.''

Now back in California again, I miss the ringing of the church bells and the stores being closed on Saturdays at 4 pm for the weekly cleaning, both inside and out.

I have beautiful memories sitting on the Lindenhof, sunshine dancing on golden leaves as they fall to the ground, the shimmering water of the Limmat framing the view of the Zunfthäuser, University, Grossmünster clear up to the lake on a lovely fall afternoon. On the way down Lindenhofgasse, in front of me, I see and hear the St. Peter's clock chiming, as if to say, ''It's later than you think!''

Yes, I am now over eighty years old. Please excuse the mistakes made in writing these memories. To this day I am still accused of writing with an accent!

I have relocated again in California. Health permitting, I am looking forward to a revisit to Switzerland!

In the meantime all I can say is: ''Thanks for the memories your collection of stories helped to stir up!

Sincerely,
Steve Courso-Hafner

THE FUZZY SIDE OF THE RIGI

by Dianne Dicks

Scientists around the world have just about perfected ways to express everything in values of O or 1. What doesn't fit into those classifications is called 'fuzzy logic'. Newcomers to Switzerland should beware that this is a very fuzzy country. Having spent over two decades living with the Swiss, I thought I had the essential elements of living in this country pretty well figured out. That was before we moved to live on Mount Rigi, smack-dab in the middle of Switzerland.

I realized there is something unusual about this place the first day we arrived while trying to dig a deep hole for our tortoise, Balthazar. He had always hibernated in a den in our previous garden. We hit upon an innocent looking Easter-egg-sized stone. Trying to remove it, we discovered it was quite determinedly connected to many other of its stony mates. We exposed whole cow-sized clumps of these rocky Easter eggs but could dig no simple hole for our dozing Balthazar. Mountains aren't supposed to be made of silly rocks like that.

I did some reading up about the place and discovered some myths about Mount Rigi claiming that some dragons, Balthazar's distant cousins, used to live here. There are also tales about *'Wildmännli'* or *'Wildlüütli'* (wild men or wild people). So far, we have seen no sign of dragons and the people in our village of Weggis don't act or appear to be very wild.

Well, that's not completely true. Only a few weeks after we got settled in on the Rigi, my husband and I were outside on our balcony one evening inhaling the crisp night air and admiring the thousands of twinkles from the sky above and on the hills around us. The Lake of Lucerne far below had disappeared into a black expanse that left us feeling as if we were perched on some asteroid in outer space.

The romance of the moment suddenly snapped into fear. A few meters from our house a whip started lashing and cracking like fireworks. We thought our imaginations had got the better of us on our asteroid. But the consistent snapping of that whip and the goose bumps on our arms were like a cruel alarm in the middle of a beautiful dream. Crime and torture were not part of the Switzerland we knew. Even my big and brave Swiss husband was turning the color of the moon. We could see nothing and expected to hear someone scream or moan but there was only the rhythmic snapping of the whip.

Before I could protest, my husband disappeared into the dark. The whipping noise stopped for a few minutes and then started again, harder and faster than ever in a steady rhythm. While I was frozen with fear and indecision, my husband returned with a smile on his face.

One of our neighbors was practicing an old folklore custom still popular in this region - snapping a whip to scare away the bad spirits of winter. Nobody believes in those bad spirits anymore. But the sport of making all that noise with those wild whips still attracts the young and not-so-young men.

A few weeks later we watched these whip-crackers stroll through the streets at *Klausjagen*, the St. Nicholas celebration held in a number of villages around the Rigi. The one in the village of Küssnacht is rather profound. As if it is not eerie enough to have dozens of whip-snappers strolling down the crowded main street of the village when all the lights are turned out, they are followed by a procession of several hundred men stepping along in slow-motion pirouettes while carrying huge and colorful, candle-lit bishops' miters on their heads. Behind them a brass band marches slowly, playing a weird cadence. Saint Nicholas is in the middle of the procession in bishop's robes. Following him are the *Trychler* (bell-ringers). Their rhythmical clanging makes your earlobes and the ground vibrate. We counted the rows of these bell ringers on parade and figured out there were over 800 of them strolling slowly around the village. Each *Trychler* lets his huge deep-tone cowbell ring and thud from one thigh to the other, step by step, in unison. At the end of the procession are the horn blowers, all playing the same bizarre note over and over again.

There must be some magic spirits around. What else could transform a modern Swiss village into a stage for practicing such eerie rituals all night long? You expect to find celebrations like that in the middle of Africa, not in the middle of Switzerland. This mountain is full of surprises and, for most of the year, only good spirits.

One of the Rigi's main problems in a country where everything is classified *der, die or das* is that the locals rarely agree to which gender this mountain belongs. A mountain is usually the masculine *der*. But some people say *die* Rigi since the name comes from *Reginen,* meaning layers of rock in plural. Others say *die* because someone started describing the Rigi as the 'Queen of the Mountains'. It must be quite shattering for a majestic mountain not to know if it's supposed to be a male *der* or a plural *die* or a female *die*. In the dialect of central Switzerland, people go *'uf d'Rigi ufe'*, or to *die* Rigi. But the people from the towns of Zug or Lucerne go *'uf e Rigi'*, therefore referring to it as *der*. After the many years I have spent struggling with the *der's, die's* and *das's* in this country, it was easy to feel at home on this fuzzy mountain. For once there is a real choice. That's freedom.

When thinking of the Alps, most people visualize boulders of granite, glaciers and eternal snow. Mount Rigi's not at all like that. It's a sprawling heap of round-rocked clumps with a cloak of green forests and meadows. It has real personality as mountains go. I wonder if a mountain, even one referred to as a Queen, ever feels like a misfit since it is so different from all the other Alps. If mountains can learn to make the best of their situation, Mount Rigi is certainly one of them.

Other mountains in Switzerland may have impressive peaks that attract attention by being significantly higher, whiter, colder and rougher than any the Rigi has. Some of these upstarts may make the Rigi look rather small and silly. But few mountains have the charisma of the Rigi. Depending upon the weather, you can see how she feels about all this.

Sometimes Mount Rigi wears a hat perched straight across her head which may not appear to be much higher than her shoulders. At other times she's got a white fluffy shawl slung daringly over one of her shoulders or even sexily sliding down one of her shapely cliffs. Sometimes, when she gets in one of her moods, she shuts herself up in fog for weeks at a time. She can be dreadful with wind and rain dashing and drumming in circles all about her, whipping the needles of her many pine and larch trees in swirls. She's quite impressive then. I tend to think that's her way of responding to those monstrous, menacing mountains she has as neighbors when they provoke her with their assaults of cold rebuffs often followed by their hot flirtations and the *Föhn*. Fortunately, usually the Rigi doesn't pay any attention to them and just keeps on basking in the sun and growing her own unique variety of plants. The real strength and weakness of this mountain is that most of the time, she doesn't act like one. She doesn't let her privileged situation go to her head. From the lake below, you look up onto massive smooth cliffs that change color, like cheeks, from pale gray to a blushing burgundy red according to her mood and her reflections of the sun, the time of day and the season. The Rigi doesn't let her clumps of Easter-egg-rocks affect her self-esteem any more than the question of her gender does.

One Sunday morning recently I was sitting out in the sun, basking in its fragrance and glow and just enjoying the peace. It was so quiet that I could only hear the purring of our lap cat. I couldn't hear the wind in the pines nor the twinkles and ripples over the expanse of the lake far below nor the birds' wings sweeping and swooping around the cliffs above. Then an earth-shaking blast almost made me fall out of my garden chair. It was the shooting of guns. This was soon followed by the puttering of Seppi's moped. I could see him far below. He flung one leg over his vehicle and took off with his *Sturmgewehr* (assault rifle) slung over one shoulder.

Seppi was going to the shooting gallery at the bottom of the mountain. Soon the cliffs roared with the ta-ta-ta-ta-ta. The echo thundered by, crashing into the rocks. My first reaction is always to wonder why in this peaceful, neutral country, we have on some Sundays to listen to these terrorizing sounds of war. But people here seem to have no such associations with these blasts they hear in the quadraphony of the Alpine sound system. Thinking of Seppi, the booming seemed harmless again.

Looking down the barrel of his rifle, Seppi's eyes do not rage with a killer's lust but twinkle with pride because he won't have to buy the round of beer later with his cronies. When they have finished shooting, for them only a brotherly sport of precision, he'll hop back on his moped with his lethal weapon slung again over his shoulder. He'll putter down to the village to meet his cronies at the local *Baiz* where they'll have a card game of *Jass* with a few crooked cigars and a shot or two of the local *Schnaps*. After that they might drop their rifles at home and change into their yodler outfits for a lovely performance for the tourists, and for themselves.

I often wonder how shocked tourists would be to know that these Alpine-flower-trimmed yodlers with their hands in their pockets and brotherhood in their beards were playfully practicing war only a few hours before. These yodlers' favorite ditty is called 'The Rigi Song'. It tells about how you can go from Lucerne to Weggis without socks or shoes. Even that ditty is a bit fuzzy.

Mountains used to be considered inhospitable, rugged and threatening barriers. Having to live and survive in them meant poverty, back-breaking work and mind-blasting isolation. In 1832 the hard-working people living on the Rigi must have thought the finely-dressed tourists were fuzzy in the head who came by steam-driven paddle boats from Lucerne to Weggis and Vitznau just to go up this mountain to see the sunrise. But soon the locals realized there was a way to earn money from these tourists' folly. They carried the tourists to the top of the Rigi in sedans on their shoulders. Good business deals have often influenced the logic of the Swiss. To cope with the continual onslaught of prominent travellers from all over the world to the Rigi, they have built two cog-wheel railways to the top, numerous ski-lifts, hotels and restaurants. Now the Rigi is not only a mountain, it's big business. Mount Rigi tolerates this bustling activity like a loving grandmother who plays along with games of her offspring.

This summer there was also a guided moonlight hike up the Rigi to view the sunrise. Moonlight hiking in the wee hours of the morning remind my husband of the maneuvers at that hour during his Swiss military training. Since he wasn't keen about it, I convinced my English friend Betty to join me. I made her feel it was an obligation for her to make up for all those generations of prominent British visitors who had been carried up the steep paths of the Rigi on somebody's shoulders. We labored up step by step, weaving up a hill that never seemed to stop. Our long line of about 100 trekkers was met at the top with *Kafi mit Schnaps* provided by the Weggis Tourist Office. We sat on the grass, keeping our eyes on the horizon. We waited, expecting to be thrilled by the sun's rays capping golden Alpine peaks along the famous 500-mile panorama.

But even efficient Swiss planning could do nothing to make the sun come up properly that morning. It sneaked up behind such thick clouds that it made us feel like somebody was pouring more milk into the soup we were in. Even a sunrise can be fuzzy if it likes, I suppose. It's obviously the Rigi's best friend.

When the Rigi and the sun are in good moods, the view here is spectacular. Steam boats transporting Rigi fans across the cool blue water below look like toys. At night these boats glow with their festive lights and seem to float in black space with the reflections of the stars in the sky and the many tiny lights twinkling in the surrounding hills. Sometimes you cannot tell where the many twinkles on the mountains stop and the stars begin. Looking down upon the lake and seeing the sky reflected, the world appears to be in a fuzzy position.

That's what can happen if you find yourself on a fuzzy mountain. You learn to be happy with the little holes you dig. You stop trying to move mountains as you stumble across ways to appreciate them and their inhabitants for their fuzzy features.

LIST OF AUTHORS AND ARTISTS

LANE ANDERSON

is a native Californian who has also lived in Texas, New Mexico and Arizona. He used to be a forestry technician for the U.S. Forest Service. His home is now a small sailboat in Santa Barbara, California, where he works as an alcohol and drug counselor for Viet Nam veterans through the Veterans Outreach Program. In his free time he explores the islands offshore in his boat. He sends cassette tapes, stories and photographs to his Swiss-American sons living in Switzerland every week, and visits them as much as he is allowed. He applied for various visas to permit him to live in Switzerland to be near his sons, but was turned down.

ANGELA ASHTON

pursued a career as a journalist before moving to Berne in 1985 with her husband and daughter. Her son was born in the same year. Born and educated in Liverpool, England, her working life as a reporter brought her into contact with a wide variety of people and situations. In England she combined the rigours of daily work with bringing up a young infant and studying for an Open University Bachelor of Arts degree. Today, she is, in the main, a homemaker but occasionally teaches English to adults. She takes part in a Bible study group with friends and believes Christianity helps her to make sense of her problems, commitments and the world in general. She enjoys attending keep-fit classes, writing children's stories, cooking and eating.

LESLIE BACHMANN

grew up in Vancouver, Canada, where she obtained a Bachelor of Education degree from the University of British Columbia in 1964. Two years later she settled into the apple orchard on the grounds of an agriculture college on the shores of Lake Geneva. There she is a mother of three, the principal's wife and is now referred to by the Old Boys as the school's ambassadress. She enjoys the people and the natural surroundings where she lives but she is equally keen on the Kingdom of Heaven within, a land she enjoys going to and helping others find. She teaches English to Women's Institute groups and to university staff as well as to prisoners.

KEN BECKER

was born and reared in Minnesota. He is a man of many hats: free-lance writer, translator, language teacher, theologian, psychological counsellor, and firewood cutter. He has been living with his Swiss wife in Buttikon, Switzerland, for the past seven years and has learned to like it there. Besides the quiet, the order, and the reliable functioning of Switzerland, he also enjoys the challenge of living with several foreign languages, though speaking Swiss-German dialect is an art he despairs of. His interests and writing projects range widely (presently including South Africa, fantasy, murder, fable, and psychological processes) and any problems are thoroughly discussed with the couple's slug-eating duck, What.

JOHN BENDIX

first came to Switzerland at age 5 to attend the Ecole d'Humanité in Goldern and has returned irregularly since then to attend school, hike, teach, folk-dance, briefly deal with psychiatric patients, and above all to try to understand a frustrating country which has meant a great deal to him. He received his B.A. from Amherst College, his M.A. from Berkeley and his Ph.D. from Indiana University in Bloomington. He teaches political science at Lewis and Clark College in Portland, Oregon, where he lives with his Swiss wife Regina and his baby daughter Claire Leah whom the relatives call Claireli. He recently finished writing a book: ''Importing Foreign Workers: A Comparison of German and American Policy'' to be published late 1990 and is currently on a study trip with students in Turkey.

RICHARD J. BLOOMFIELD

spent his senior high school year in Berne in 1967 and returned to his native St. Paul, Minnesota, to study Germanics at Macalester College and then theology at Bethel Theological Seminary. You could take Richard out of Europe but you can't take Europe out of Richard. His studies, teaching experiences and two pastorates in the USA were punctuated by his visits to Switzerland, Austria and Germany. In 1981 he was offered and accepted the call to be the pastor of two Reformed parishes in S-chanf and La Punt in the Engadine valley where he learned Romansch but not how to ski. He is now pastor of the Reformed Parish in St. Gall. Not long after accepting this call he fell in love with a church board member and on New Year's Eve in 1988 their marriage ceremony was filled with laughter.

GEORGE BLYTHE

originally came from Nottingham, England, but emigrated three times and still can't make up his mind where he belongs. First he emigrated to Montreal where he became interested in journalism and language, then to Germany where he worked as a translator, and finally (?) to Switzerland where translating and editing promoted interests in the life sciences and later in psychiatry, on which he published a bilingual glossary. Now in early retirement after some twenty years editing company house journals and books, he hopes to have more time for other, less esoteric, publishing ventures.

JEAN BONJOUR

was born in a lucky place, Fortuna, California. She grew up in a small town in Oregon and became an elementary school teacher in Bend, Oregon, before earning a B.A. in Psychology at Stanford University in California. She served in the U.S. Air Force in World War II in England, France and Germany. Later, while attending the University of Geneva, she met her Swiss husband. They were transferred by an airline company to Zurich, Bombay, Frankfurt and back to Zurich. Her book for children with a story about an elephant was published while they lived in India. Back in Zurich, she joined the Creative Writer's Group of a women's club and wrote verse and stories for club bulletins. She is an avid 'peasant style' painter and enjoys living wherever she is.

ROGER BONNER

was born in Geneva in 1943 and moved with his family to Los Angeles, California, at the age of 6. He lived there till he was 21. The danger of being drafted into the Viet Nan War persuaded him to return to his native country, where he was quickly drafted into the Swiss Army. Afterwards he had to start from scratch, learn Swiss German and decide what to do with his life. He worked in supermarkets and became a really top vegetable and fruit salesman. He decided to give up this promising career and study languages instead. He now teaches in-company English courses and works as a freelance translator in Basle. Unfortunately he can't earn a living writing love poetry. He has had a book of poetry published and occasionally pours his whole soul into short stories. He sometimes believes in miracles, but none has happened to him yet.

CLAIRE BONNEY

graduated from St. Lawrence University in northern New York. She came to Switzerland in 1977 on a Thomas J. Watson Fellowship to study Swiss Carnival and maskmaking. It was only by enrolling at the University of Zurich that the Swiss foreign police could be convinced that she was indeed a serious scholar. As a result, she became just that and completed her *Lizentiat* in art history, folklore and ethnology. She is now married to a Swiss journalist and is Curator of the Museum of Architecture in Basle. She's homesick every day.

JOSEPH CARUSO

grew up in New York where his Italian ancestors had emigrated and adapted so well that they stopped playing *boccia* and speaking Italian at home. Now living in Zurich with a name like Caruso makes the Swiss assume he is Italian. Unlike a lot of Italians in Switzerland, he doesn't wait on tables but provides a lot of the artwork in lively Swiss publications. Thanks to his Swiss wife and two children, he has no trouble coping with Swiss German. His own firm, CGD Computer Graphic Design AG designed this book and he made the sketches throughout it. As an artist working so much with computers, he is convinced the machine can be only as creative as the man or woman using it and that computers enable artists to enter new worlds. Besides being a businessman, illustrator and cartoonist, he is active in the American business community in Zurich.

CHRIS CORBETT

was born in England and emigrated with his parents to California when he was two years old. He grew up in 'the Prune Capital of the World' which today is known as Silicon Valley. He owned and operated a publishing business in Los Angeles and also worked in the film industry there on a number of TV shows, on an Academy Award winning documentary and a Walt Disney project. Seeking the continental charm, he moved to Switzerland in 1985 with his Swiss wife and son. He now works at the European headquarters of an American multi-national firm near Zurich helping executives with their information needs and producing an in-house newsletter. He is active in the American community in Zurich and enjoys photography.

STEVE COURSO-HAFNER

was born in Zurich in 1909 and lived with his grandmother at Lindenhofstrasse 1 until the age of 14 when he joined his family in California. After finishing school he became associated with motion picture studios as a 'make-up-man'. Later he became vice-president of a large cosmetic firm and after 20 years left this firm to open his own chain of beauty schools in California. He was appointed by the Govenor of California, at that time Ronald Reagan, to the State Board of Cosmetology. He returned to Switzerland in 1970 to open a factory for a cosmetic firm which did not materialize. He and his wife have been living in California again since 1975.

DIANNE DICKS

had her first intercultural shock when she left her native Indiana to attend Rollins College in Florida which was filled with New Englanders who teased her about her accent. She came to Switzerland on a two and one-half month exchange program in 1961. Now she has lived here over two and one-half decades. She worked in the Basle region as a translator and in-company English teacher before moving in 1988 with her family and translation office to Weggis where the view is the greatest distraction. She may have lost some of her Hoosier twang but now she gets teased about her accent in *Schwizerdütsch*. Not speaking English at home with her Swiss husband and her two children has made her fond of teaching English, writing about intercultural experiences and trying to encourage others to write too. Collecting stories about living in Switzerland started out as a hobby.

BRIAN FAIRMAN

was born in Carshalton, a suburb of London, and in spite of Hitler's many 'birthday presents' which were regularly dropped around his home, he survived. After a grammar school education he went into the motor insurance business and also studied the works of Monty Python as a keen sense of humour was necessary to survive the experience of motorists describing their accidents! A semi-pro musician, in 1985 he married his second wife, a Swiss from the German-speaking region, who became the road crew for his band which was soon ''probably the tidiest rock 'n' roll band in England.'' He now lives in the village of Blonay and is working on the design of the world's first combined lawnmower/hang-glider.

STEVEN GREGORIS

was born, raised and everything else in Toronto, Canada. After having made the mistake of wandering just a bit too far from home, he was snapped up by a young Swiss female and willingly (in fact, very willingly) dragged to one of the world's most prosperous countries to live. Together they are the embarrassingly happy parents of two wonderful kids. Besides teaching English he spends an inordinate amount of time trying to figure out what 'Swiss' means while simultaneously trying to take life as seriously as everyone says he should.

MAVIS GUINARD

was born an American but grew up in Europe and South America. After graduating from a New England college, she returned to Argentina, first working as girl Friday and interpreter for a foreign correspondent, then as a reporter on a Buenos Aires newspaper. After deadlines came marriage and babies. Her French husband's transfer to Switzerland gave them a whole new country to explore by hiking, skiing and discovering offbeat museums. After their three daughters no longer needed her help with their *devoirs*, she went back to her typewriter, translating books, writing features and earning bylines in a variety of newspapers and specialty publications.

PATRICIA HIGHSMITH

is an American born in Texas and educated in New York. She had a job for about a year then embarked on a free-lance writing career with short stories and novels. She lived for long or short periods in Mexico, Italy, France, England and now lives in Switzerland in the Ticino. She is best known perhaps for the Hitchcock "Strangers on a Train" film from her first book of the same name and for the Tom Ripley series (four so far) the first of which was filmed with Alain Delon as the amoral Tom, the third with Dennis Hopper as the protagonist and called "The American Friend". Her latest book of short stories is "Tales of Natural and Unnatural Catastrophes", having to do with ecology, more to do with politics and religion, the two topics we are not supposed to bring up at polite dinner parties. She lives alone except for two cats, and prefers villages to cities as dwelling places.

KRIS JENSON

was born precocious and stubborn in Phoenix, Arizona. She was held there in curiosity for 18 years. She learned French which did not help much in preparing her for a year as an exchange student in Lucerne where they speak a dialect vaguely resembling German. An intensive German course for a month and her compulsion for self-expression helped her to achieve limited eloquence. The rolling, emerald, construction crane-dotted landscape, relative physical safety from crime and pollution, the Lucerne *Fasnacht*, friends and host families, and the fun of making Swiss necks swivel will surely lure her back for a long visit, despite the frustrations of feeling like a clumsy, unpunctual bog in a well-oiled, rich Swiss society. She's been accepted to attend Wellesley College in Boston where she intends to take folly and physics seriously.

DREW KEELING

is an American who moved to Zurich in 1986 to search for the Holy Grail. Instead he has found less potent elixirs such as Radio 24, the Sfr. 100 *Halbpreis-Abonnement* of the SBB and *Birchermuesli*. His most notable failures to date include a) an inability to disguise himself as a gnome, b) an inability to yodel and c) an inability to attain the skiing skill of the average Swiss three-year-old.

MUTHANA KUBBA

was born and bred in Baghdad, Iraq. He read engineering at Imperial College, University of London where he obtained his honours degree in Electrical Engineering and a Ph.D. in Communications. Returning home in the troubled early sixties, he joined the College of Engineering at the University of Baghdad where he spent 16 years on the staff, becoming head of the Department and an Assistant Professor. He emigrated to Switzerland in 1978 and started his own trading company. He now heads a multinational company dealing with luxury limousines. Married with three (almost) grown up children, he divides his time between the quiet Canton of Zug, exciting London and demanding Bremen interspersed with occasional visits home in romantic Baghdad.

JAN LANE

was born in Wisconsin but considers California her heart's home. She holds a B.F.A. in Theatre Arts, a California teaching credential and a masters degree in education. She feels fortunate to have worked professionally as an actress, counsellor, teacher, sculptor and administrator. She has built up three businesses - a pre-school, a small art gallery and a college of massage therapy. Before marrying a German-speaking Swiss and moving to Switzerland in 1982, she was coordinator of the refugee children's program at the Indochinese Center in Portland, Oregon. At present she teaches English in Locarno. She finds that single life for a middle-aged foreign-born woman living in the Ticino is rather limited but dodging wild drivers provides lots of excitement.

ADHAM LOUTFI

grew up in California. His father's career with the airline industry and mother's love of travel assured that he too was bitten by the travel bug at an early age. Alternating trips overseas with study, he managed to earn his B.A. in International Studies at Earlham College in Indiana and his Master's from the School for International Training in Vermont. He now leads groups of unsuspecting American college students on the Experiment in International Living's semester abroad program, most recently to Zurich. His goal this week is to get everyone in the world on a first-name basis with each other.

STANLEY MASON

has lived in Switzerland for many years without being assimilated and is now a near-recluse who chiefly tends his two gardens. Always something of an outsider, he was born high up in the Canadian Rockies but brought up in the English Midlands where his father was a coal miner. He went to Oxford on a scholarship, moved to Switzerland unwillingly as a teacher, but married a *Ticinese* girl and has since stayed put. He has published two books of poetry, a four-volume English textbook, a play which won an award in California, and a translation of Albrecht von Haller's major poem *"Die Alpen"*. After working for twenty years in engineering and twenty in art publishing, he now provides the English that appears in three leading Swiss magazines and in his spare time (if any) translates German poetry into English.

MARI MUELLER

grew up in Paradise Valley, Arizona, and recently graduated from the University of the Pacific in Stockton, California, and hopes to go on to law school this year. She came to Switzerland on an exchange program for several months in 1989 living with a Swiss family in Oberrieden. That stay allowed her to meet some of her relatives in Switzerland as well as enjoy skiing, traveling, music and reading. Her grandfather was a Swiss citizen of Niederbipp and her father holds both American and Swiss passports.

KATE MÜHLETHALER

was born in Cheshire, England. After leaving school she took a secretarial course and then went on to train as a teacher. On finishing her probationary year in a primary school, she went to work as head teacher in a Day Care Centre for Pre-school children in the USA. She came to live in Switzerland in 1972 and has been teaching English at "all kinds of places" for about 15 years. She lives with her husband, daughter, and a stray cat at about 725 m in the Jura mountains and enjoys venturing down every year for the Carnival.

KARLA NOELL

spent her formative years in Greenwich Village, New York City. In 1959 she graduated from Western College for Women in Oxford, Ohio, and since then has travelled around the world, throughout South America, Africa, Turkey and Russia with her Hungarian-born husband. In 1971 they moved with their two sons to Lausanne where she later matriculated at the University of Lausanne obtaining an equivalency in history and expertise in all the English grammar anyone would ever want to know. She now teaches English and writes short stories.

ALEX PORTER

was born in Manhattan, New York, while his Swiss parents were living there. He grew up near Lucerne where he also completed his apprenticeship as a structural draftsman. Interested in becoming a magician, he attended the Art Academy in Bath, England, and the Pantomime School in Ilg near Zurich. His one-man-performances throughout Switzerland in small theaters are described as a mixture of seriousness, foolishness, magic and poetry.

IRENE RITTER

has now lived longer in Lucerne, Switzerland, than in her home city of Manchester, England. Following the study of Modern Languages, she worked in Spanish at the European Service of the British Broadcasting Corporation, in French at the Embassy in London and, with English and German added, over the Channel at the Lucerne Tourist Office. Two (consecutive) Swiss husbands and two children later, she finally put down roots and gained insight into the Swiss way of life. Since then she has been lecturing, broadcasting and writing in English about this country and its people. She is the author of 'Swiss Magic', a book of episodes of Swiss history and folklore. She soothes her nerves with a good novel and loves to travel whenever possible.

ANN ROBERT

first came to Switzerland in 1960 when her father was posted to the British Embassy in Berne. She graduated from Neuchâtel University and became an assistant in Medieval French there. During that time she met her future husband at a students' ski camp. They lived a while in Paris then in Princeton. After three years in the USA, they settled in Corcelles, near Neuchâtel. Her husband's job as a Maths Professor has enabled her to spend several semesters with him in Canada, Brazil and California. They have three children and although she marked her occupation as 'housewife' on the last census sheet, she spends most of her time on other things than housework. She is in charge of the Corcelles Public Library and president of the local parish council. Her only regret about living in Switzerland is that she has proved incapable of teaching her two younger children to speak English.

JANET RÜSCH

was born and educated in Lancashire in England. She worked 11 years for the Inland Revenue and while doing her duty for Queen and Country she met her Swiss husband in London. She accompanied him back to Schaffhausen where she once timidly answered an advertisement in the local paper for an English teacher with grave misgivings and a pounding heart. She's now been teaching English at all levels for 17 years. She is a founder member of what has become Switzerland's most significant association for English teachers and enjoys attending their various courses and workshops. She finds horse riding exhilarating as it provides time for reflection and new ideas for English lessons.

GAY SCOTT O'CONNOR

is a painter and sculptor. She works under the professional name 'GAY' and uses the intense colours inspired by her Jamaican childhood. A multi-national, she is Jamaican by birth and upbringing, British through her father and Swiss by marriage. She has lived in Switzerland for nearly eighteen years, not always in the same place

208

but always within sight of the Lake of Zurich. She has no problem pronouncing *Chuchichästli*, but refuses to ski, skate or sled. In spite of her name, no, she isn't. Her parents named her Gay in a more innocent age. This considerably muddles the Swiss, however, who know it in one sense only. It also confuses computers and most of them have decided she must be a man. Gay lives with her three teenage children, various cats and hundreds of books in Wollerau in the Canton of Schwyz.

DAVID SPEICHER

already mixed fun, team spirit and serious hard work at the University of Toledo, Ohio, as a basketball player while earning his MBA. Afterwards in 1977 he had two goals: to play professional basketball and to explore Europe. He played with teams in Belgium, Italy and later around Lausanne in Switzerland where he met his life's team-mate, a French-speaking Swiss woman who later became his wife. Now 'retired' from professional basketball, he uses his business studies and knowledge of three European languages in marketing at an American company in the Canton of Zug where ceilings are high enough for him, his wife and their son. He's learned to accept the fact that there are some parts of Switzerland (in Appenzell, for example) where he would never be able to stand tall.

SUSAN STAFFORD

was born and grew up in the village of Gerrards Cross, not far from Windsor Castle in the south of England. She has lived in Switzerland (first in Zurich, then in Basle) for 20 years and works as a technical translator. In her spare time she writes poetry, studies popular psychology (i.e. how to cope with neurotic quirks) and is involved in amateur dramatics. She made her debut singing and dancing in a musical, which is rather like jumping in at the deep end.

CATHERINE P. STUDER

is Swiss and has been living in Switzerland most of her life. She is also American as she was born in the USA and lived there until she was eight years old. Twenty years later she had the opportunity to spend a post-doctoral year at the State University of New York in Stony Brook, Long Island, where she met her future Swiss husband. They now live with their two sons in Baselland. As a goodwill ambassador between Switzerland and the USA, she regularly writes a column for a newspaper in New York about Swiss affairs. Recently she has become interested in and involved with American families whose ancestors emigrated from Switzerland to the USA in the 18th and 19th centuries.

SUSAN M. TIBERGHIEN

thought she'd always be a New Yorker until she went to the University of Grenoble for graduate work and fell in love with a Frenchman. Giving up plans for a career in publishing, she married him and lived in various places in Europe before settling down with their six French-speaking children in Geneva. When her children started leaving home, she went back to writing regularly in her mother-tongue. She is the leader of a women's writers workshop in Geneva which meets regularly. Many of her short stories and essays have been published in periodicals in America and in Europe. She is a member of International PEN and the Authors Guild of America. She recently edited ''Offshoots'', a literary review for her writers' workshop.

BARRY TUNICK

is an American who has been a Los Angeles resident for most of his 55 years. Since 1980 he has co-constructed the L.A. Times Sunday crossword puzzle. He considers his 15 summers visiting his wife's family in rural Switzerland among his happiest times and finds that Cormoret in the Bernese Jura between Biel and La Chaux-de-Fonds has all the stereotypes about Switzerland. On or between its borders are a chocolate factory, a Gruyére cheese dairy and a factory making parts for the watch industry. He finds the Swiss there refreshingly free of their stereotypes of being formal, insincerely polite and unfriendly.

SUSAN TUTTLE-LAUBE

was born in New Jersey where her Swiss father had emigrated and married her German mother. She is therefore a dual citizen with two passports. Now living in Switzerland, she feels like an American disguised as a Swiss *Hausfrau*. Her efforts to do the American-Super-Mom-Career-Woman thing are often combined with bribes of chocolate to her two young children or with promises that they can take turns pushing the return key on her typewriter. Literally between the children and housework, she does translations and co-edits a newsletter in English for newcomers to Switzerland. Last summer 14 pumpkins grew in her garden in Wettingen. She does not iron the sheets.

GILLIAN USTER

was born in South Africa of South African/English/Danish parentage in 1947. Described as an 'experiment' and often referred to as 'being vaccinated with a gramophone needle', she matriculated and talked her way onto the staff of a daily newspaper as a cub reporter and photographer at the age of 17. She spent 14 years working on various newspapers and magazines covering everything from marriages to murders. She met her Swiss husband during the course of her duties. After a whirlwind courtship she followed him to Switzerland where they were married in 1978. They then made their home in Tokyo for several years where their son was born and later moved to Kuala Lumpur, Malaysia. Six years ago they settled in Baar, near Zug in Switzerland. A sense of humour, plenty of friends and activities, including being president of an international group of women in Zug, have kept her going.

MASAKO S. UZAWA

had youthful dreams of becoming a writer as she grew up in Hokkaido, the pastoral northern island of Japan. An English major at a college in Tokyo paved her way to winning a Fullbright scholarship in 1951 to study social work at the University of North Carolina in the USA where she met a Swiss chemist who later became her husband. They have been living in the Basle region since 1959 and have three grown-up children. Through the years in Switzerland she has worked as a free-lance interpreter, translator, tourist guide and done occasionally volunteer social work. She is able to combine all these interests when she helps a Japanese paraplegic group who come to Switzerland to enjoy winter sports with their Swiss friends. She still enjoys writing in her leisure time in Japanese or English as a form of expression.

SUSIE VEREKER

though born in England, has been moving round the world since she was three years old, first as an army officer's daughter and then as a diplomat's wife. She has worked in publishing in London, au paired in Germany, typed in Aden, taught English in Surrey, and raised children in Australia, Greece and Thailand. With her British husband, she has been living in a beautiful Genevois village since early 1987. She works as a volunteer, producing a club magazine in Geneva, where she is also a member of a women writers' group. She is sad that the family's time in Switzerland is ticking to a close, as it has been one of the happiest episodes of her life.

DON WELLS

is a native of California and spent forty years broadcasting profes-sional and college sports in various cities in the U.S. He was a radio and television 'voice' for the Chicago White Sox and Los Angeles Angels baseball teams. He also had assignments in the National Football League and various university athletic conferences. During World War II, he spent three years in the United States Army and a good part of that military service was in Europe. He and his native Californian wife are now permanent Swiss residents. He likes to quote a line Pablo Picasso once poster-painted: "It takes one a long time to become young." The Wells' stong concern for family and others leads to that late-in-years' youthful feeling.

HEIDRUN WEST

was born in Sudetenland which is now Czechoslovakia. Starting her life as a refugee, she has lived in Germany, England, Scotland, the United States and Switzerland. Through moving she has acquired different passports, a mixture of accents, a British husband and an American B.A. She also has two almost grown-up sons - one British, one American. Realizing that roots cannot be found but have to be made, she has become an addicted gardener - of plants and people.

CORNELIA ZIEGLER

was born in Croydon, England. After studying art in London she went to Munich to continue studying and worked on graphic designs and animated films. After a few years in Berne in graphic art, advertising and film animation, she moved to Basle in 1972 where she now has her own free-lance studio. Her commissions involve book illustrations, advertising, painting theatre backcloths, designing costumes, sketching townscapes of Basle and giving drawing lessons. She feels like she is becoming more Swiss all the time and appreciates not having to be afraid walking around Swiss towns armed only with her sketchbook which becomes an invitation and not a shield. She loves the challenge of using a 'line' that dances like a dancer, kicks like a football player or makes your mouth water when you see a sketch of a menu or makes you understand the love a blind man has for his guide dog. Learning the language of the 'line' enables her to seek ways to express exciting, unfathomable realms.

TEACHERS' TIPS

by Dianne Dicks

The following exercises may be helpful in getting groups to discuss their own intercultural experiences. English teachers can use them to liven up English lessons and encourage students to read the stories in 'Ticking Along Too' outside of class. Please do not use these stories to test comprehension, analyse grammar rules or otherwise take the fun out of learning a language. The stories in this book and these exercises are meant to be fun and thought-provoking and to help get discussions going about intercultural encounters.

1. PREDICT THE STORY FROM THE TITLE

Ask students in pairs to guess what the following stories are probably about by looking at the titles. Have them write a few sentences with short descriptions. Good titles for this purpose are:

Sweeping Differences
An Inconvenience Off Bahnhofstrasse
Musical Chairs
Echoes
Bus Stop Blues
Behind Those Closed Curtains
Serving Swiss Time
Dead On Time
An Unforgettable Great Myth
Afloat Together
A New Commandment
The Word Starts with an 'S'
Pinches of Culinary Swissness
Fanfare

Each pair then reports to the class what they think the story is about. Outside of class, the students will read the story to confirm if their guesses were right.

2. PREDICT THE WORDS TO BE FOUND

Ask students to select one title and to make a list of 10 to 15 words they might expect to find in that article. Then have the students read that article quickly and see if any of their expected words occur.

After one of the above exercises you might want to ask students to select one of the stories they are most curious about and have them read it as homework and tell the class briefly about it the next lesson.

3. PREDICT THE SOLUTION TO A PROBLEM

Elicit from students briefly what they think the story 'Behind Those Closed Curtains' is about. Then have students read silently the first page of this story. In a brief discussion with the class, confirm that they get the gist of the story so far. Then have students in pairs predict what happens next and write this down in a few sentences. Then have the pairs of students report their ideas to the whole class. Afterwards give students the second page of the story to read silently and quickly. Did anyone guess correctly how the story would develop?

4. A STORY PUZZLE

Divide your class into groups of 5. Each person in the group gets a paragraph of the story 'An Unforgettable Great Myth' on a slip of paper. Each reads their paragraph out loud and together they decide the order of the story. You could also cut out each of the 15 sentences and pass these on slips to 15 students who try to figure out the order of the sentences. Get your students to keep reading the texts on their slips out loud to each other until they can stand in a row according to the order of their sentences.

5. TEXT FOR DICTATION

Divide your class into teams at one end of the room. Have the text of 'Swiss Humor?' at the other end of the room. Each team will write down part of this poem. The first team to complete their part wins. Each team member runs to look at the text, quickly memorizes a line and runs back to dictate it as clearly and as carefully as possible to the other team members. Then another one of the team runs to the text for the next line and dictates it to the others.

Because students will be writing quickly, spelling should not count. After the last line has been dictated, each team's members should compare what they have written and help each other understand the text well enough for it to be read afterwards to the whole class. This exercise helps even shy students practice pronouncing English words and also to distinguish sounds and how several words sometimes sound like one.

6. WHAT HAVE WE DONE TO THE SWISS?

Have several pairs of students make lists of 'English' influences upon Swiss culture. Have rest of class in pairs make list of 'Swiss' influences upon the world. Then get class in two groups to help get their lists as long as possible. Then have each student with list of English influences exchange ideas with a student with list of Swiss influences.

Another classroom project that could be stimulated by the article 'What Have We Done to the Swiss?' is to discuss if the use of English is causing the Swiss to commit 'cultural suicide'. Keep lists of English words used in local shops, on local ads, posters, sales slogans and product names.

Get your students in teams to find the best translations in your students' mother-tongue for the following English words:

leasing	talk show
long-drink	crash
fast food	smog
public relations or PR	Yuppie-look
multiple choice	skinhead
quiz	dealer
floppy disk	goodwill
single	sexy
display	jet-set
interview	doping
job sharing	intercity
hit	jumbo
shopping	jogging

7. GET YOUR CLASS INTO PAIRS

To get your class into pairs, pass out one part of a title to each student. Students walk around reading out the words on their slips of paper and listening to each other for suitable matching parts. Pairs of students keep reading off their titles until the whole class agrees which pairs have the probable titles.

Dead ...	... On Time
Abseiling ...	... Down the Garden
Tangibles ...	... and Intangibles
Musical ...	... Chairs
Does Your ...	... Husband Yodel?
The Word...	... Starts with an 'S'
Behind Those ...	... Closed Curtains
Hairpin...	... Bends
We Can ...	... Work It Out
From Hollywood to ...	... an Alpine Hamlet

8. SPEED READING

When using English in real-life situations, it is not necessary to understand every word. Help your students learn to cope with this situation. Use any story for this exercise but 'Kantonsschule Romance' is particularly suitable here, especially with teenagers.

First have your students go through the story and underline as quickly as possible all words which they do NOT immediately understand. They should not read the story for content but only go through the words quickly. It does not matter if even half the words in the story are crossed out.

Afterwards they should read the story as quickly as possible looking only at the words not underlined. Stop them after a few minutes and try to elicit the contents of the story by asking simple questions like "Where does the story take place?" "Who is Markus?" "Does the writer like Markus?" Have your students guess as much as possible about the content of the story. In the end, ask them if they think this is a true story. Why or why not. What two words on the first page of the story probably do not exist in the English language?

If your class gets the gist of the story, that's more than enough. If they enjoy talking about it, they might voluntarily look up a few of the words they originally crossed out. Somehow students don't forget what THEY want to learn.

9. GET YOUR CLASS TALKING

The following exercise provides a reason for your students to express agreement and disagreement and allows them to formulate their personal values. Give each student a copy of the questionnaire and allow them a few minutes to read through it quickly and circle the mark indicating their opinions. Afterwards, in groups of four, have students compare answers and discuss those they disagree strongly about. Caution: these statements are taken out of context and do not necessarily express the opinion of the author of the story.

Statements 1 through 16 and the articles they come from are suitable for intermediate students learning English. Statements 17 through 30 are suitable for more advanced students. The more interested your students are in wanting to read the article, the easier the article will be for them to understand.

This exercise is particularly suitable for getting discussions going in intercultural workshops.

Circle your opinion as follows:

++ means 'I agree strongly'
+ means 'I agree'
0 means 'I'm neutral'
- means 'I disagree'
-- means 'I disagree strongly'

---

1. In Switzerland we do not put our feet on streetcar cushions.
from 'Headaches 403 - 408'

++ + 0 - --

---

2. Thou shalt not laugh in church!
from 'A New Commandment'

++ + 0 - --

---

3. "If I'd known what Swiss mountain passes are like," he said, "we'd have come by train."
from 'Hairpin Bends'

++ + 0 - --

---

4. I dread the idea of sounding 'cute' with my errors. I don't want to be tedious or make people have to work hard to understand me.
from 'Cawfee and Rösti'

++ + 0 - --

---

5. Swiss people seem reserved at first and hesitant to make friends.
from 'Under the Swiss Roof'

++ + 0 - --

---

6. To understand people in Switzerland and especially how they act on some days, therefore, you must realize how they can be affected by the *Föhn*.
from 'Pinches of Culinary Swissness'

++ + 0 - --

---

7. Mountain walking is obviously a part of Swiss life in which everyone should participate.
from 'Haven't We Passed Those Cows Before?'

++ + 0 - --

---

8. Being a daughter-in-law can be tricky at the best of times.
from 'Sweeping Differences'

++ + 0 - --

9. When the Swiss want to sell something successfully to their countrymen, they proudly stamp it, in large letters, 'Swiss Made'.
from 'Dead On Time'

++ + 0 - --

10. When a young child is undergoing the natural process of learning its mother tongue, it can learn several other languages at the same time without difficulty.
from 'The Language of Play'

++ + 0 - --

11. I can't help myself or anyone else by trying too hard to fit in, and losing part of myself in the process.
from 'On Fitting In'

++ + 0 - --

12. Restrooms in Switzerland have posed more problems or challenges to me than I ever could have imagined.
from 'An Inconvenience Off Bahnhofstrasse'

++ + 0 - --

13. There is still a strong tradition (in Switzerland) of not being extravagant and wasteful.
from 'An Inconvenience Off Bahnhofstrasse'

++ + 0 - --

14. It is not comfortable to feel at home in a place you do not belong.
from 'Familiar Distance'

++ + 0 - --

15. The majority of women with young children have to be full-time homemakers
from 'From Housewife to Hausfrau'

++ + 0 - --

16. Swiss people are just as reluctant to make friends with other Swiss, sometimes even more so, than they are with foreigners.
from 'Learning the Ropes in Heidi's Playground'

++ + 0 - --

17. Switzerland is a grand place to spend the golden years of our lives.

from 'From Hollywood to an Alpine Hamlet'

++ + 0 - --

---

18. For the Swiss, *Hochdeutsch* lends a formality to any situation that makes a truly genial and relaxed conversation impossible.

from 'Summer with Swiss Sons'

++ + 0 - --

---

19. When young Swiss get away from their *Ordnung*-laden homes, they like to cut loose a good bit.

from 'A Summer with Swiss Sons'

++ + 0 - --

---

20. Just as the English can never learn to say *Chuchichäschtli*, the German Swiss hardly ever manage to pronounce certain English consonants.

from 'Pratfalls on the Language Frontier'

++ + 0 - --

---

21. (Switzerland) is so well-organized, punctual and hygienic that nothing crazy and irrational can happen in it.

from 'Meeting Mephisto'

++ + 0 - --

---

22. The local dialect is rooted so deep in those born and raised here that 'foreigners' can usually be spotted the moment they open their mouths.

from 'Do You Speak Schwizerdütsch'

++ + 0 - --

---

23. My wife thinks that by buying all these things, they're satisfying a desire to turn their earnings into something tangible, something more concrete than a bankbook to show for their toil.

from 'Tangibles and Intangibles'

++ + 0 - --

24. If the Swiss don't put their new residents on mountaintops, their more habitable regions can indeed get cramped
from 'Afloat Together'

++ + 0 - --

25. Spotless hotels, trains and streets depend on foreign help for the dirty work.
from 'How Switzerland Became Clean'

++ + 0 - --

26. I realised, however, that, in most cases, the reluctance to communicate was not due to downright unfriendliness, but a certain shyness
from 'A Morning Ride'

++ + 0 - --

27. If even easy-walking-distance neighbours do not ring up and ask if they can pop in for a minute around 6pm, it is because they (each of the parties concerned) don't need this brief pick-up.
from 'Leisure Time: How Do the Swiss Spend Theirs'

++ + 0 - --

28. There is almost a growing dependence on English words, causing the Swiss to neglect their own languages and even commit cultural suicide.
from 'What Have We Done to the Swiss'

++ + 0 - --

29. I believe the origin of the strong independent streak in Swiss communities...has a great deal to do with the past natural constraints under which natives lived.
from 'Familiar Distance'

++ + 0 - --

30. The main difference between a British housewife and a Swiss *Hausfrau* stems from a difference in the education system of each country.
from 'From Housewife to Hausfrau'

++ + 0 - --

AN INVITATION

to all readers

Still Ticking Along with the Swiss

Reading this book may have reminded you of your own favorite experience with the Swiss, an experience that changed your life or made you smile or just think twice. Have you ever been embarrassed or misunderstood because you could not speak a Swiss language? Maybe you have some special knowledge about the Swiss that would be entertaining or informative for others to learn about. Perhaps reading this book has inspired you to pull out some poetry or short stories that have been tucked away into a drawer. Have you got a story, article, poem or sketch for the next edition of this book?

Now that two collections have been published with mostly stories from 'foreigners' in Switzerland about the Swiss, maybe it's time there is a collection of stories in English written by the Swiss about the 'foreigners' they meet in Switzerland?

If you would like to share your experiences with others who are interested in intercultural encounters, write to Dianne Dicks, c/o Bergli Books Ltd, CH-6353 Weggis, Switzerland.